MASS EFFECT™

INVASION

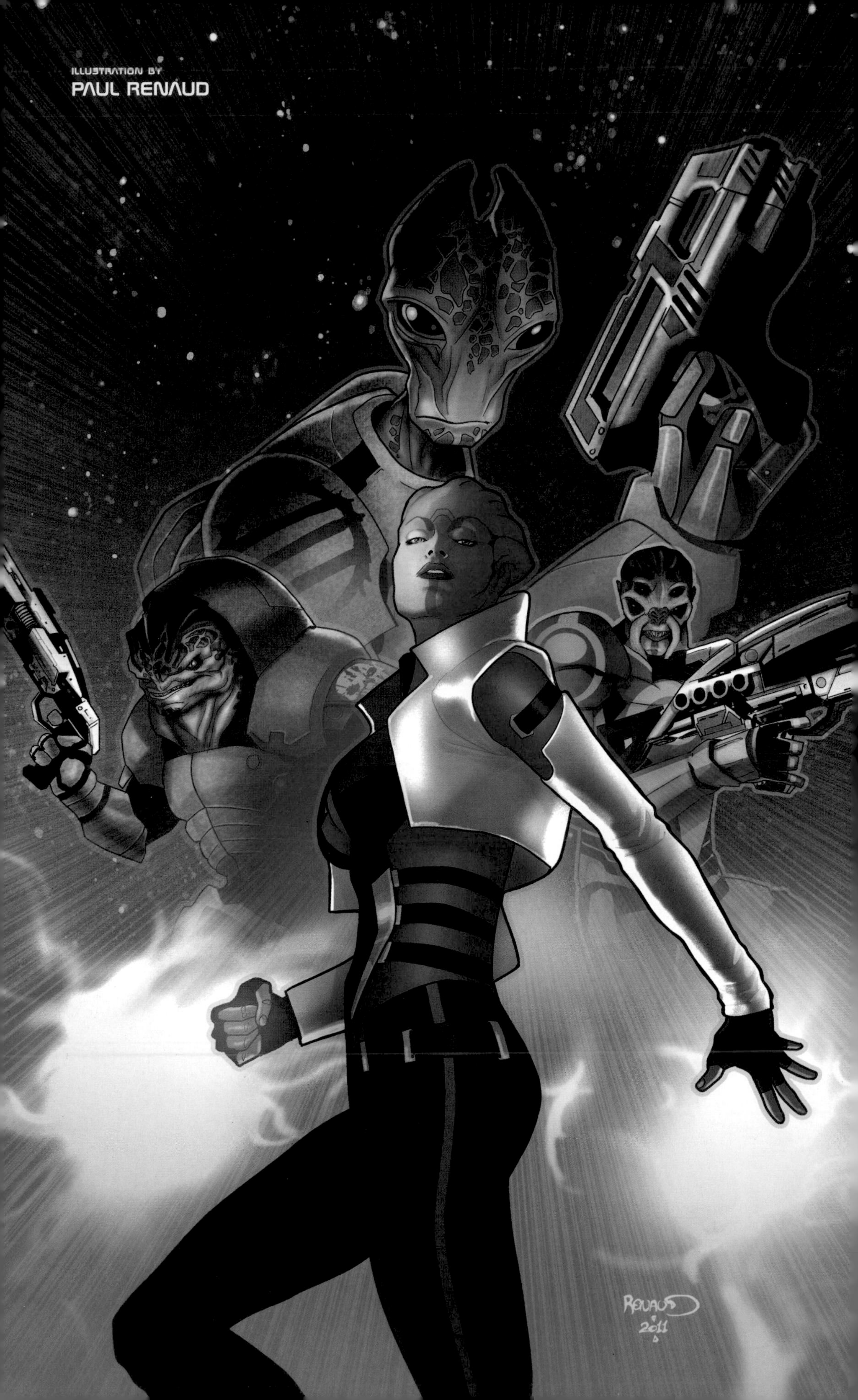
RENAUD
2011

ILLUSTRATION BY
PAUL RENAUD

MASS EFFECT™
INVASION

STORY
MAC WALTERS

SCRIPT
JOHN JACKSON MILLER

ART
OMAR FRANCIA

COLORS
MICHAEL ATIYEH

LETTERING
MICHAEL HEISLER

DARK HORSE BOOKS®

PUBLISHER
MIKE RICHARDSON

ASSISTANT EDITOR
BRENDAN WRIGHT

EDITOR
DAVE MARSHALL

DESIGNER
STEPHEN REICHERT

MASS EFFECT: INVASION

This volume collects issues #1 through #4 of the Dark Horse comic-book series *Mass Effect: Invasion*, as well as a short story from the Dark Horse Digital Store.

To my gaming group—Bob, Robbie, and Michael—with thanks for their support over the years.
—**John Jackson Miller**

For my Dad! I couldn't be more thankful to the man who taught me curiosity and love for creation and art! Thank you for always being so present in my life! This book, like my whole career, is for you!
—**Omar Francia**

For my girls, Megan and Audrey. I love you.
—**Michael Atiyeh**

Special thanks to BioWare, including:
DEREK WATTS, Art Director; CASEY HUDSON, Executive Producer; AARYN FLYNN, Studio GM,
BioWare Edmonton; RAY MUZYKA and GREG ZESCHUK, BioWare Co-Founders

Published by Dark Horse Books
A division of Dark Horse Comics, Inc.
10956 SE Main Street | Milwaukie, OR 97222

DarkHorse.com | MassEffect.com

LIBRARY OF CONGRESS CATALOGING-IN-PUBLICATION DATA

Walters, Mac.
Mass effect : invasion / story, Mac Walters ; script, John Jackson Miller ; art, Omar Francia ; colors, Michael Atiyeh ; lettering, Michael Heisler ; cover art, Massimo Carnevale ; back cover art, Paul Renaud. -- 1st ed.
p. cm.
ISBN 978-1-59582-867-5
1. Graphic novels. I. Miller, John Jackson. II. Francia, Omar. III. Atiyeh, Michael. IV. Title. V. Title: Invasion.
PN6727.W277M35 2012
741.5'943--dc23
2011040611

First standard edition: April 2012
ISBN 978-1-59582-867-5

Custom hardcover edition: April 2012
ISBN 978-1-59582-943-6

1 3 5 7 9 10 8 6 4 2
Printed at Midas Printing International, Ltd., Huizhou, China

MIKE RICHARDSON President and Publisher • NEIL HANKERSON Executive Vice President • TOM WEDDLE Chief Financial Officer • RANDY STRADLEY Vice President of Publishing • MICHAEL MARTENS Vice President of Book Trade Sales • ANITA NELSON Vice President of Business Affairs • MICHA HERSHMAN Vice President of Marketing • DAVID SCROGGY Vice President of Product Development • DALE LAFOUNTAIN Vice President of Information Technology • DARLENE VOGEL Senior Director of Print, Design, and Production • KEN LIZZI General Counsel • DAVEY ESTRADA Editorial Director • SCOTT ALLIE Senior Managing Editor • CHRIS WARNER Senior Books Editor • DIANA SCHUTZ Executive Editor • CARY GRAZZINI Director of Print and Development • LIA RIBACCHI Art Director • CARA NIECE Director of Scheduling

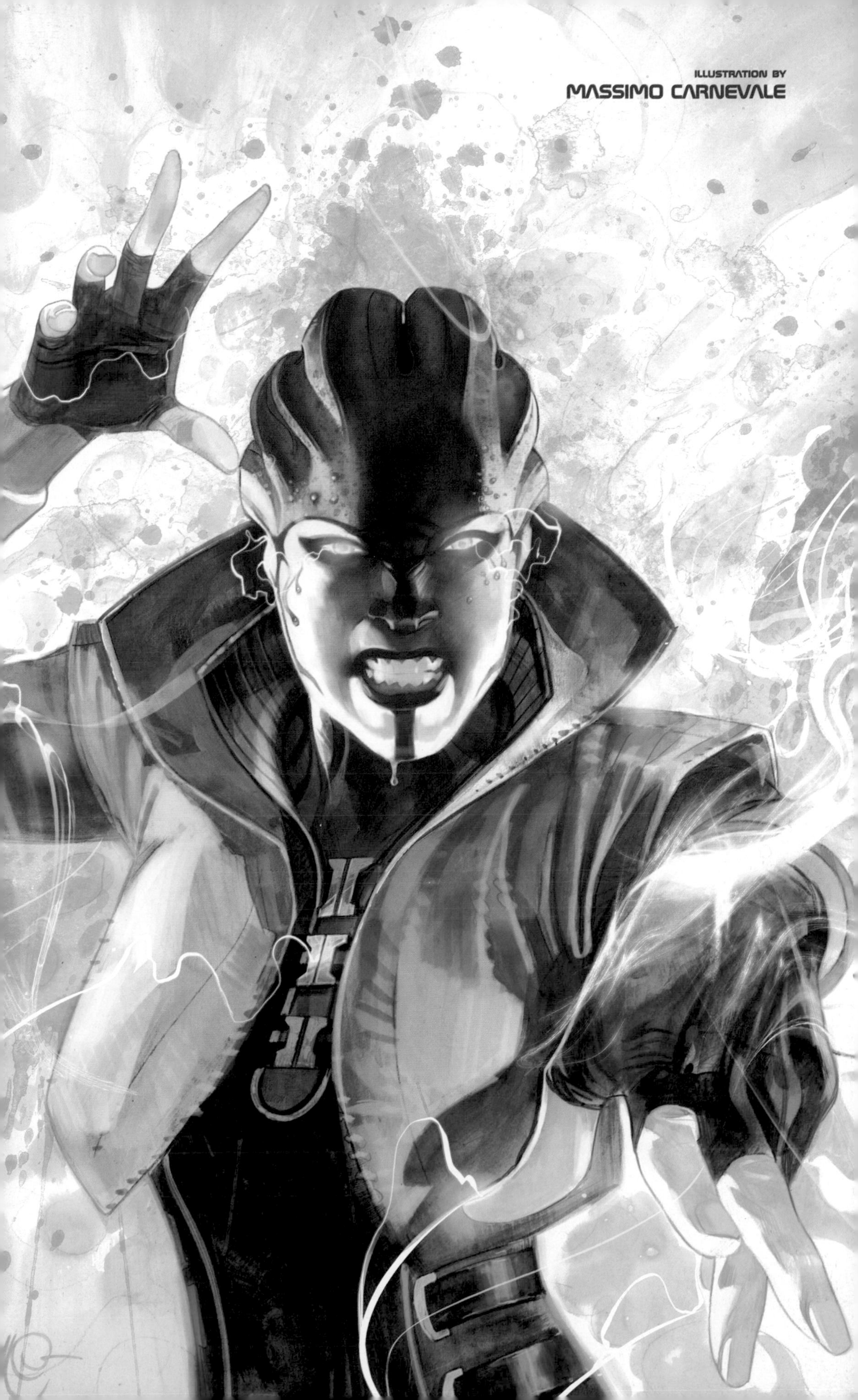

ILLUSTRATION BY
MASSIMO CARNEVALE

Omega stands alone. Beyond the reach of galactic politics, the space station has provided a home for commerce unwelcome elsewhere for years—all its criminal gangs fearing its leader, the powerful asari biotic Aria T'Loak.

But there are those who do not respect Aria's rule—or anything else. Following Commander Shepard's successful expedition against the mysterious Collector menace, the prohuman organization Cerberus establishes bases beyond the Omega 4 relay to investigate the alien threat.

When Cerberus's experiments with Reaper technologies go wrong, a new threat emerges from the relay, ready to wreak destruction on an unsuspecting galaxy. The first stop on the path to utter destruction: Omega, which stands, as always, alone . . .

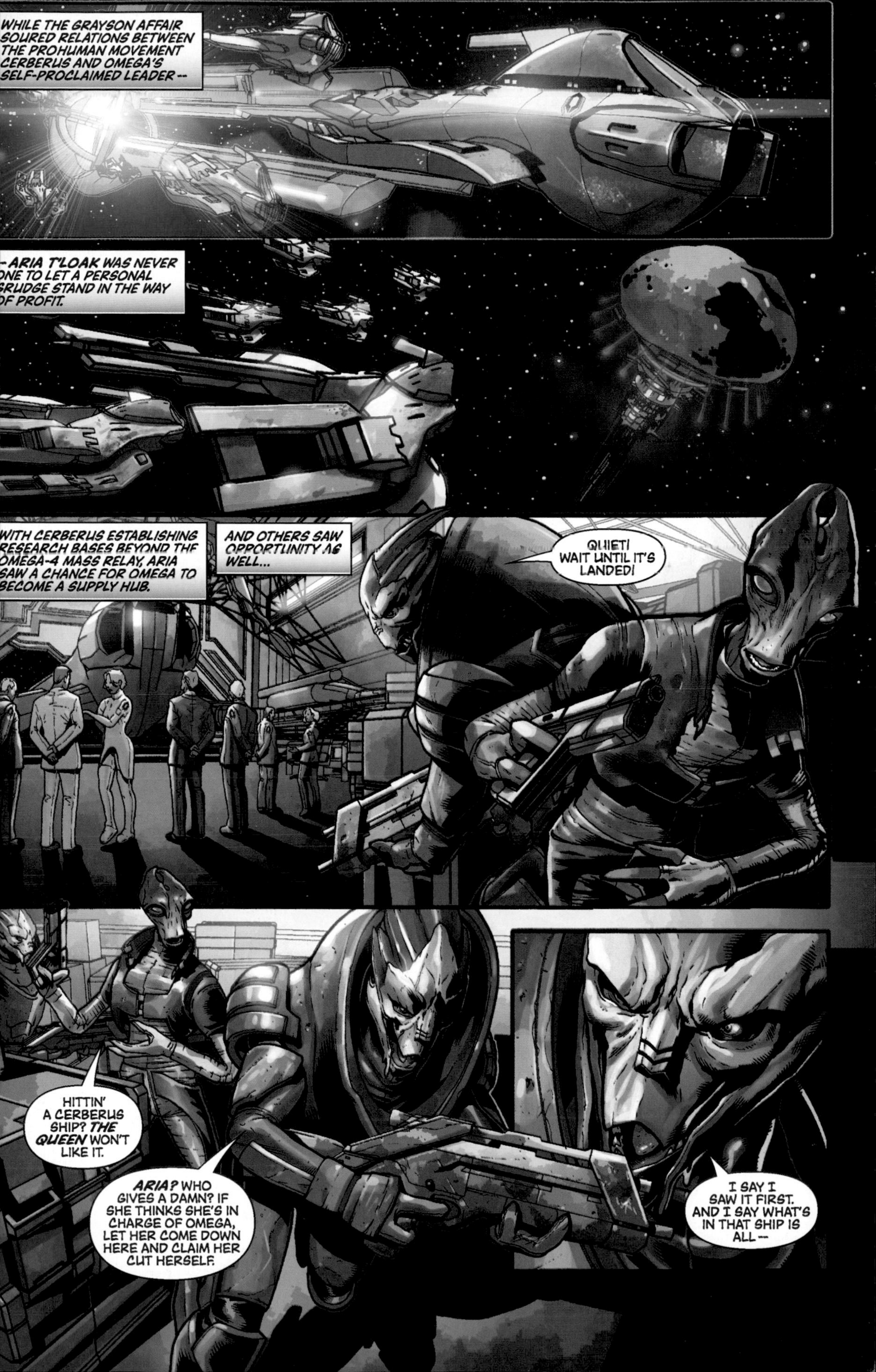

WHILE THE GRAYSON AFFAIR SOURED RELATIONS BETWEEN THE PROHUMAN MOVEMENT CERBERUS AND OMEGA'S SELF-PROCLAIMED LEADER --
-- ARIA T'LOAK WAS NEVER ONE TO LET A PERSONAL GRUDGE STAND IN THE WAY OF PROFIT.
WITH CERBERUS ESTABLISHING RESEARCH BASES BEYOND THE OMEGA-4 MASS RELAY, ARIA SAW A CHANCE FOR OMEGA TO BECOME A SUPPLY HUB.
AND OTHERS SAW OPPORTUNITY AS WELL...
QUIET! WAIT UNTIL IT'S LANDED!
HITTIN' A CERBERUS SHIP? THE QUEEN WON'T LIKE IT.
ARIA? WHO GIVES A DAMN? IF SHE THINKS SHE'S IN CHARGE OF OMEGA, LET HER COME DOWN HERE AND CLAIM HER CUT HERSELF.
I SAY I SAW IT FIRST. AND I SAY WHAT'S IN THAT SHIP IS ALL --

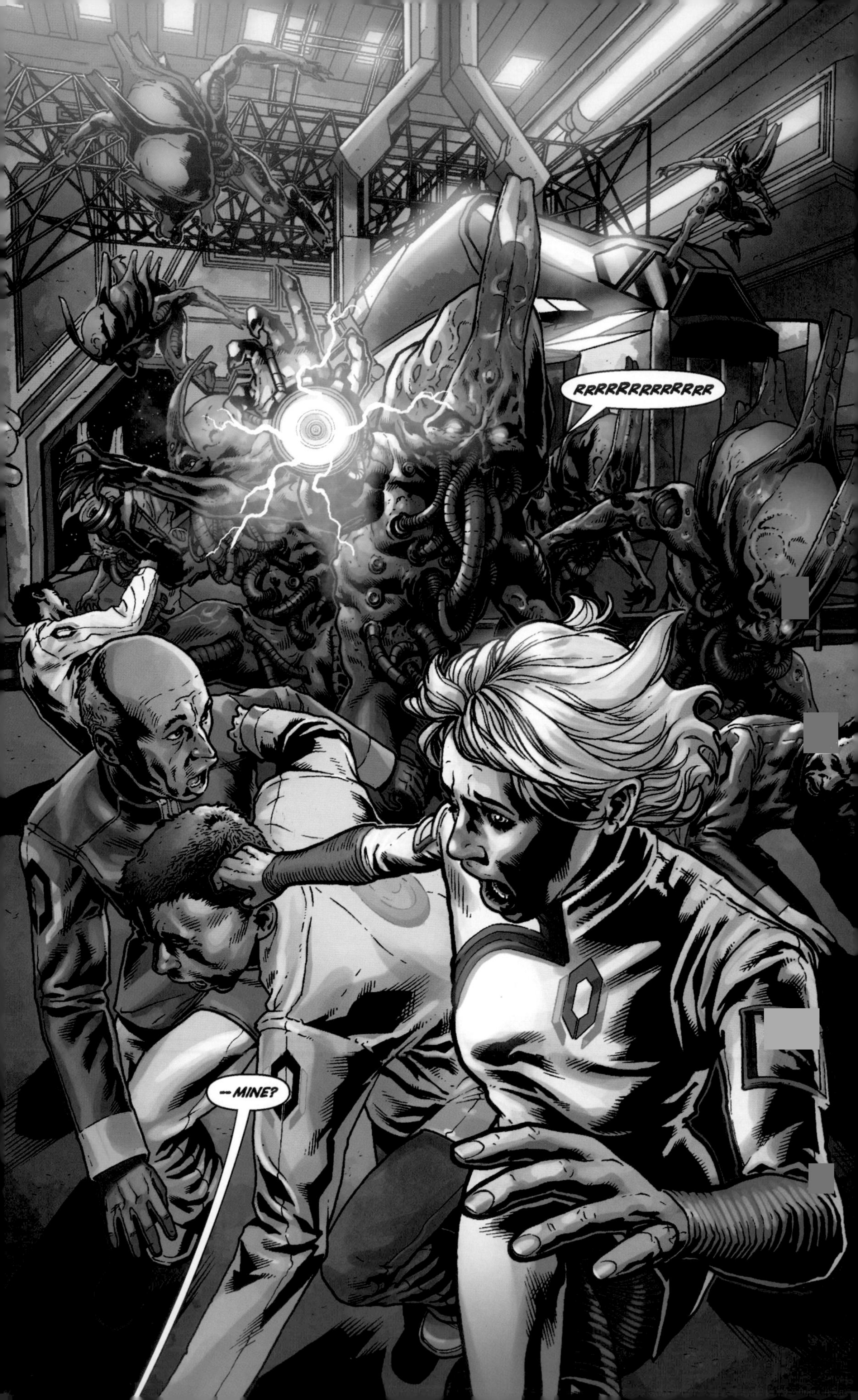
RRRRRRRRRRRR
--MINE?

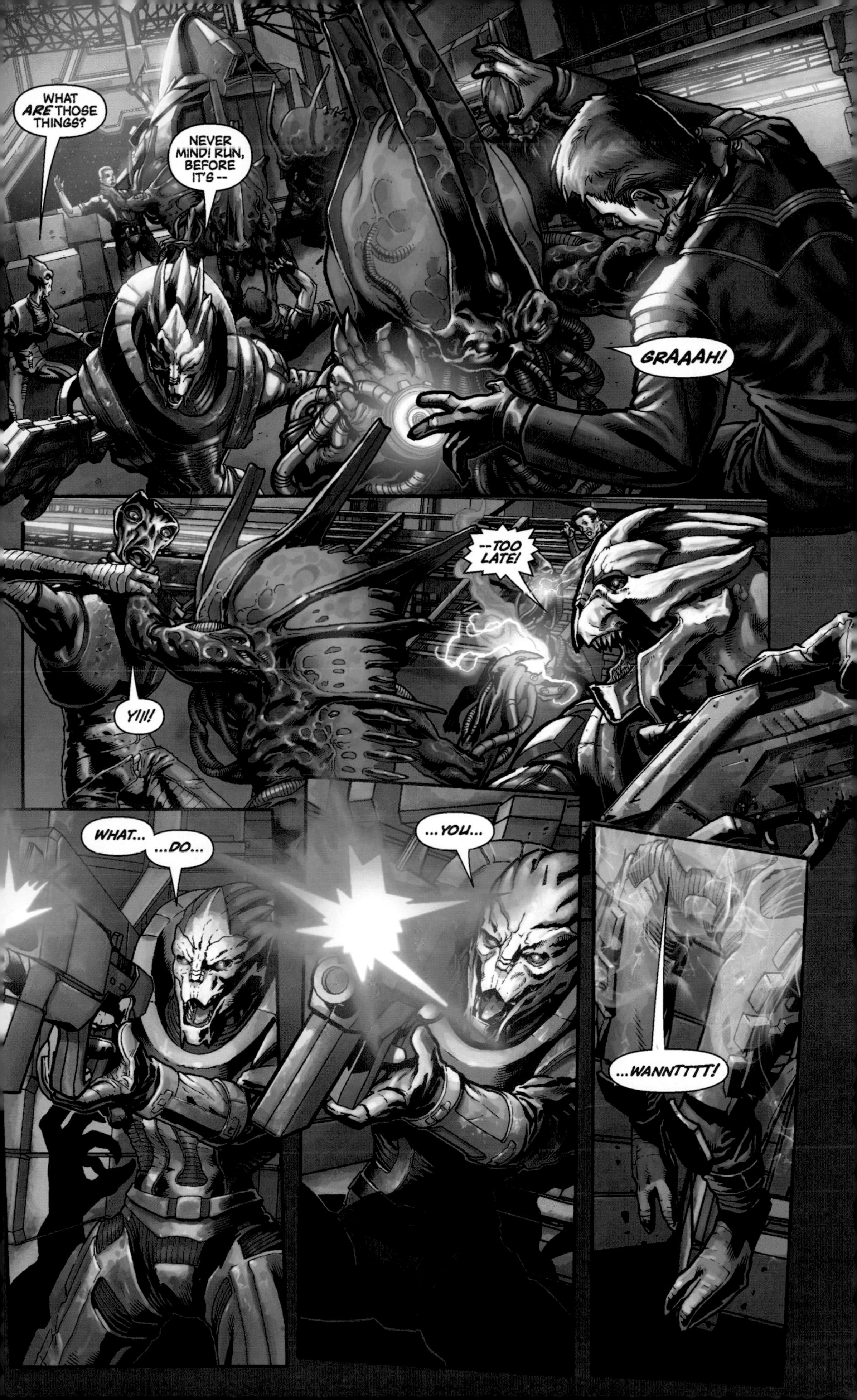
WHAT *ARE* THOSE THINGS?
NEVER MIND! RUN, BEFORE IT'S --
GRAAAH!
--TOO LATE!
YIII!
WHAT...
...DO...
...YOU...
...WANNTTTT!

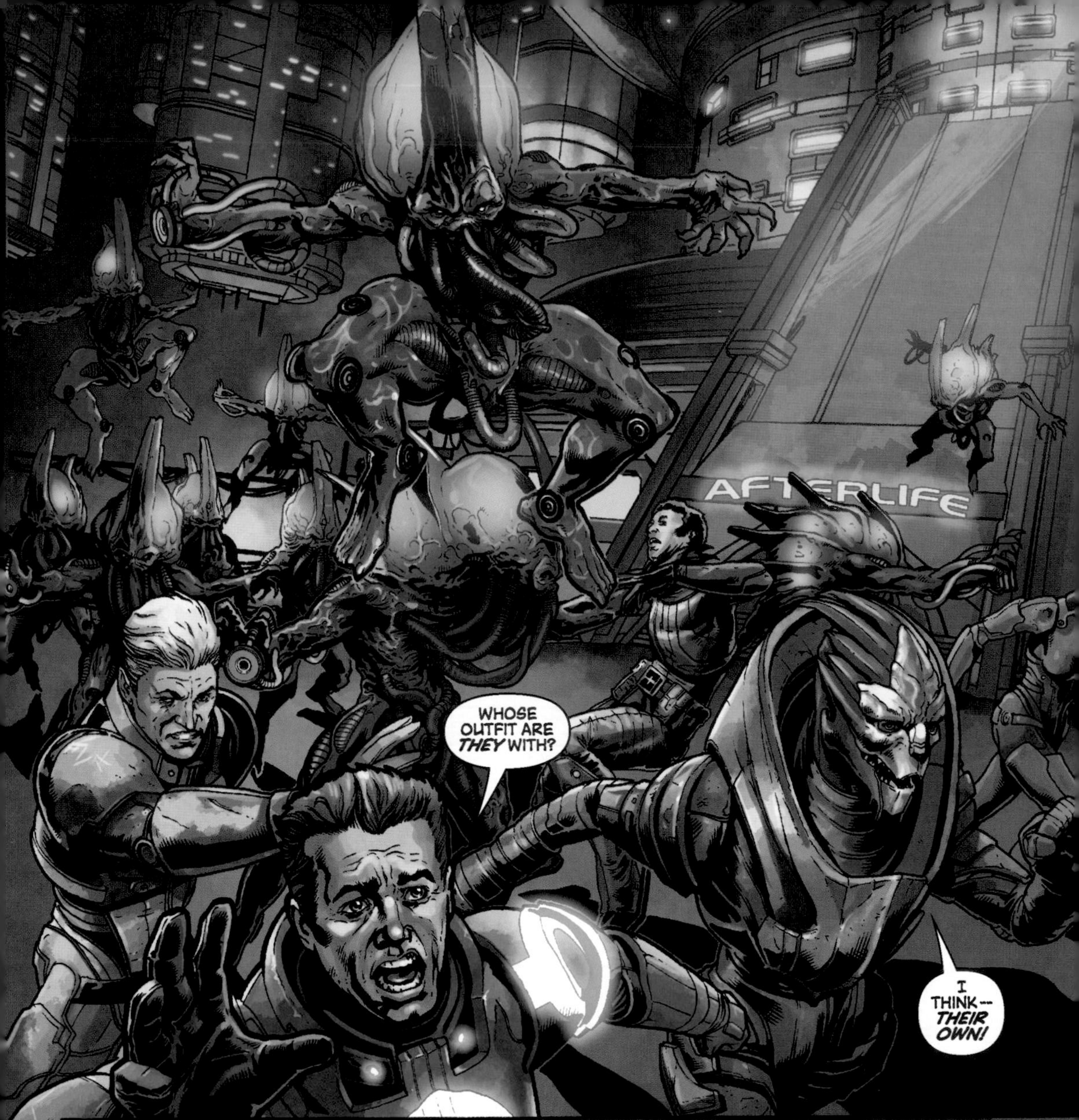
AFTERLIFE
WHOSE OUTFIT ARE *THEY* WITH?
I THINK-- *THEIR OWN!*
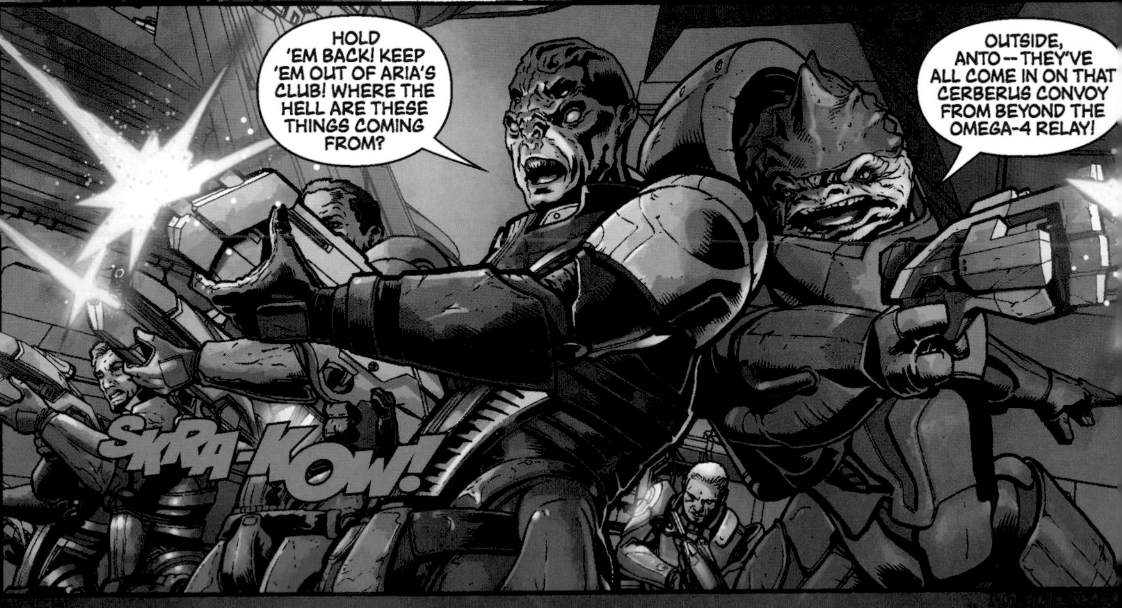
HOLD 'EM BACK! KEEP 'EM OUT OF ARIA'S CLUB! WHERE THE HELL ARE THESE THINGS COMING FROM?
OUTSIDE, ANTO -- THEY'VE ALL COME IN ON THAT CERBERUS CONVOY FROM BEYOND THE OMEGA-4 RELAY!
SKRA-KOW!

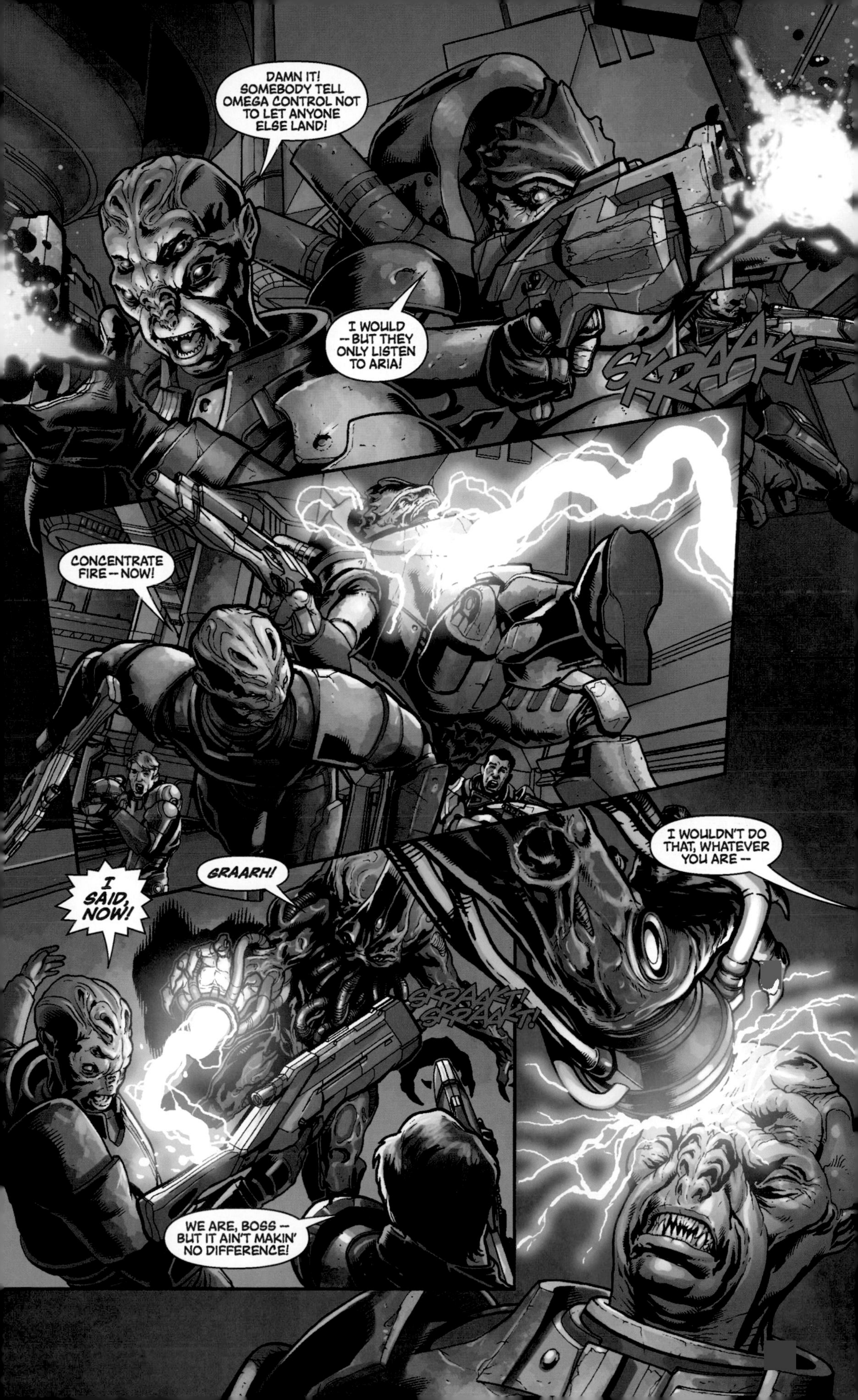
DAMN IT! SOMEBODY TELL OMEGA CONTROL NOT TO LET ANYONE ELSE LAND!
I WOULD --BUT THEY ONLY LISTEN TO ARIA!
SKRAAKT
CONCENTRATE FIRE--NOW!
I WOULDN'T DO THAT, WHATEVER YOU ARE--
GRAARH!
I SAID, NOW!
SKRAAKT! SKRAAKT!
WE ARE, BOSS -- BUT IT AIN'T MAKIN' NO DIFFERENCE!

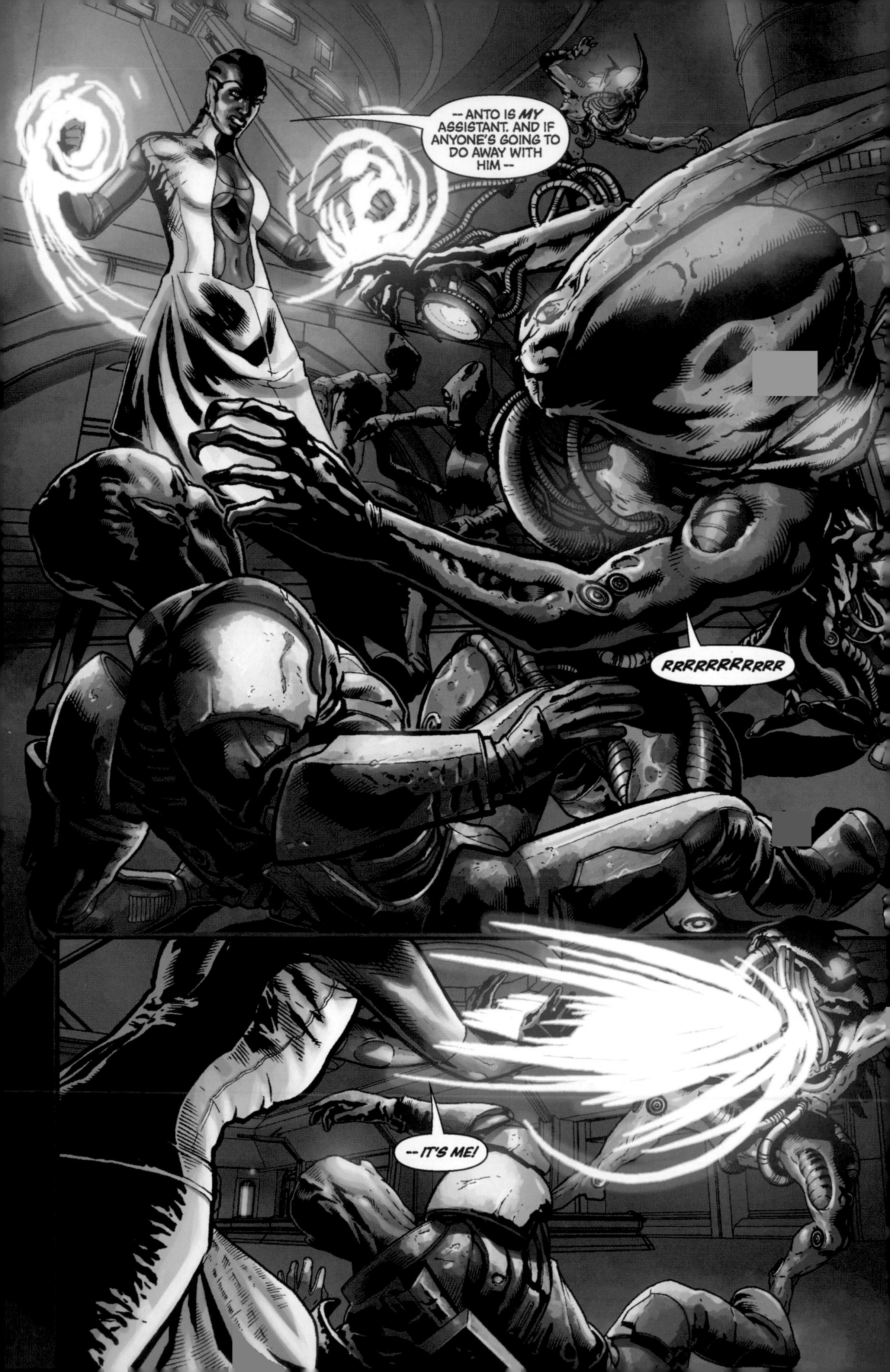
-- ANTO IS MY ASSISTANT. AND IF ANYONE'S GOING TO DO AWAY WITH HIM --
RRRRRRRRRRR
-- IT'S ME!

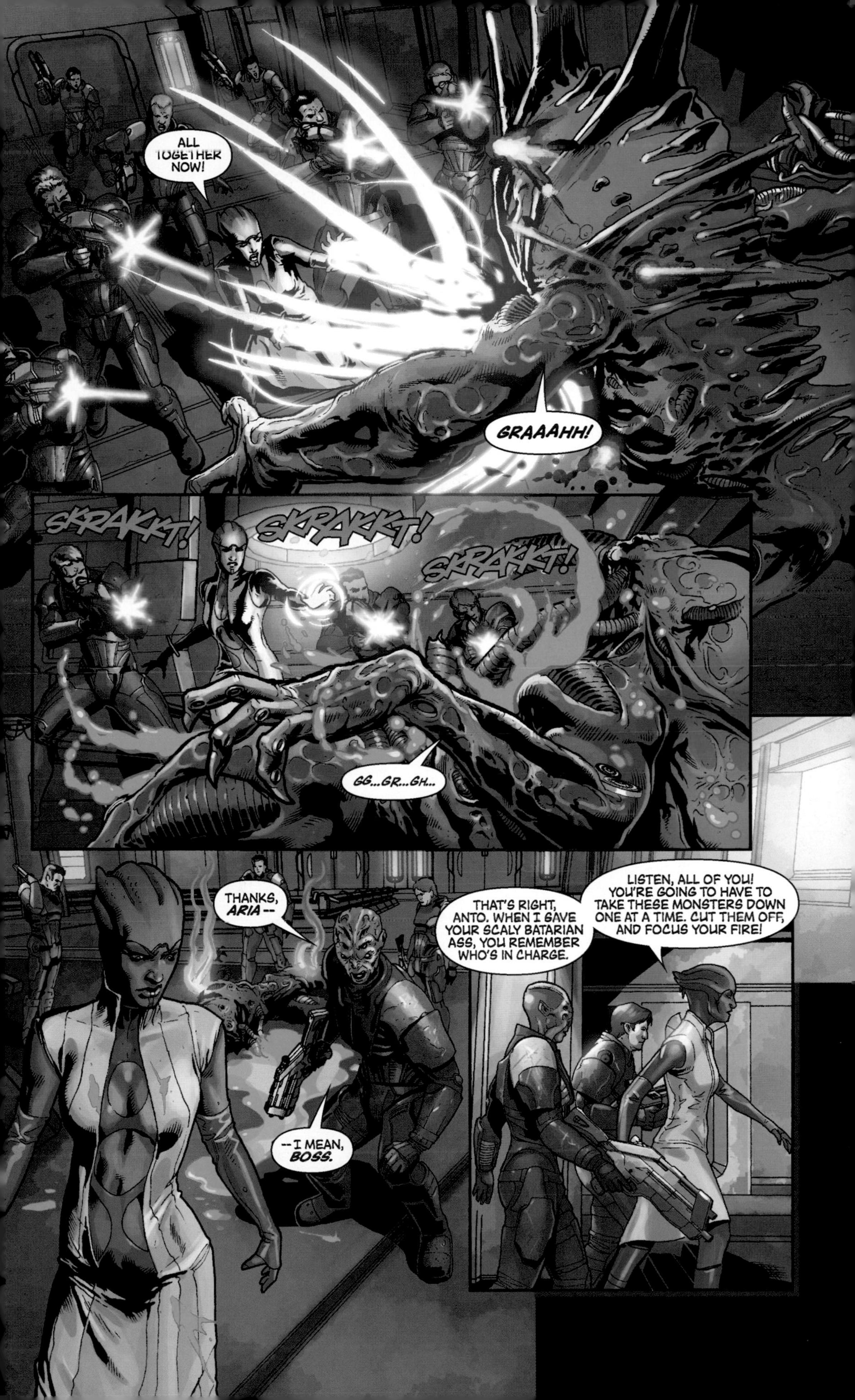
ALL TOGETHER NOW!
GRAAAHH!
SKRAKKT!
SKRAKKT!
SKRAKKT!
GG...GR...GH...
THANKS, ARIA--
--I MEAN, BOSS.
THAT'S RIGHT, ANTO. WHEN I GAVE YOUR SCALY BATARIAN ASS, YOU REMEMBER WHO'S IN CHARGE.
LISTEN, ALL OF YOU! YOU'RE GOING TO HAVE TO TAKE THESE MONSTERS DOWN ONE AT A TIME. CUT THEM OFF, AND FOCUS YOUR FIRE!

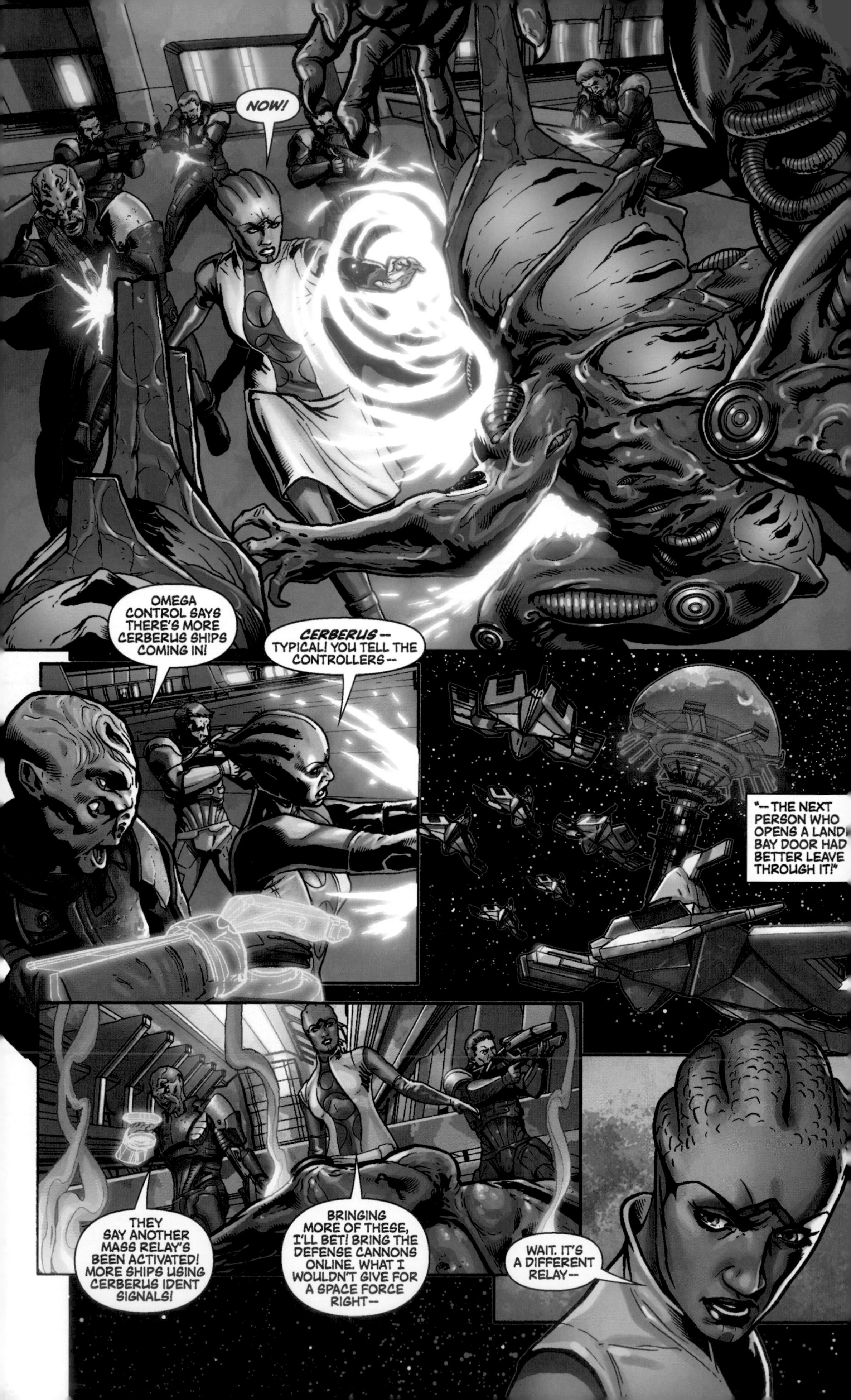
NOW!
OMEGA CONTROL SAYS THERE'S MORE CERBERUS SHIPS COMING IN!
CERBERUS -- TYPICAL! YOU TELL THE CONTROLLERS --
"-- THE NEXT PERSON WHO OPENS A LAND BAY DOOR HAD BETTER LEAVE THROUGH IT!"
THEY SAY ANOTHER MASS RELAY'S BEEN ACTIVATED! MORE SHIPS USING CERBERUS IDENT SIGNALS!
BRINGING MORE OF THESE, I'LL BET! BRING THE DEFENSE CANNONS ONLINE. WHAT I WOULDN'T GIVE FOR A SPACE FORCE RIGHT--
WAIT. IT'S A DIFFERENT RELAY--

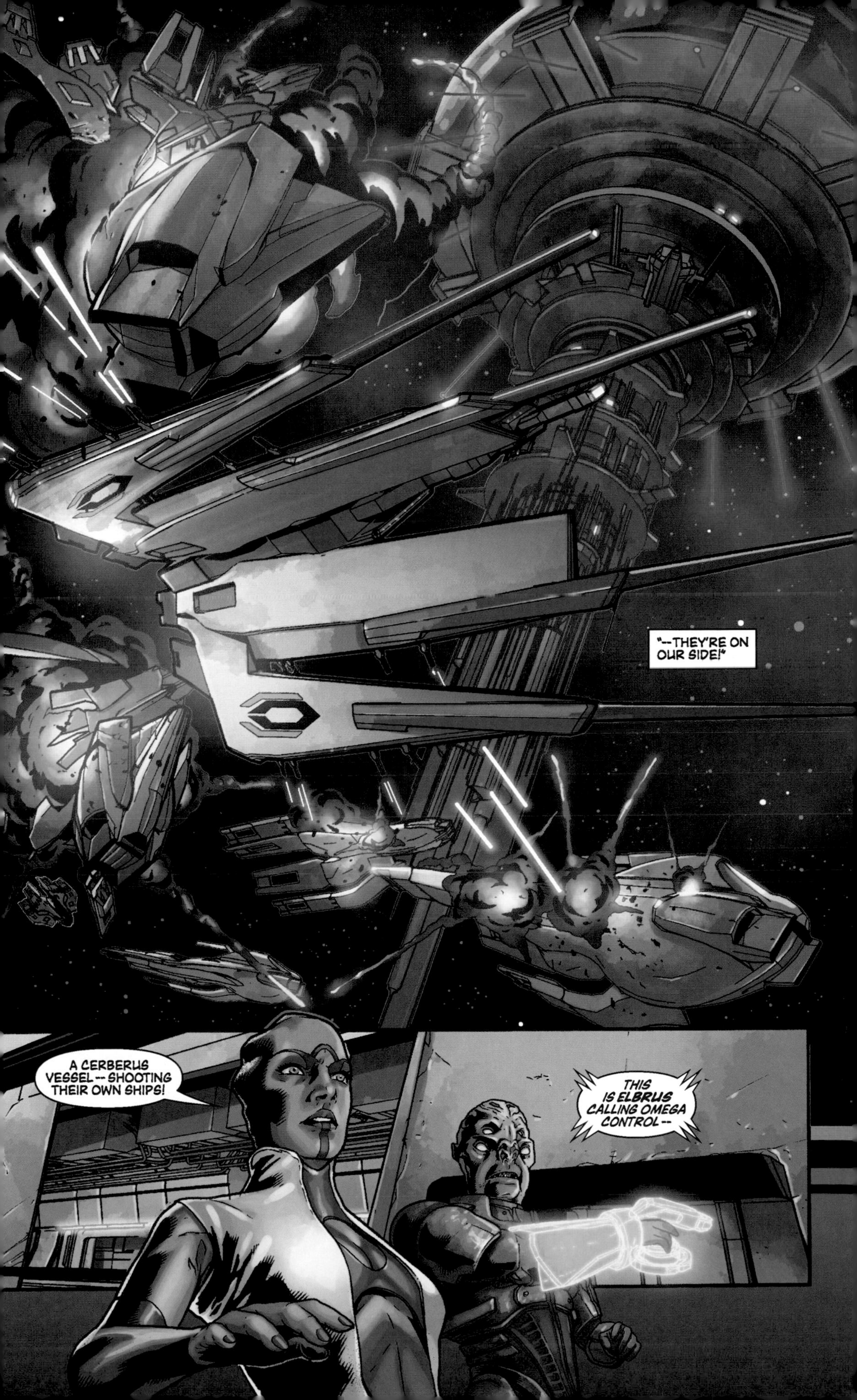
"--THEY'RE ON OUR SIDE!"
A CERBERUS VESSEL -- SHOOTING THEIR OWN SHIPS!
THIS IS ELBRUS CALLING OMEGA CONTROL --

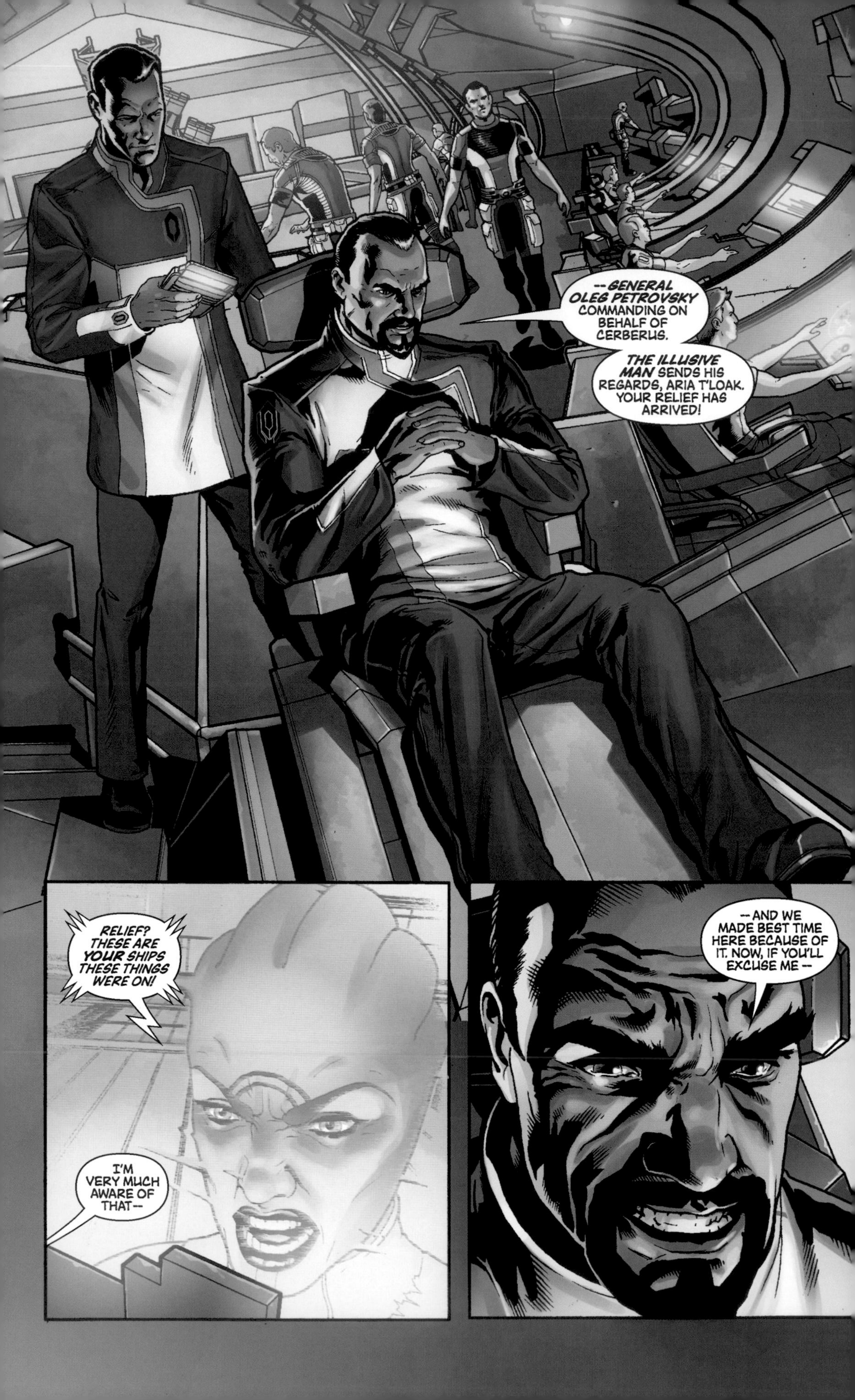
--GENERAL OLEG PETROVSKY COMMANDING ON BEHALF OF CERBERUS.
THE ILLUSIVE MAN SENDS HIS REGARDS, ARIA T'LOAK. YOUR RELIEF HAS ARRIVED!
RELIEF? THESE ARE YOUR SHIPS THESE THINGS WERE ON!
I'M VERY MUCH AWARE OF THAT--
--AND WE MADE BEST TIME HERE BECAUSE OF IT. NOW, IF YOU'LL EXCUSE ME --

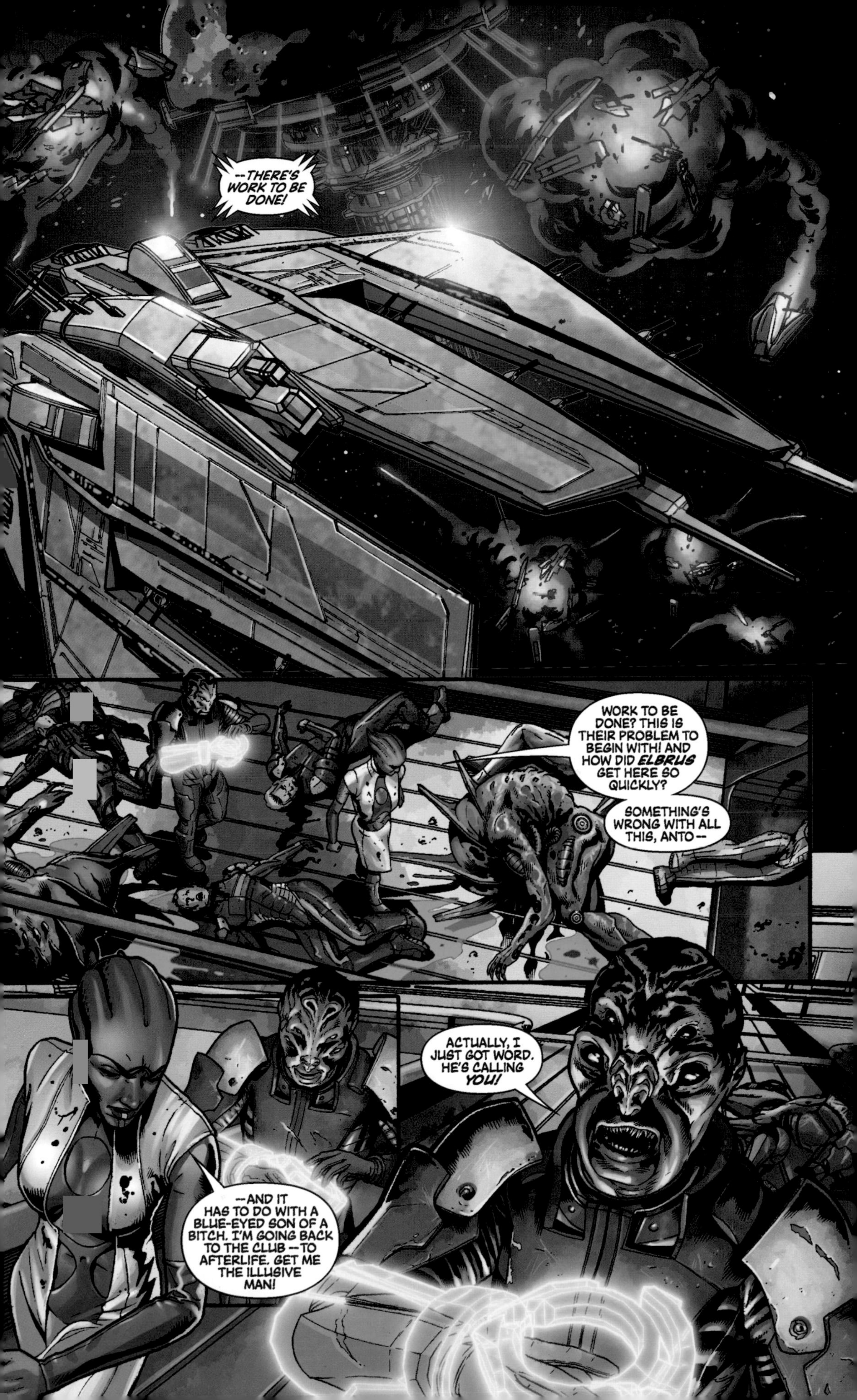
--THERE'S WORK TO BE DONE!
WORK TO BE DONE? THIS IS THEIR PROBLEM TO BEGIN WITH! AND HOW DID ELBRUS GET HERE SO QUICKLY?
SOMETHING'S WRONG WITH ALL THIS, ANTO--
ACTUALLY, I JUST GOT WORD. HE'S CALLING YOU!
--AND IT HAS TO DO WITH A BLUE-EYED SON OF A BITCH. I'M GOING BACK TO THE CLUB --TO AFTERLIFE. GET ME THE ILLUSIVE MAN!

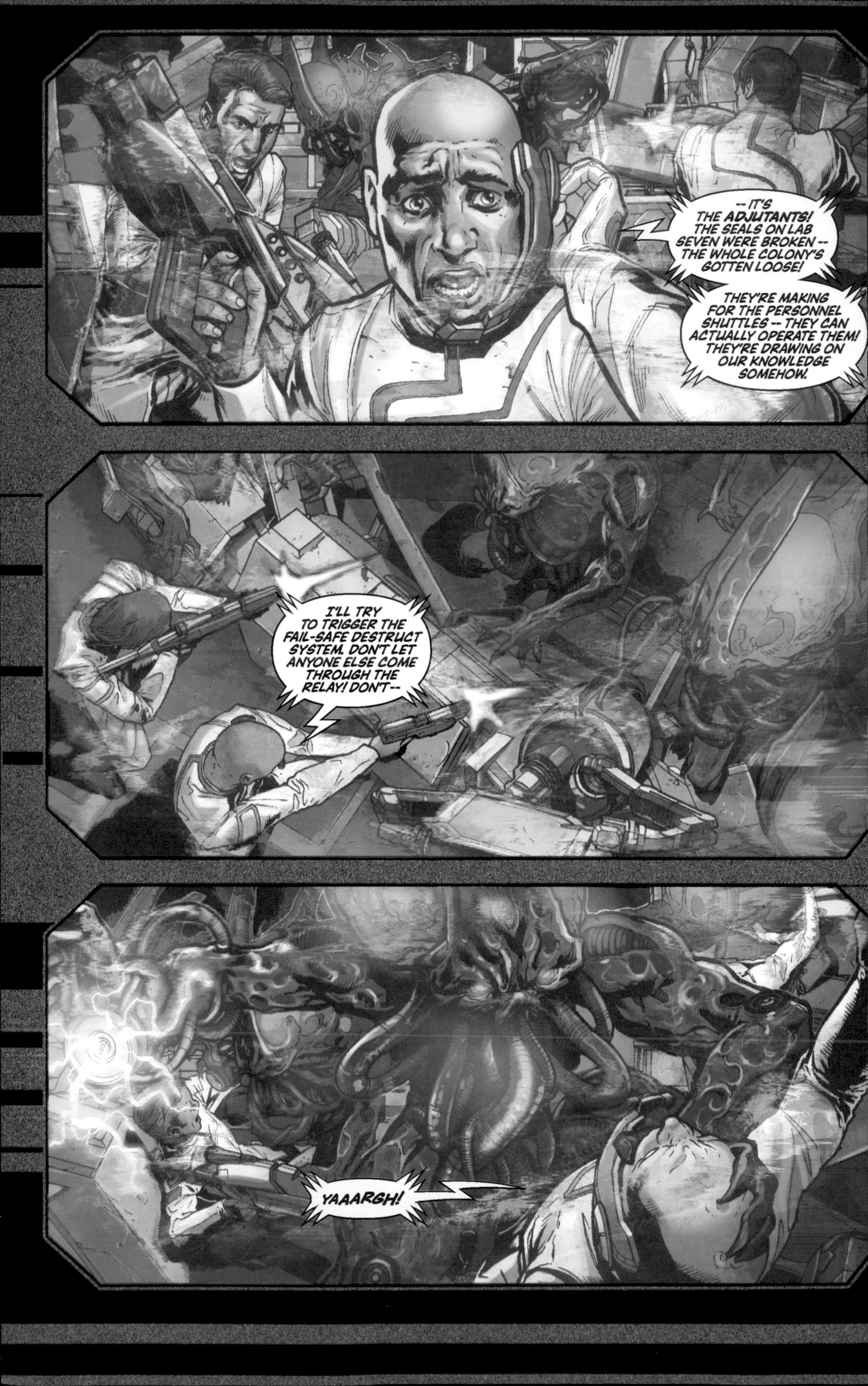
-- IT'S THE ADJUTANTS! THE SEALS ON LAB SEVEN WERE BROKEN -- THE WHOLE COLONY'S GOTTEN LOOSE!
THEY'RE MAKING FOR THE PERSONNEL SHUTTLES -- THEY CAN ACTUALLY OPERATE THEM! THEY'RE DRAWING ON OUR KNOWLEDGE SOMEHOW.
I'LL TRY TO TRIGGER THE FAIL-SAFE DESTRUCT SYSTEM. DON'T LET ANYONE ELSE COME THROUGH THE RELAY! DON'T--
YAAARGH!

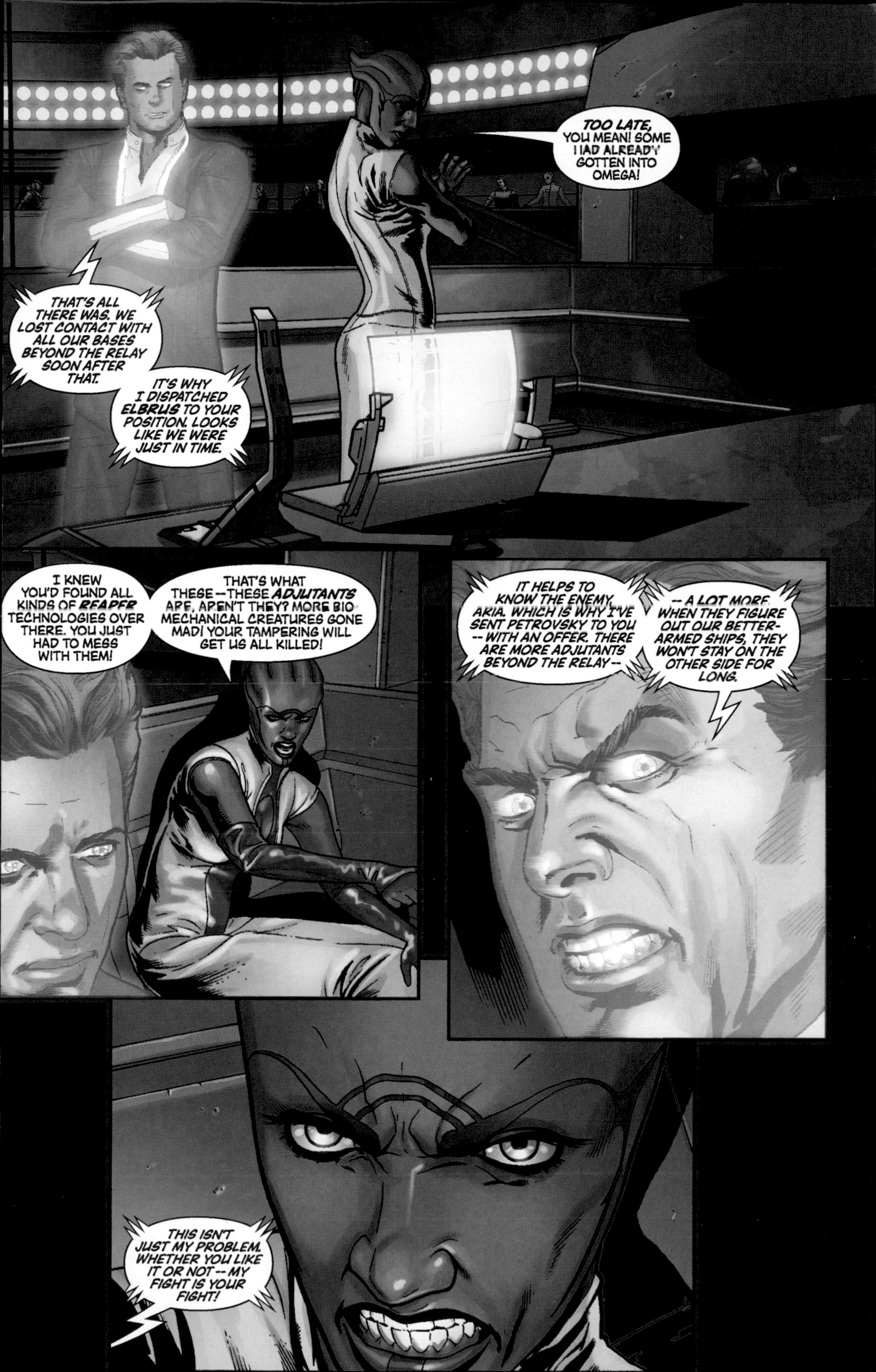
THAT'S ALL THERE WAS. WE LOST CONTACT WITH ALL OUR BASES BEYOND THE RELAY SOON AFTER THAT.
TOO LATE, YOU MEAN! SOME HAD ALREADY GOTTEN INTO OMEGA!
IT'S WHY I DISPATCHED ELBRUS TO YOUR POSITION. LOOKS LIKE WE WERE JUST IN TIME.
I KNEW YOU'D FOUND ALL KINDS OF REAPER TECHNOLOGIES OVER THERE. YOU JUST HAD TO MESS WITH THEM!
THAT'S WHAT THESE -- THESE ADJUTANTS ARE, AREN'T THEY? MORE BIO MECHANICAL CREATURES GONE MAD! YOUR TAMPERING WILL GET US ALL KILLED!
IT HELPS TO KNOW THE ENEMY, ARIA. WHICH IS WHY I'VE SENT PETROVSKY TO YOU -- WITH AN OFFER. THERE ARE MORE ADJUTANTS BEYOND THE RELAY --
-- A LOT MORE. WHEN THEY FIGURE OUT OUR BETTER-ARMED SHIPS, THEY WON'T STAY ON THE OTHER SIDE FOR LONG.
THIS ISN'T JUST MY PROBLEM. WHETHER YOU LIKE IT OR NOT -- MY FIGHT IS YOUR FIGHT!

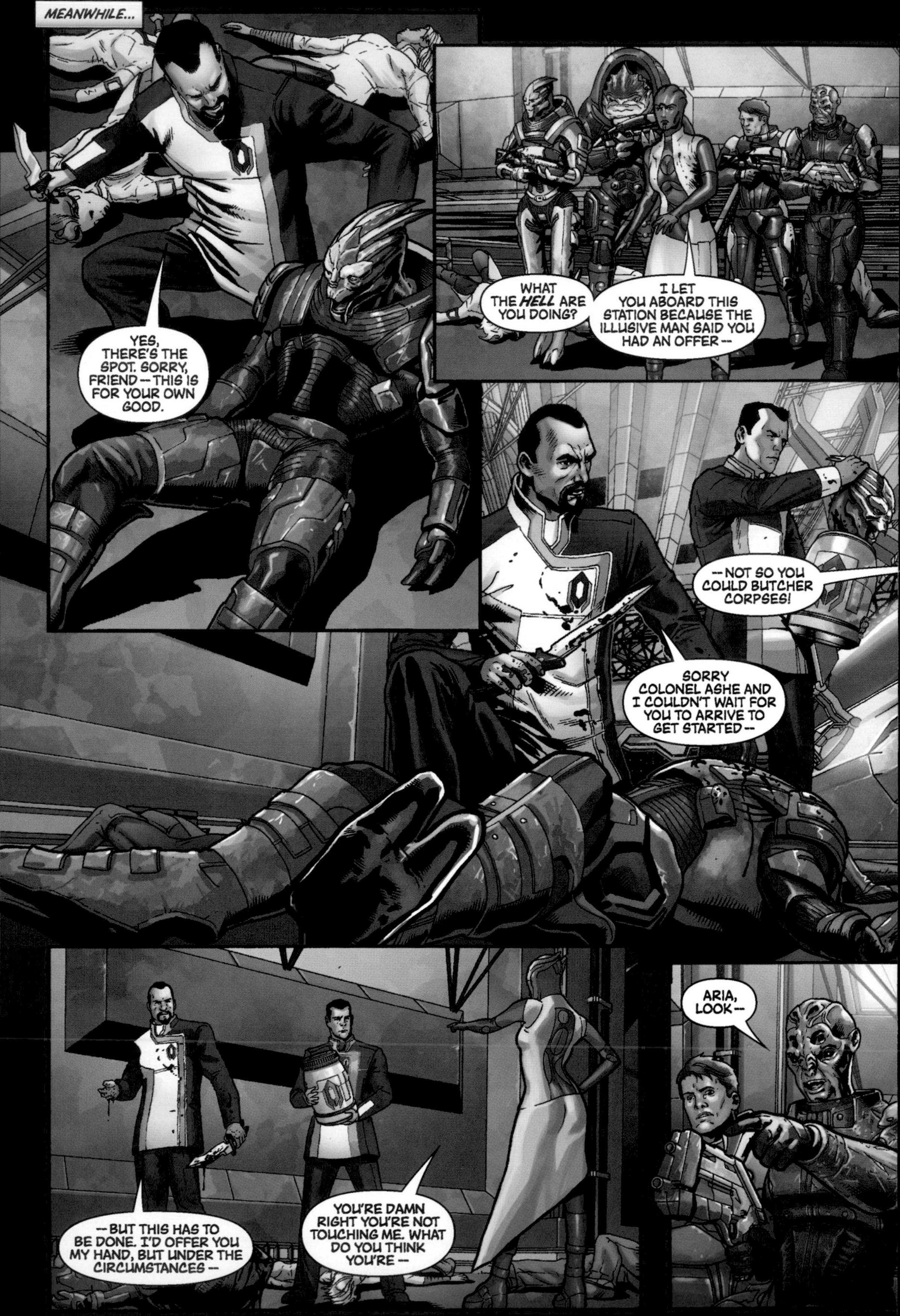
MEANWHILE...
YES, THERE'S THE SPOT. SORRY, FRIEND -- THIS IS FOR YOUR OWN GOOD.
WHAT THE HELL ARE YOU DOING?
I LET YOU ABOARD THIS STATION BECAUSE THE ILLUSIVE MAN SAID YOU HAD AN OFFER --
-- NOT SO YOU COULD BUTCHER CORPSES!
SORRY COLONEL ASHE AND I COULDN'T WAIT FOR YOU TO ARRIVE TO GET STARTED --
-- BUT THIS HAS TO BE DONE. I'D OFFER YOU MY HAND, BUT UNDER THE CIRCUMSTANCES --
YOU'RE DAMN RIGHT YOU'RE NOT TOUCHING ME. WHAT DO YOU THINK YOU'RE --
ARIA, LOOK --

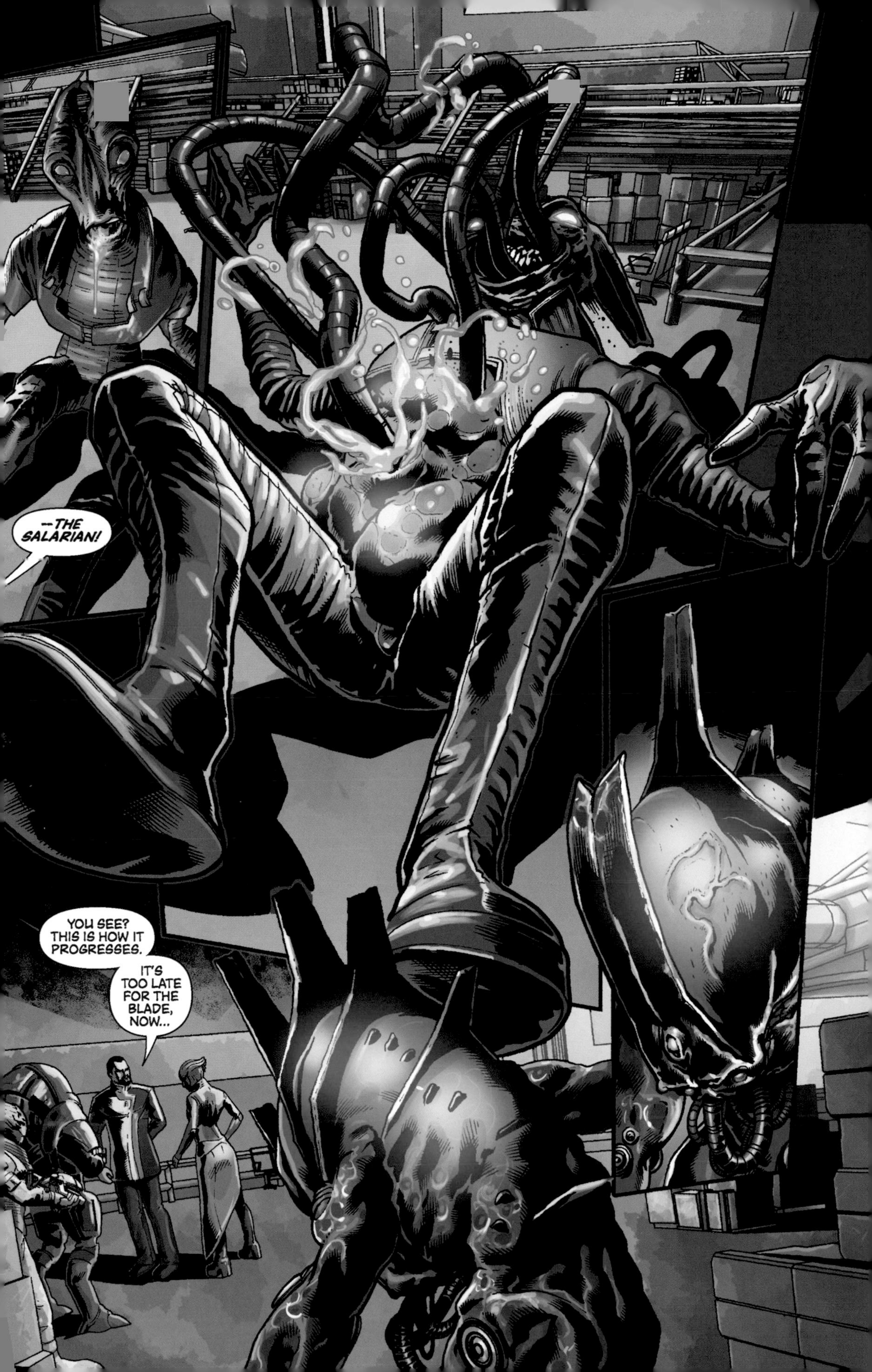
--THE SALARIAN!
YOU SEE? THIS IS HOW IT PROGRESSES.
IT'S TOO LATE FOR THE BLADE, NOW...

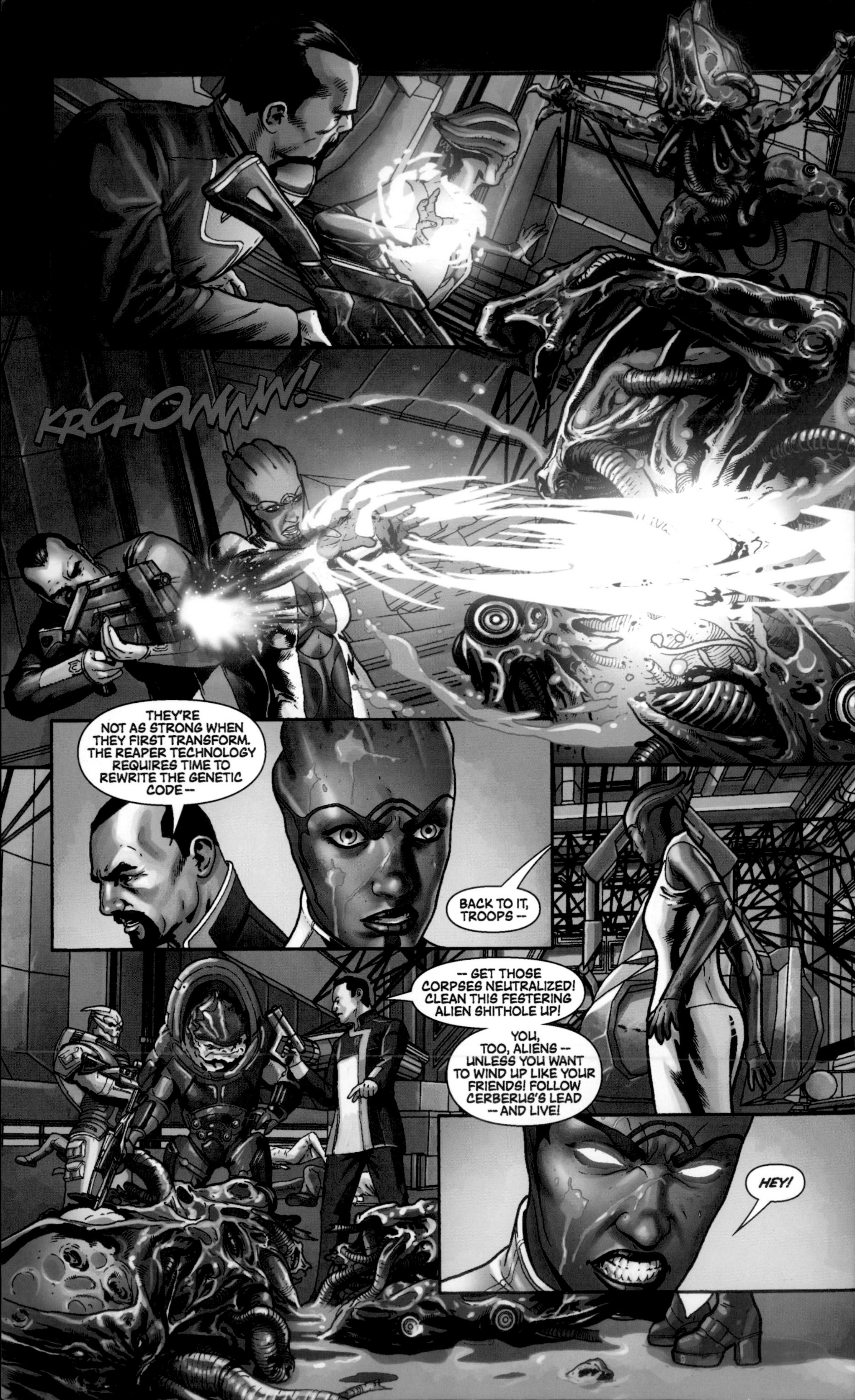
KRCHOWWW!
THEY'RE NOT AS STRONG WHEN THEY FIRST TRANSFORM. THE REAPER TECHNOLOGY REQUIRES TIME TO REWRITE THE GENETIC CODE --
BACK TO IT, TROOPS --
-- GET THOSE CORPSES NEUTRALIZED! CLEAN THIS FESTERING ALIEN SHITHOLE UP!
YOU, TOO, ALIENS -- UNLESS YOU WANT TO WIND UP LIKE YOUR FRIENDS! FOLLOW CERBERUS'S LEAD -- AND LIVE!
HEY!

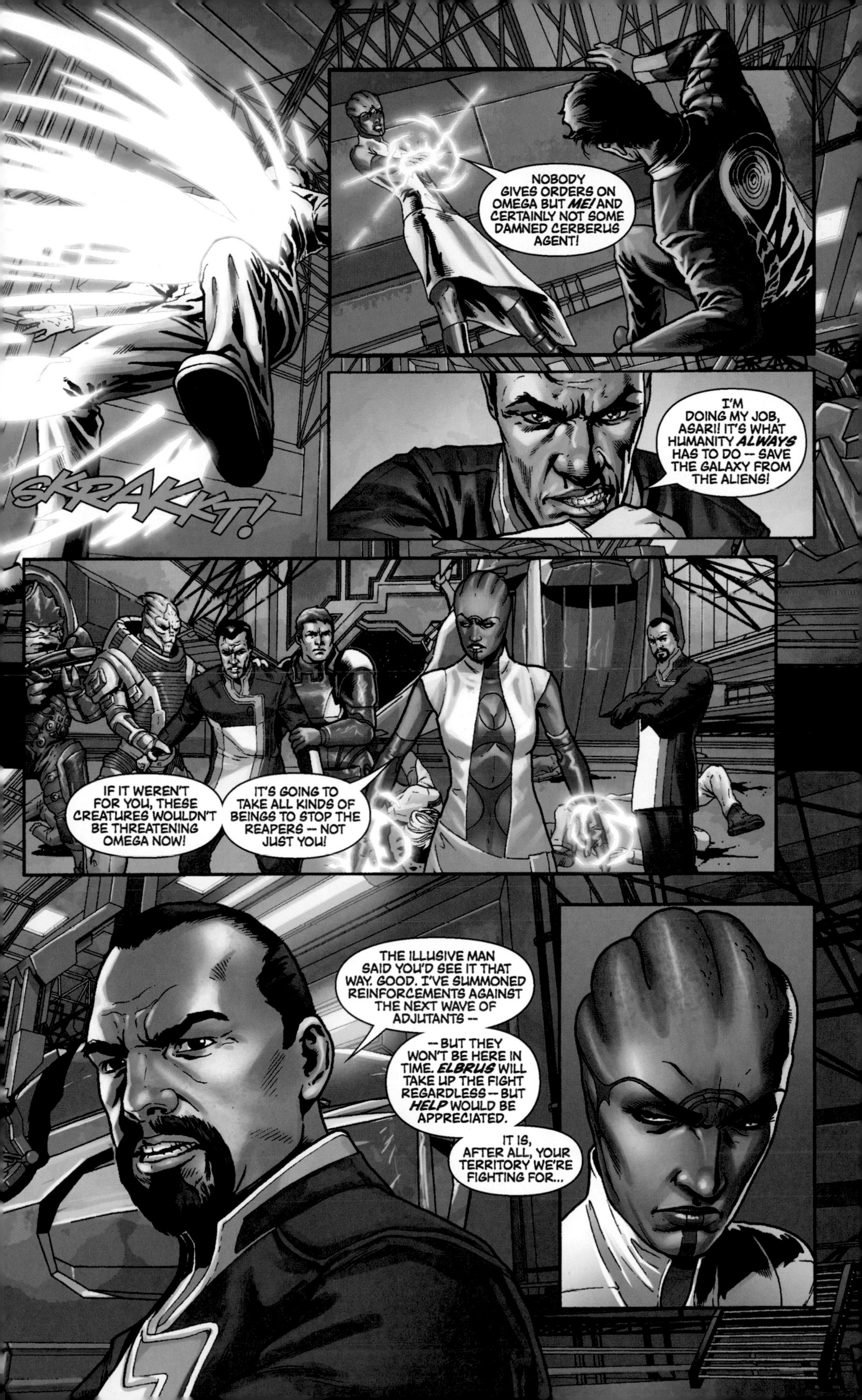
NOBODY GIVES ORDERS ON OMEGA BUT ME! AND CERTAINLY NOT SOME DAMNED CERBERUS AGENT!
SKRAKKT!
I'M DOING MY JOB, ASARI! IT'S WHAT HUMANITY ALWAYS HAS TO DO -- SAVE THE GALAXY FROM THE ALIENS!
IF IT WEREN'T FOR YOU, THESE CREATURES WOULDN'T BE THREATENING OMEGA NOW!
IT'S GOING TO TAKE ALL KINDS OF BEINGS TO STOP THE REAPERS -- NOT JUST YOU!
THE ILLUSIVE MAN SAID YOU'D SEE IT THAT WAY. GOOD. I'VE SUMMONED REINFORCEMENTS AGAINST THE NEXT WAVE OF ADJUTANTS --
-- BUT THEY WON'T BE HERE IN TIME. ELBRUS WILL TAKE UP THE FIGHT REGARDLESS -- BUT HELP WOULD BE APPRECIATED.
IT IS, AFTER ALL, YOUR TERRITORY WE'RE FIGHTING FOR...

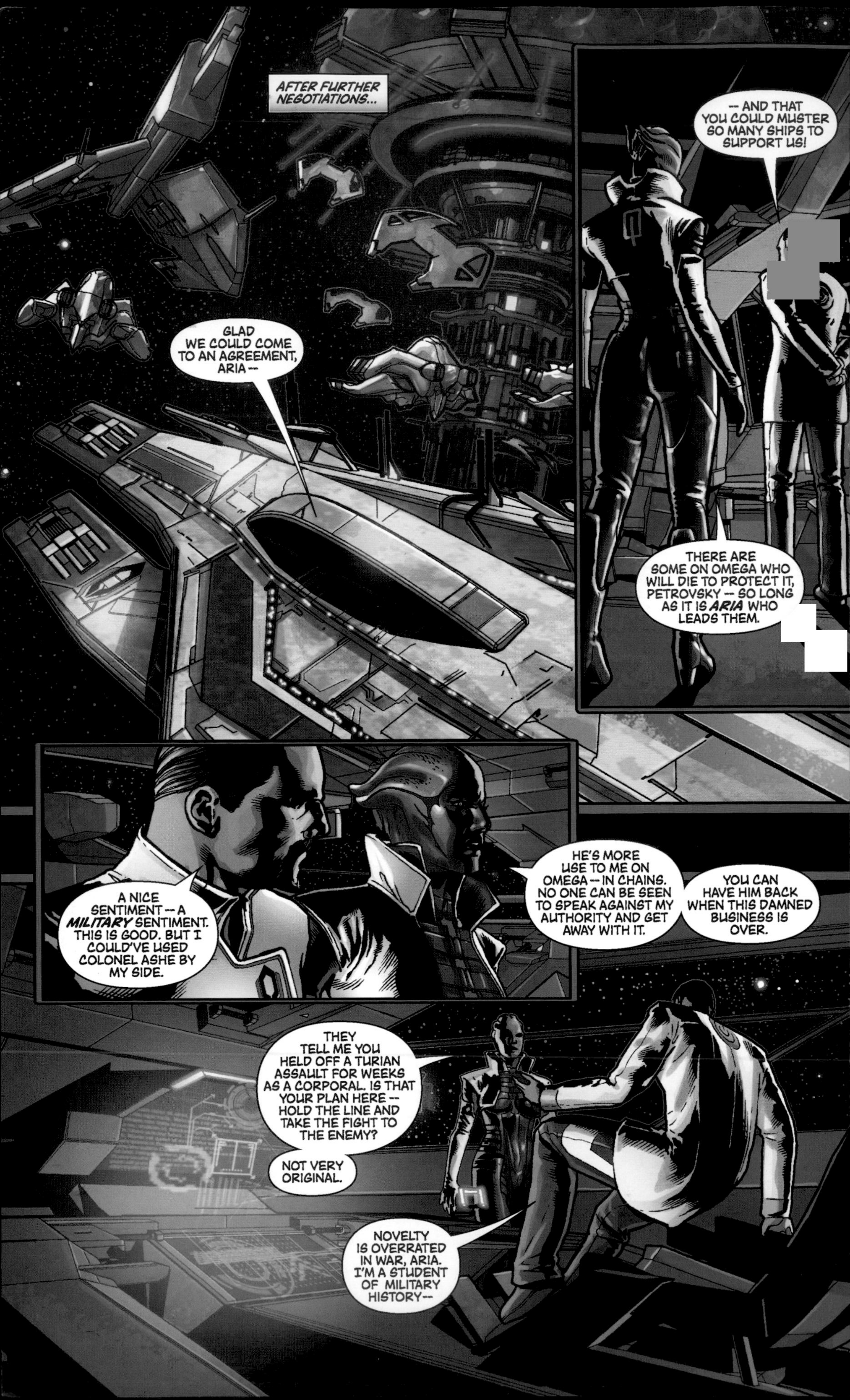
AFTER FURTHER NEGOTIATIONS...
GLAD WE COULD COME TO AN AGREEMENT, ARIA --
-- AND THAT YOU COULD MUSTER SO MANY SHIPS TO SUPPORT US!
THERE ARE SOME ON OMEGA WHO WILL DIE TO PROTECT IT, PETROVSKY -- SO LONG AS IT IS ARIA WHO LEADS THEM.
A NICE SENTIMENT -- A MILITARY SENTIMENT. THIS IS GOOD. BUT I COULD'VE USED COLONEL ASHE BY MY SIDE.
HE'S MORE USE TO ME ON OMEGA -- IN CHAINS. NO ONE CAN BE SEEN TO SPEAK AGAINST MY AUTHORITY AND GET AWAY WITH IT.
YOU CAN HAVE HIM BACK WHEN THIS DAMNED BUSINESS IS OVER.
THEY TELL ME YOU HELD OFF A TURIAN ASSAULT FOR WEEKS AS A CORPORAL. IS THAT YOUR PLAN HERE -- HOLD THE LINE AND TAKE THE FIGHT TO THE ENEMY?
NOT VERY ORIGINAL.
NOVELTY IS OVERRATED IN WAR, ARIA. I'M A STUDENT OF MILITARY HISTORY--

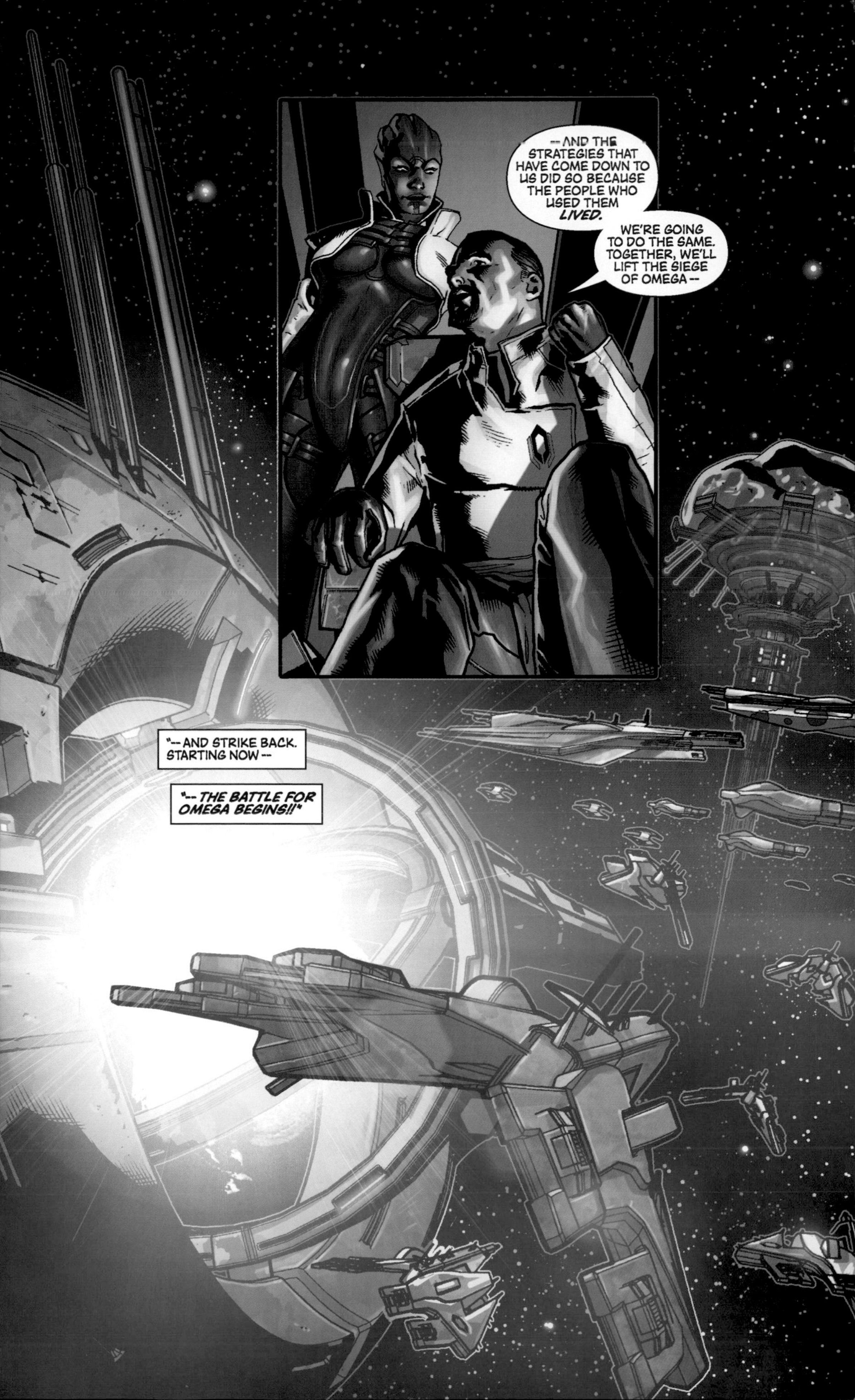
--AND THE STRATEGIES THAT HAVE COME DOWN TO US DID SO BECAUSE THE PEOPLE WHO USED THEM *LIVED.*
WE'RE GOING TO DO THE SAME. TOGETHER, WE'LL LIFT THE SIEGE OF OMEGA --
"-- AND STRIKE BACK. STARTING NOW --
"-- THE BATTLE FOR OMEGA BEGINS!!"

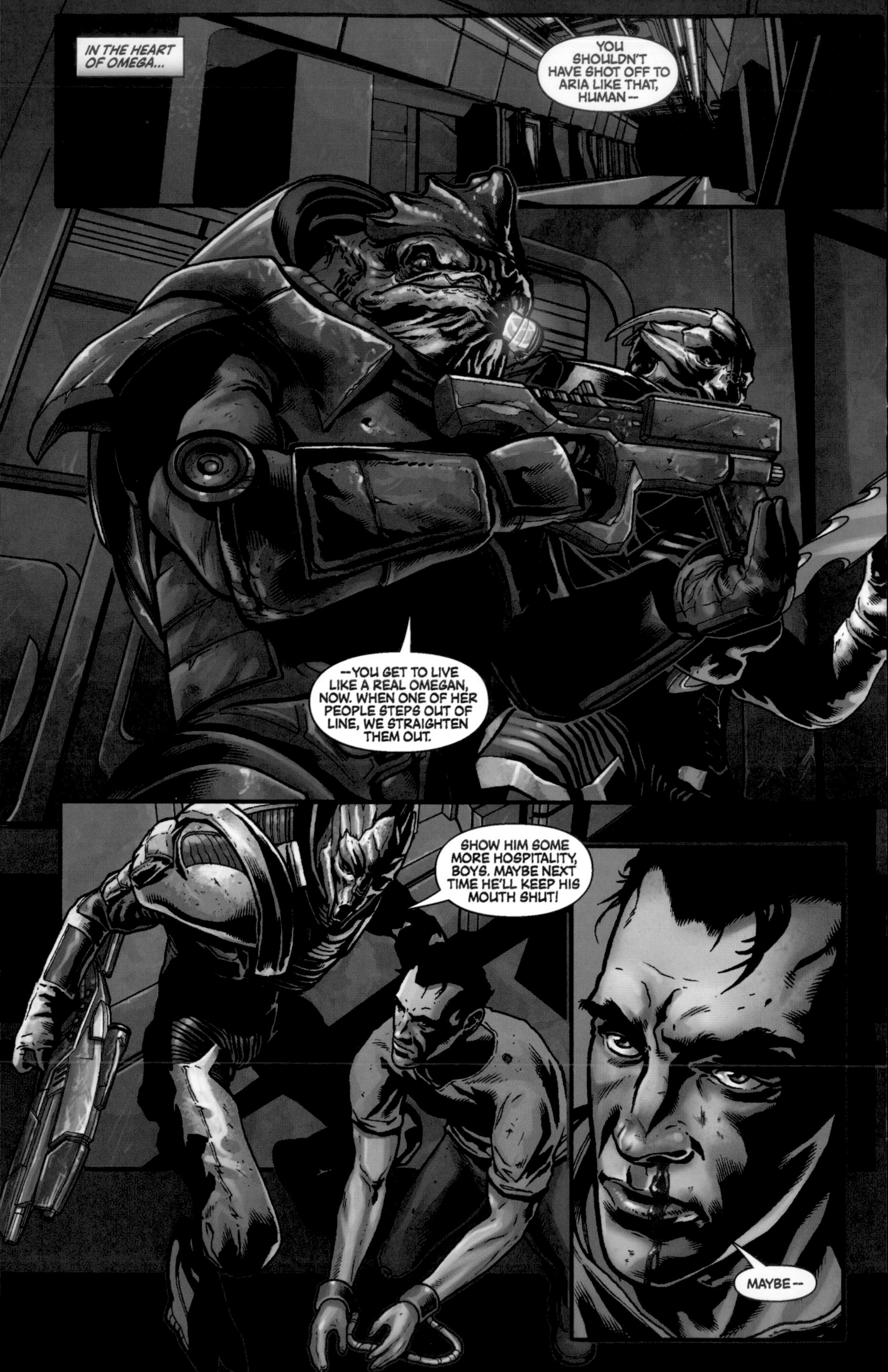
IN THE HEART OF OMEGA...
YOU SHOULDN'T HAVE SHOT OFF TO ARIA LIKE THAT, HUMAN --
--YOU GET TO LIVE LIKE A REAL OMEGAN, NOW. WHEN ONE OF HER PEOPLE STEPS OUT OF LINE, WE STRAIGHTEN THEM OUT.
SHOW HIM SOME MORE HOSPITALITY, BOYS. MAYBE NEXT TIME HE'LL KEEP HIS MOUTH SHUT!
MAYBE --

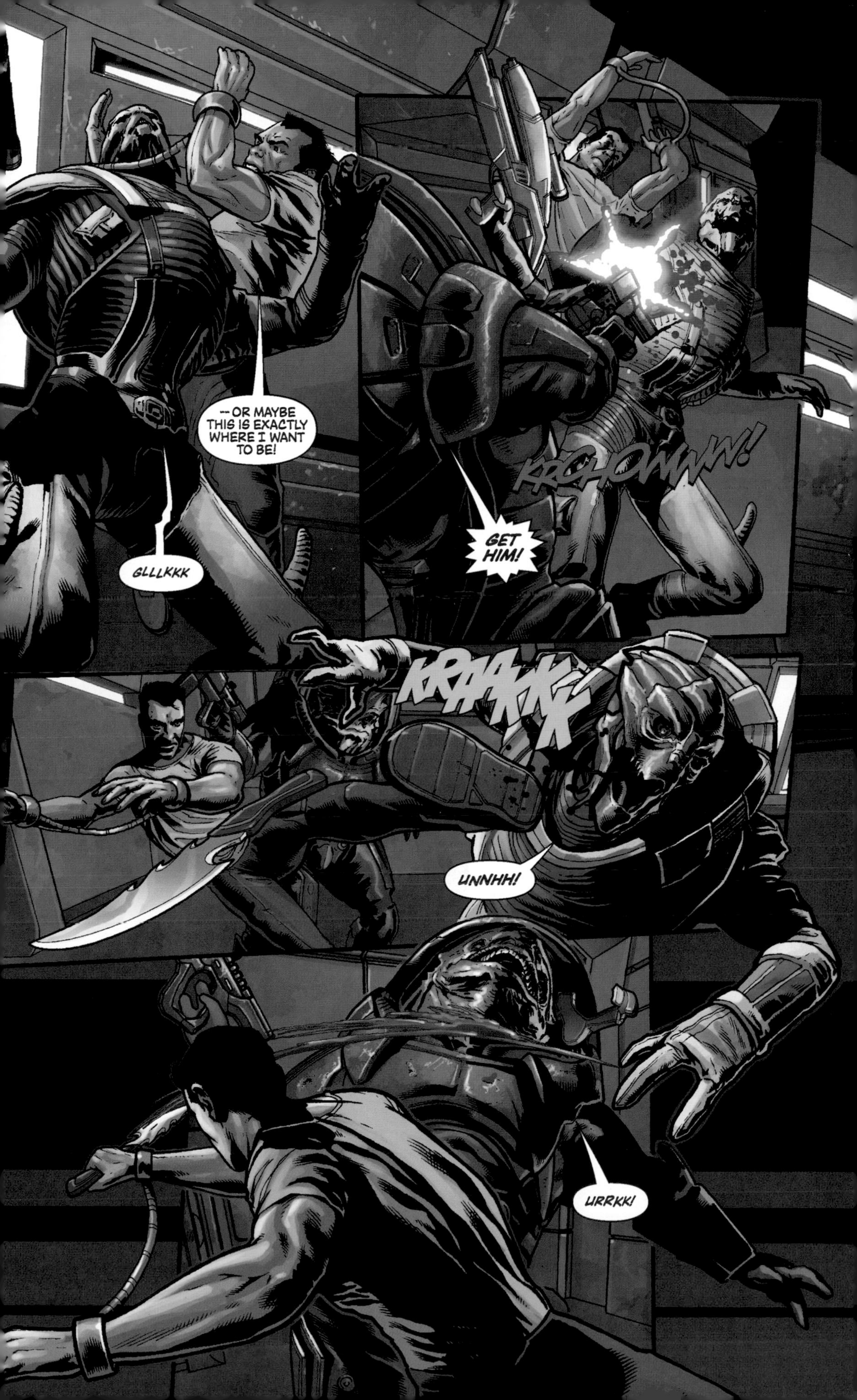
--OR MAYBE THIS IS EXACTLY WHERE I WANT TO BE!
GLLLKKK
KRCHOWWW!
GET HIM!
KRAAKKK
UNNHH!
URRKK!

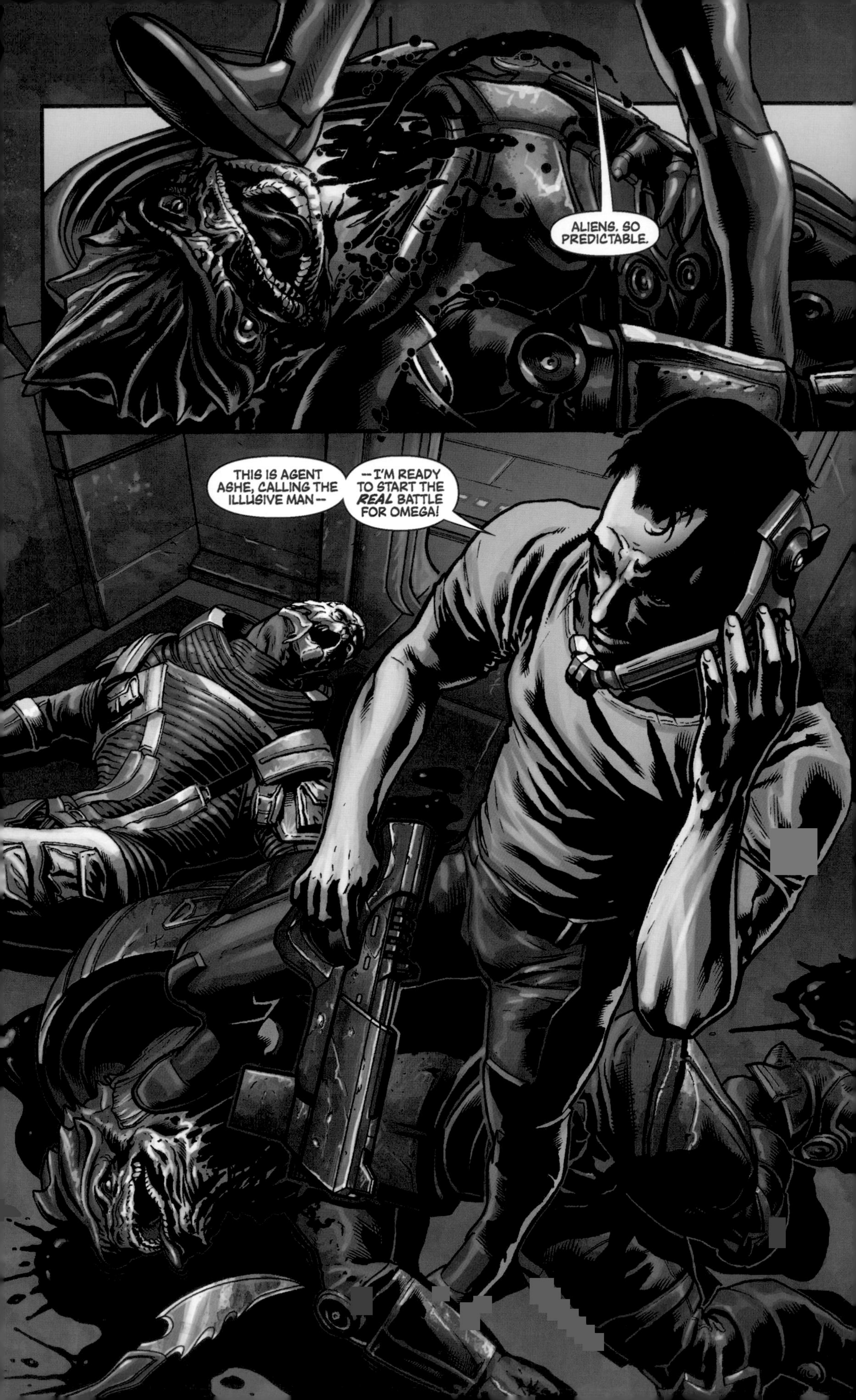
ALIENS. SO PREDICTABLE.
THIS IS AGENT ASHE, CALLING THE ILLUSIVE MAN --
-- I'M READY TO START THE *REAL* BATTLE FOR OMEGA!

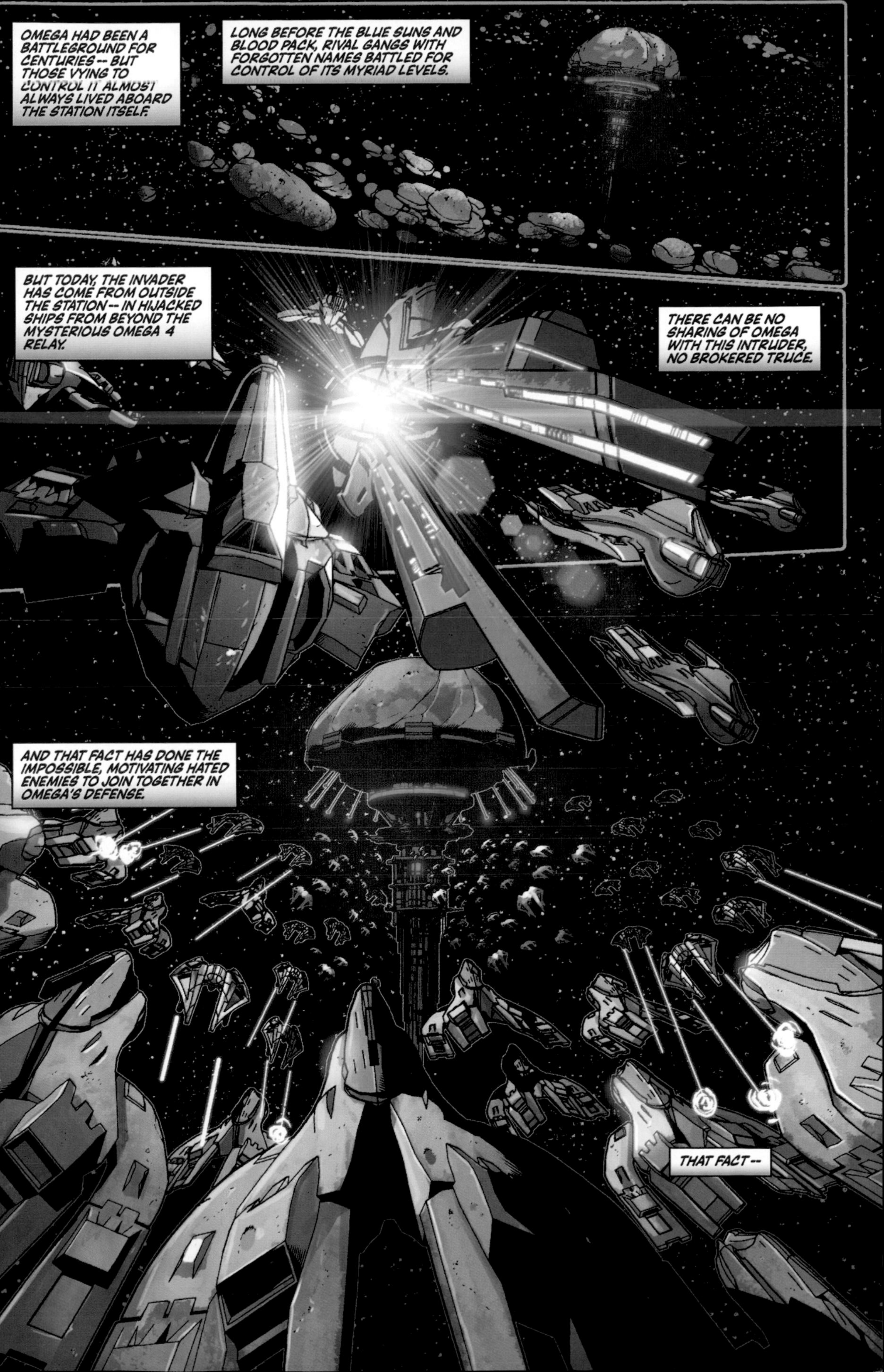
OMEGA HAD BEEN A BATTLEGROUND FOR CENTURIES -- BUT THOSE VYING TO CONTROL IT ALMOST ALWAYS LIVED ABOARD THE STATION ITSELF.
LONG BEFORE THE BLUE SUNS AND BLOOD PACK, RIVAL GANGS WITH FORGOTTEN NAMES BATTLED FOR CONTROL OF ITS MYRIAD LEVELS.
BUT TODAY, THE INVADER HAS COME FROM OUTSIDE THE STATION -- IN HIJACKED SHIPS FROM BEYOND THE MYSTERIOUS OMEGA 4 RELAY.
THERE CAN BE NO SHARING OF OMEGA WITH THIS INTRUDER, NO BROKERED TRUCE.
AND THAT FACT HAS DONE THE IMPOSSIBLE, MOTIVATING HATED ENEMIES TO JOIN TOGETHER IN OMEGA'S DEFENSE.
THAT FACT --

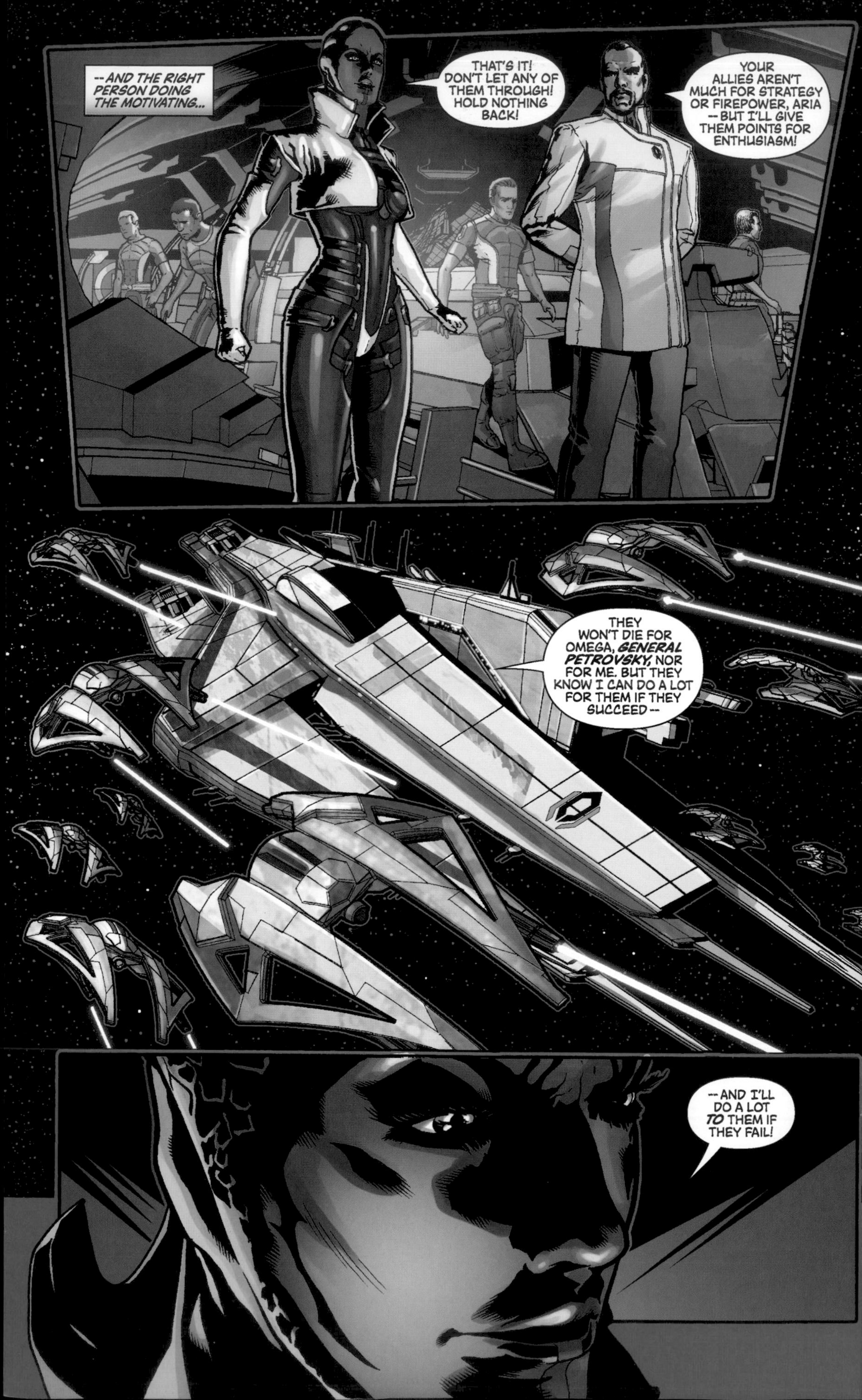
--AND THE RIGHT PERSON DOING THE MOTIVATING...
THAT'S IT! DON'T LET ANY OF THEM THROUGH! HOLD NOTHING BACK!
YOUR ALLIES AREN'T MUCH FOR STRATEGY OR FIREPOWER, ARIA --BUT I'LL GIVE THEM POINTS FOR ENTHUSIASM!
THEY WON'T DIE FOR OMEGA, *GENERAL PETROVSKY,* NOR FOR ME. BUT THEY KNOW I CAN DO A LOT FOR THEM IF THEY SUCCEED --
--AND I'LL DO A LOT *TO* THEM IF THEY FAIL!

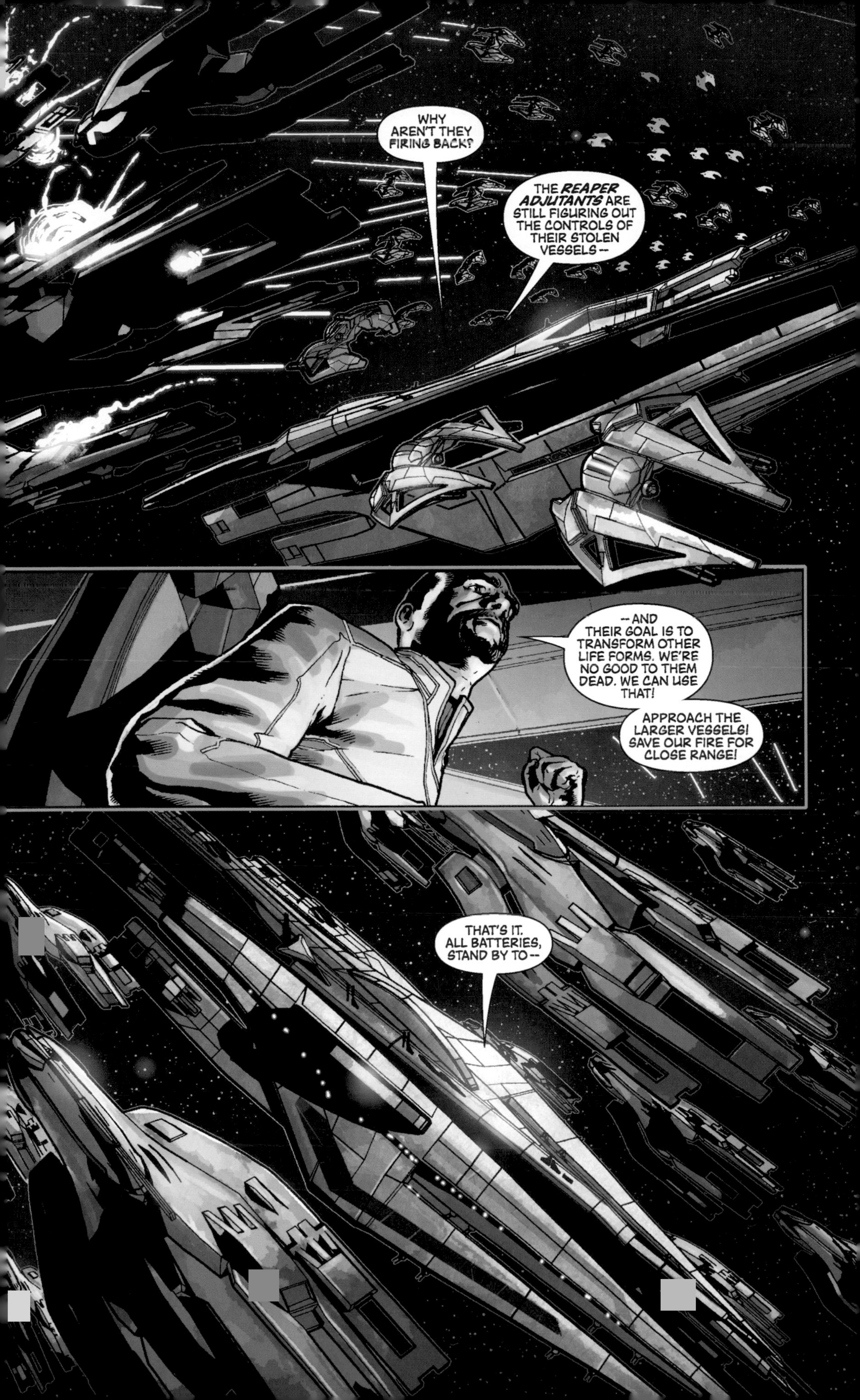
WHY AREN'T THEY FIRING BACK?
THE *REAPER ADJUTANTS* ARE STILL FIGURING OUT THE CONTROLS OF THEIR STOLEN VESSELS --
-- AND THEIR GOAL IS TO TRANSFORM OTHER LIFE FORMS. WE'RE NO GOOD TO THEM DEAD. WE CAN USE THAT!
APPROACH THE LARGER VESSELS! SAVE OUR FIRE FOR CLOSE RANGE!
THAT'S IT. ALL BATTERIES, STAND BY TO --

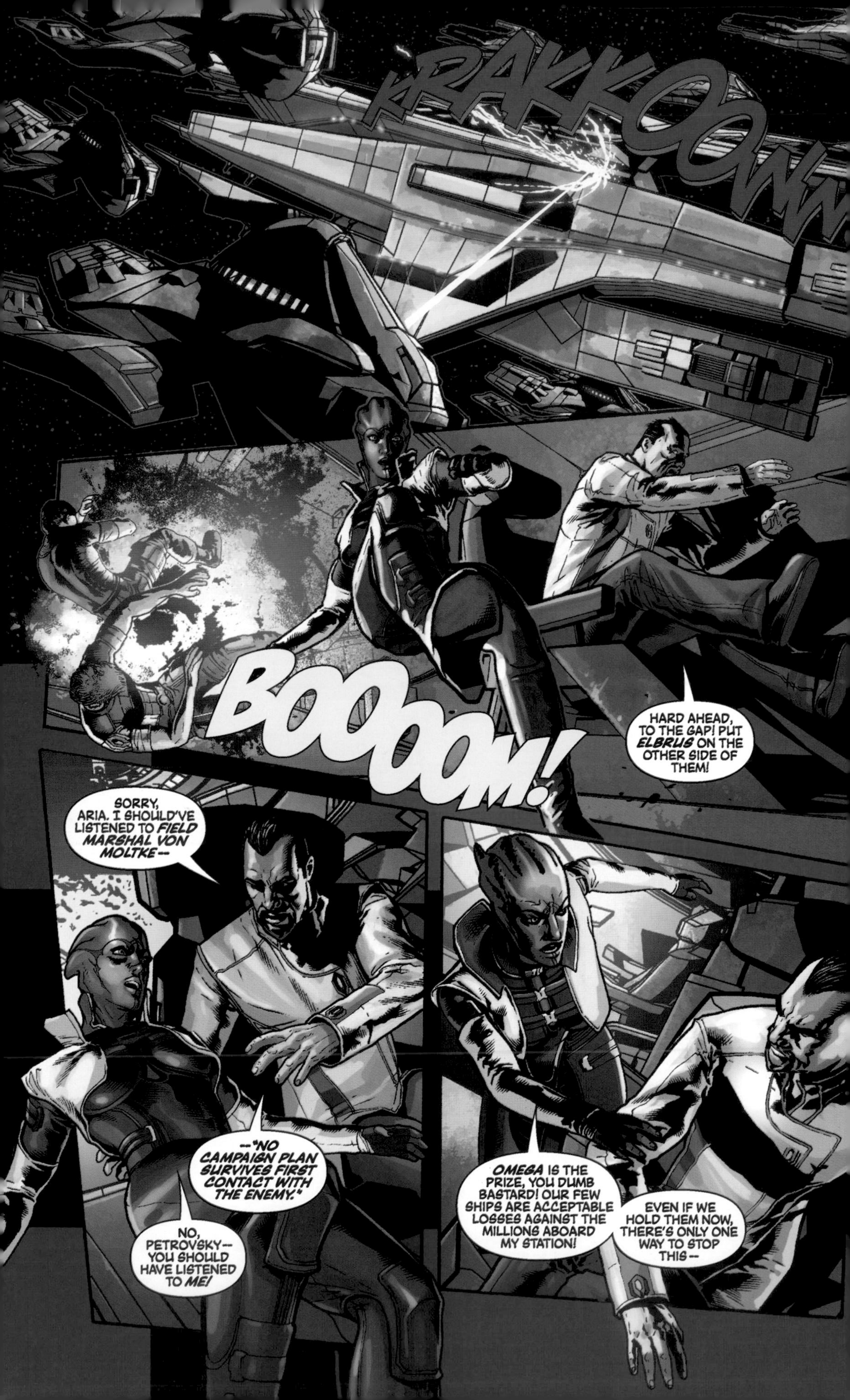
KRAKKOOWW
BOOOOM!
HARD AHEAD, TO THE GAP! PUT ELBRUS ON THE OTHER SIDE OF THEM!
SORRY, ARIA. I SHOULD'VE LISTENED TO FIELD MARSHAL VON MOLTKE--
--"NO CAMPAIGN PLAN SURVIVES FIRST CONTACT WITH THE ENEMY."
NO, PETROVSKY-- YOU SHOULD HAVE LISTENED TO ME!
OMEGA IS THE PRIZE, YOU DUMB BASTARD! OUR FEW SHIPS ARE ACCEPTABLE LOSSES AGAINST THE MILLIONS ABOARD MY STATION!
EVEN IF WE HOLD THEM NOW, THERE'S ONLY ONE WAY TO STOP THIS--

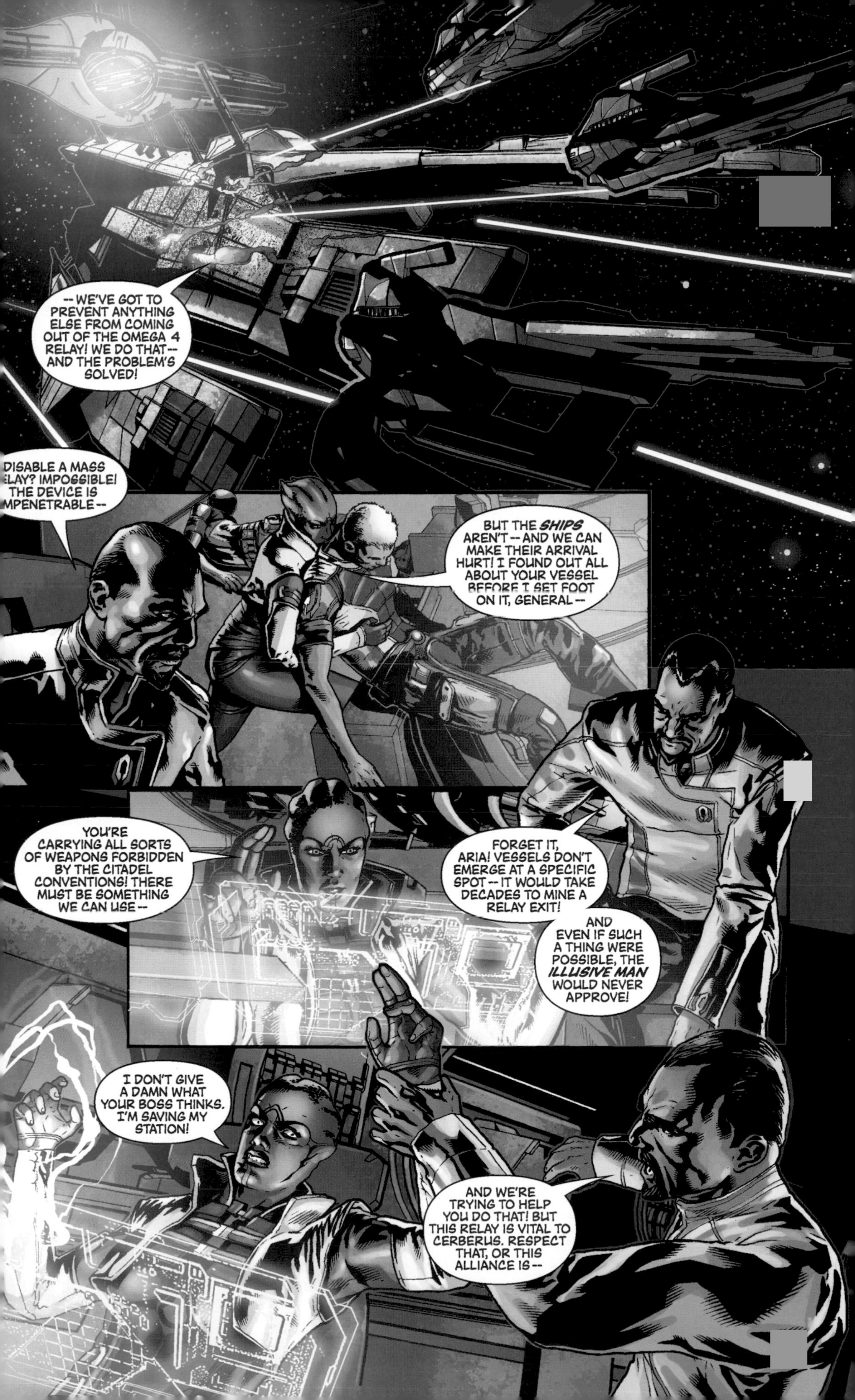
-- WE'VE GOT TO PREVENT ANYTHING ELSE FROM COMING OUT OF THE OMEGA 4 RELAY! WE DO THAT -- AND THE PROBLEM'S SOLVED!
DISABLE A MASS ELAY? IMPOSSIBLE! THE DEVICE IS MPENETRABLE --
BUT THE *SHIPS* AREN'T -- AND WE CAN MAKE THEIR ARRIVAL HURT! I FOUND OUT ALL ABOUT YOUR VESSEL BEFORE I SET FOOT ON IT, GENERAL --
YOU'RE CARRYING ALL SORTS OF WEAPONS FORBIDDEN BY THE CITADEL CONVENTIONS! THERE MUST BE SOMETHING WE CAN USE --
FORGET IT, ARIA! VESSELS DON'T EMERGE AT A SPECIFIC SPOT -- IT WOULD TAKE DECADES TO MINE A RELAY EXIT!
AND EVEN IF SUCH A THING WERE POSSIBLE, THE *ILLUSIVE MAN* WOULD NEVER APPROVE!
I DON'T GIVE A DAMN WHAT YOUR BOSS THINKS. I'M SAVING MY STATION!
AND WE'RE TRYING TO HELP YOU DO THAT! BUT THIS RELAY IS VITAL TO CERBERUS. RESPECT THAT, OR THIS ALLIANCE IS --

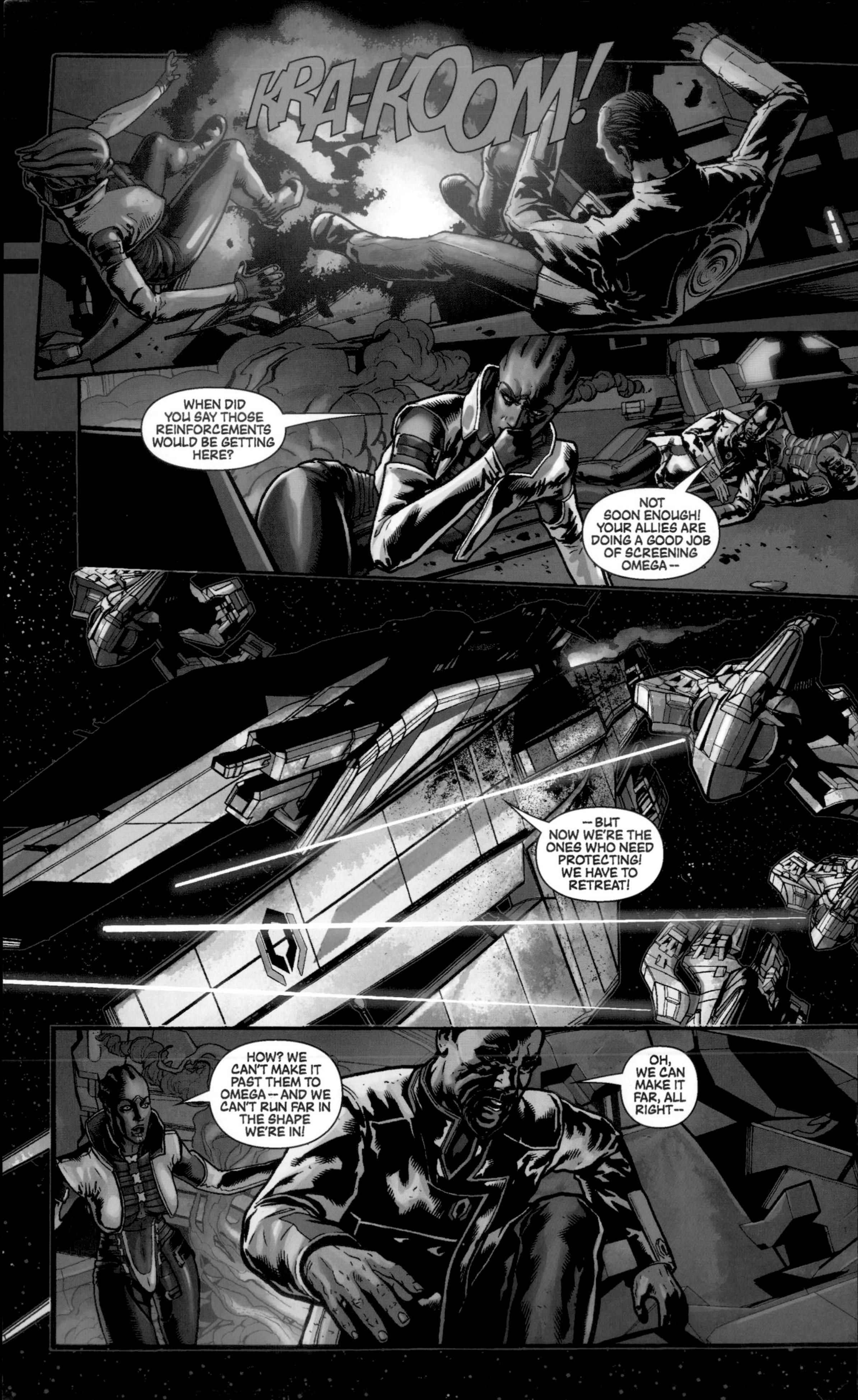
KRA-KOOM!
WHEN DID YOU SAY THOSE REINFORCEMENTS WOULD BE GETTING HERE?
NOT SOON ENOUGH! YOUR ALLIES ARE DOING A GOOD JOB OF SCREENING OMEGA --
-- BUT NOW WE'RE THE ONES WHO NEED PROTECTING! WE HAVE TO RETREAT!
HOW? WE CAN'T MAKE IT PAST THEM TO OMEGA -- AND WE CAN'T RUN FAR IN THE SHAPE WE'RE IN!
OH, WE CAN MAKE IT FAR, ALL RIGHT --

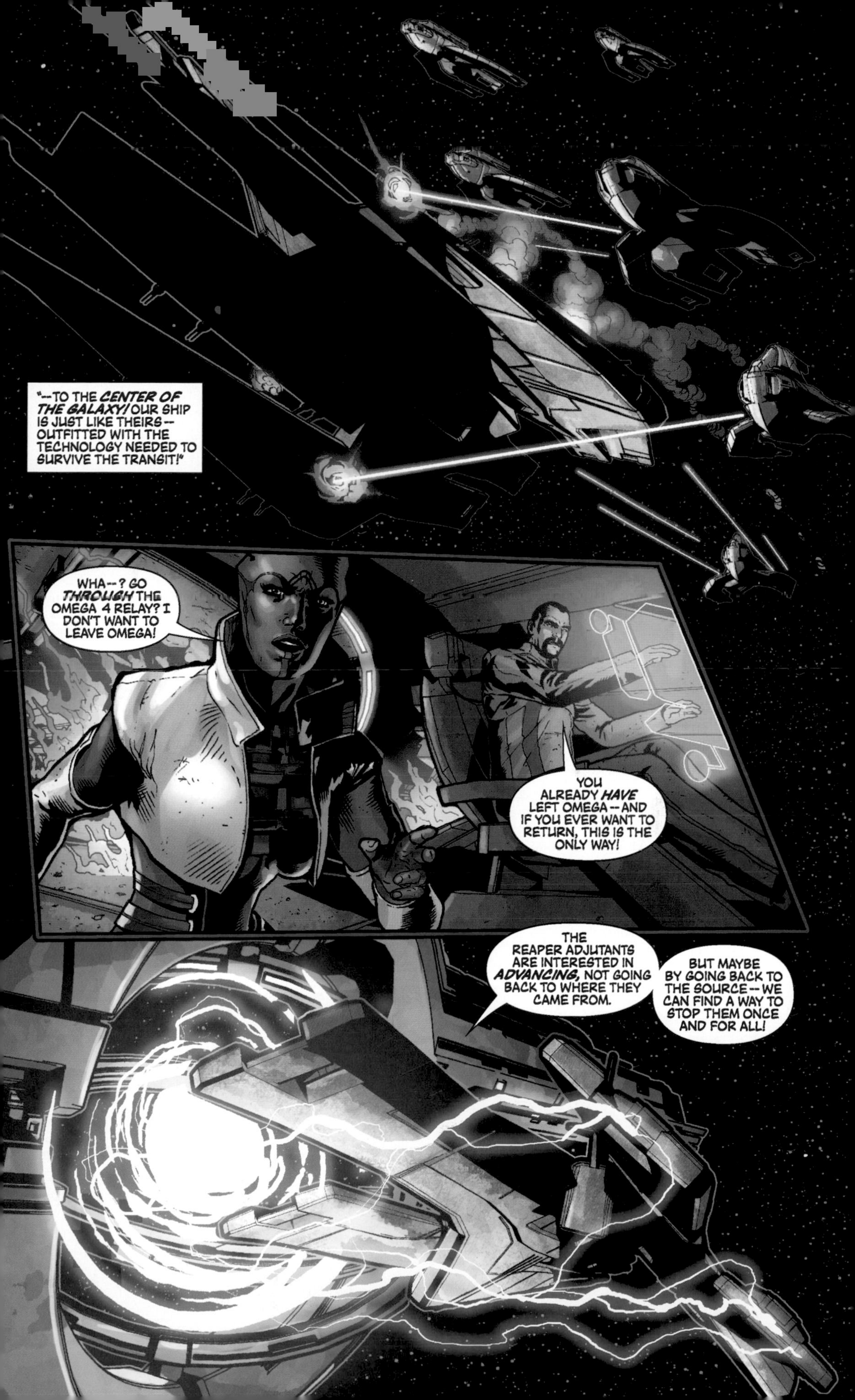
"--TO THE CENTER OF THE GALAXY! OUR SHIP IS JUST LIKE THEIRS -- OUTFITTED WITH THE TECHNOLOGY NEEDED TO SURVIVE THE TRANSIT!"
WHA--? GO THROUGH THE OMEGA 4 RELAY? I DON'T WANT TO LEAVE OMEGA!
YOU ALREADY HAVE LEFT OMEGA -- AND IF YOU EVER WANT TO RETURN, THIS IS THE ONLY WAY!
THE REAPER ADJUTANTS ARE INTERESTED IN ADVANCING, NOT GOING BACK TO WHERE THEY CAME FROM.
BUT MAYBE BY GOING BACK TO THE SOURCE -- WE CAN FIND A WAY TO STOP THEM ONCE AND FOR ALL!

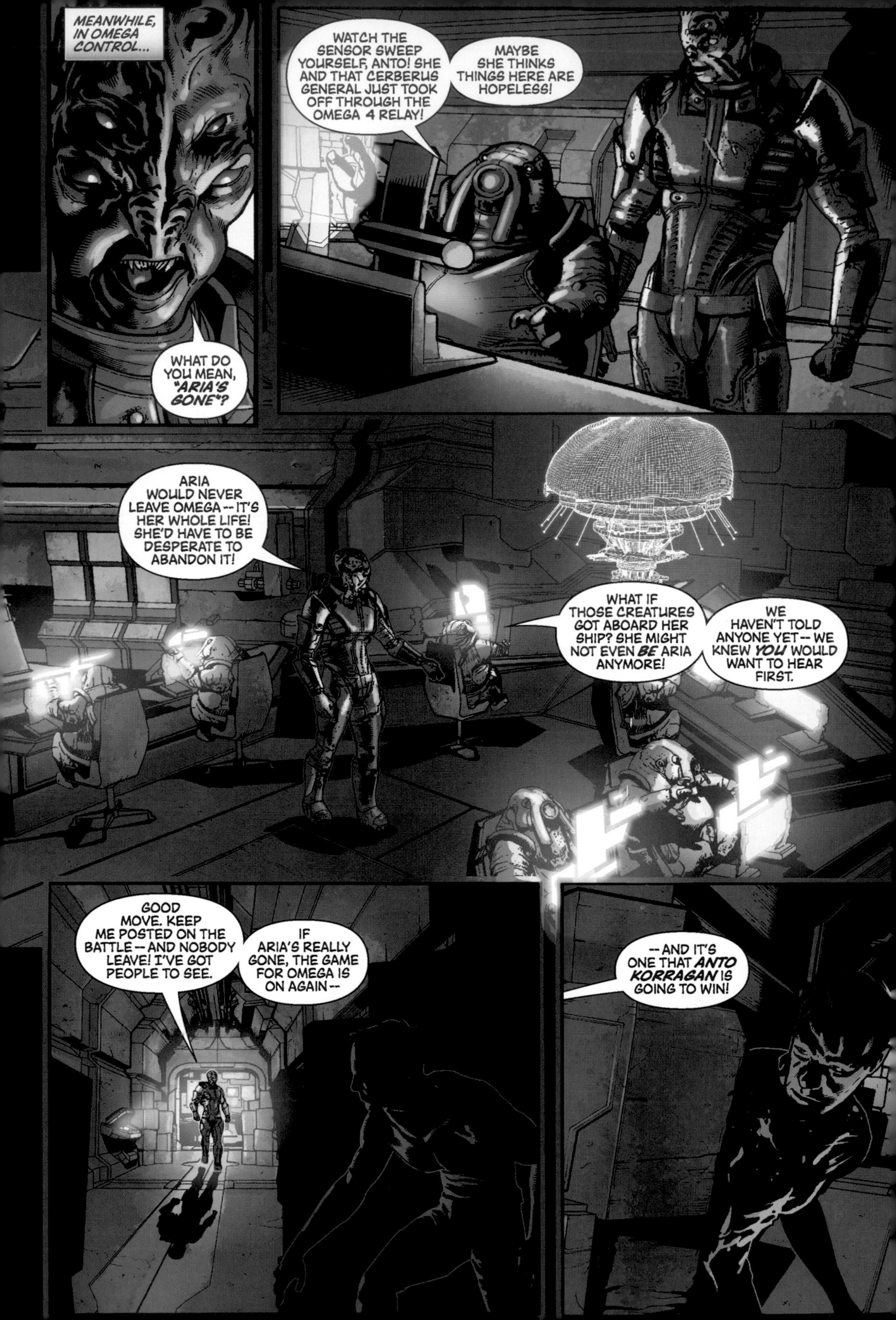
MEANWHILE, IN OMEGA CONTROL...
WHAT DO YOU MEAN, "ARIA'S GONE"?
WATCH THE SENSOR SWEEP YOURSELF, ANTO! SHE AND THAT CERBERUS GENERAL JUST TOOK OFF THROUGH THE OMEGA 4 RELAY!
MAYBE SHE THINKS THINGS HERE ARE HOPELESS!
ARIA WOULD NEVER LEAVE OMEGA -- IT'S HER WHOLE LIFE! SHE'D HAVE TO BE DESPERATE TO ABANDON IT!
WHAT IF THOSE CREATURES GOT ABOARD HER SHIP? SHE MIGHT NOT EVEN BE ARIA ANYMORE!
WE HAVEN'T TOLD ANYONE YET -- WE KNEW YOU WOULD WANT TO HEAR FIRST.
GOOD MOVE. KEEP ME POSTED ON THE BATTLE -- AND NOBODY LEAVE! I'VE GOT PEOPLE TO SEE.
IF ARIA'S REALLY GONE, THE GAME FOR OMEGA IS ON AGAIN --
-- AND IT'S ONE THAT ANTO KORRAGAN IS GOING TO WIN!

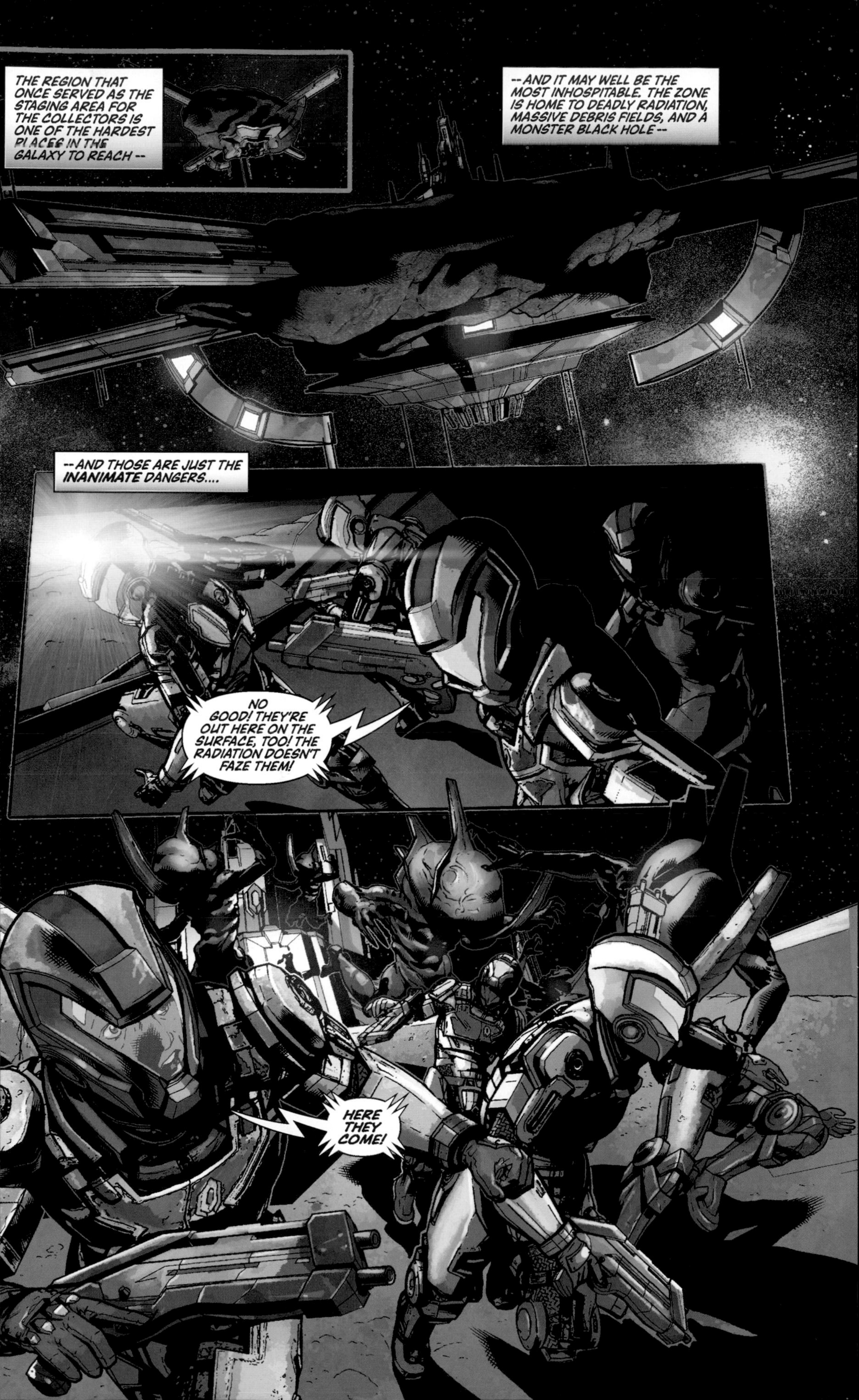
THE REGION THAT ONCE SERVED AS THE STAGING AREA FOR THE COLLECTORS IS ONE OF THE HARDEST PLACES IN THE GALAXY TO REACH --
--AND IT MAY WELL BE THE MOST INHOSPITABLE. THE ZONE IS HOME TO DEADLY RADIATION, MASSIVE DEBRIS FIELDS, AND A MONSTER BLACK HOLE --
--AND THOSE ARE JUST THE INANIMATE DANGERS....
NO GOOD! THEY'RE OUT HERE ON THE SURFACE, TOO! THE RADIATION DOESN'T FAZE THEM!
HERE THEY COME!

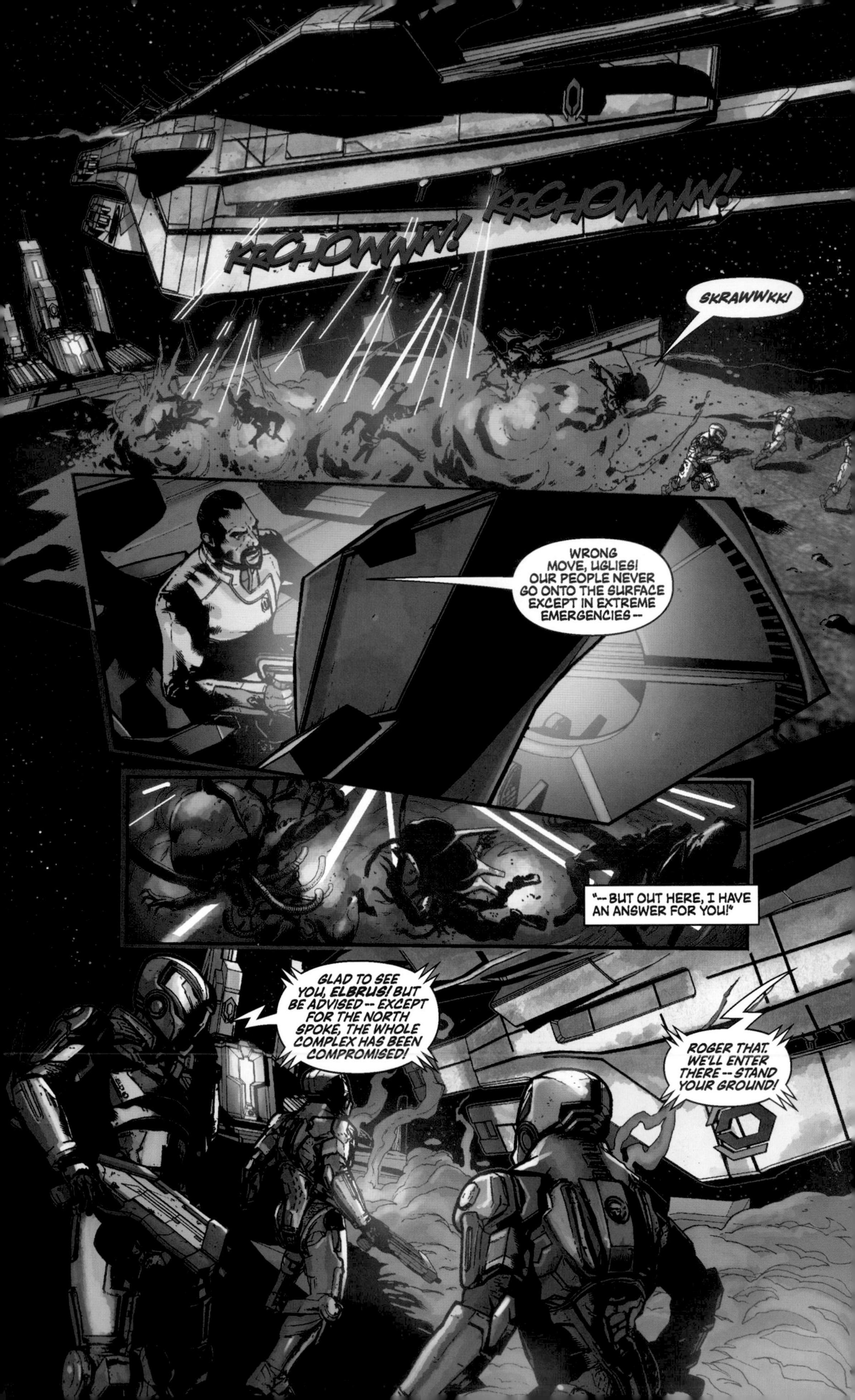
KRCHOWWW!
KRCHOWWW!
SKRAWWKK!
WRONG MOVE, UGLIES! OUR PEOPLE NEVER GO ONTO THE SURFACE EXCEPT IN EXTREME EMERGENCIES --
"-- BUT OUT HERE, I HAVE AN ANSWER FOR YOU!"
GLAD TO SEE YOU, ELBRUS! BUT BE ADVISED -- EXCEPT FOR THE NORTH SPOKE, THE WHOLE COMPLEX HAS BEEN COMPROMISED!
ROGER THAT. WE'LL ENTER THERE -- STAND YOUR GROUND!

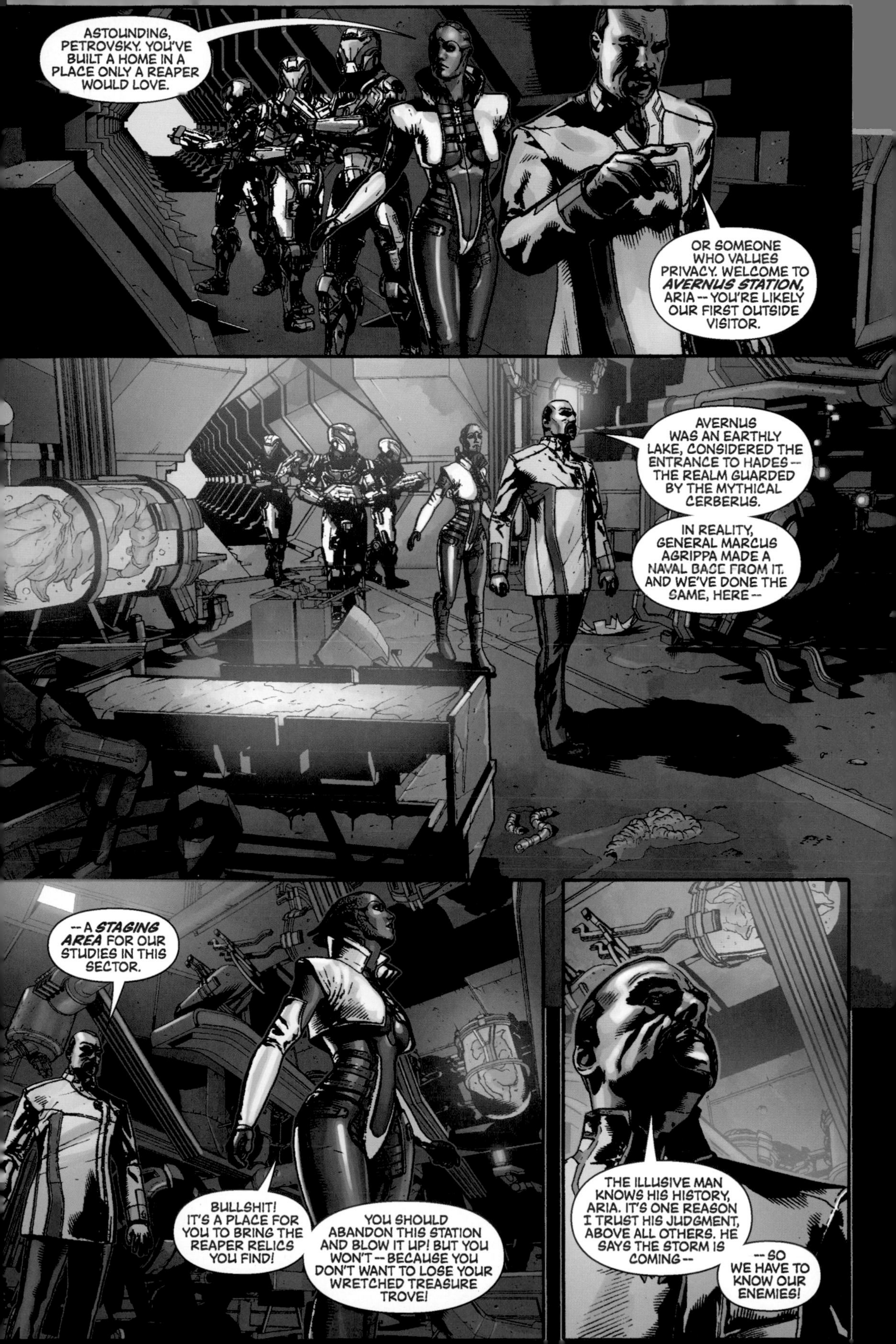
ASTOUNDING, PETROVSKY. YOU'VE BUILT A HOME IN A PLACE ONLY A REAPER WOULD LOVE.
OR SOMEONE WHO VALUES PRIVACY. WELCOME TO AVERNUS STATION, ARIA -- YOU'RE LIKELY OUR FIRST OUTSIDE VISITOR.
AVERNUS WAS AN EARTHLY LAKE, CONSIDERED THE ENTRANCE TO HADES -- THE REALM GUARDED BY THE MYTHICAL CERBERUS.
IN REALITY, GENERAL MARCUS AGRIPPA MADE A NAVAL BASE FROM IT. AND WE'VE DONE THE SAME, HERE --
-- A STAGING AREA FOR OUR STUDIES IN THIS SECTOR.
BULLSHIT! IT'S A PLACE FOR YOU TO BRING THE REAPER RELICS YOU FIND!
YOU SHOULD ABANDON THIS STATION AND BLOW IT UP! BUT YOU WON'T -- BECAUSE YOU DON'T WANT TO LOSE YOUR WRETCHED TREASURE TROVE!
THE ILLUSIVE MAN KNOWS HIS HISTORY, ARIA. IT'S ONE REASON I TRUST HIS JUDGMENT, ABOVE ALL OTHERS. HE SAYS THE STORM IS COMING --
-- SO WE HAVE TO KNOW OUR ENEMIES!

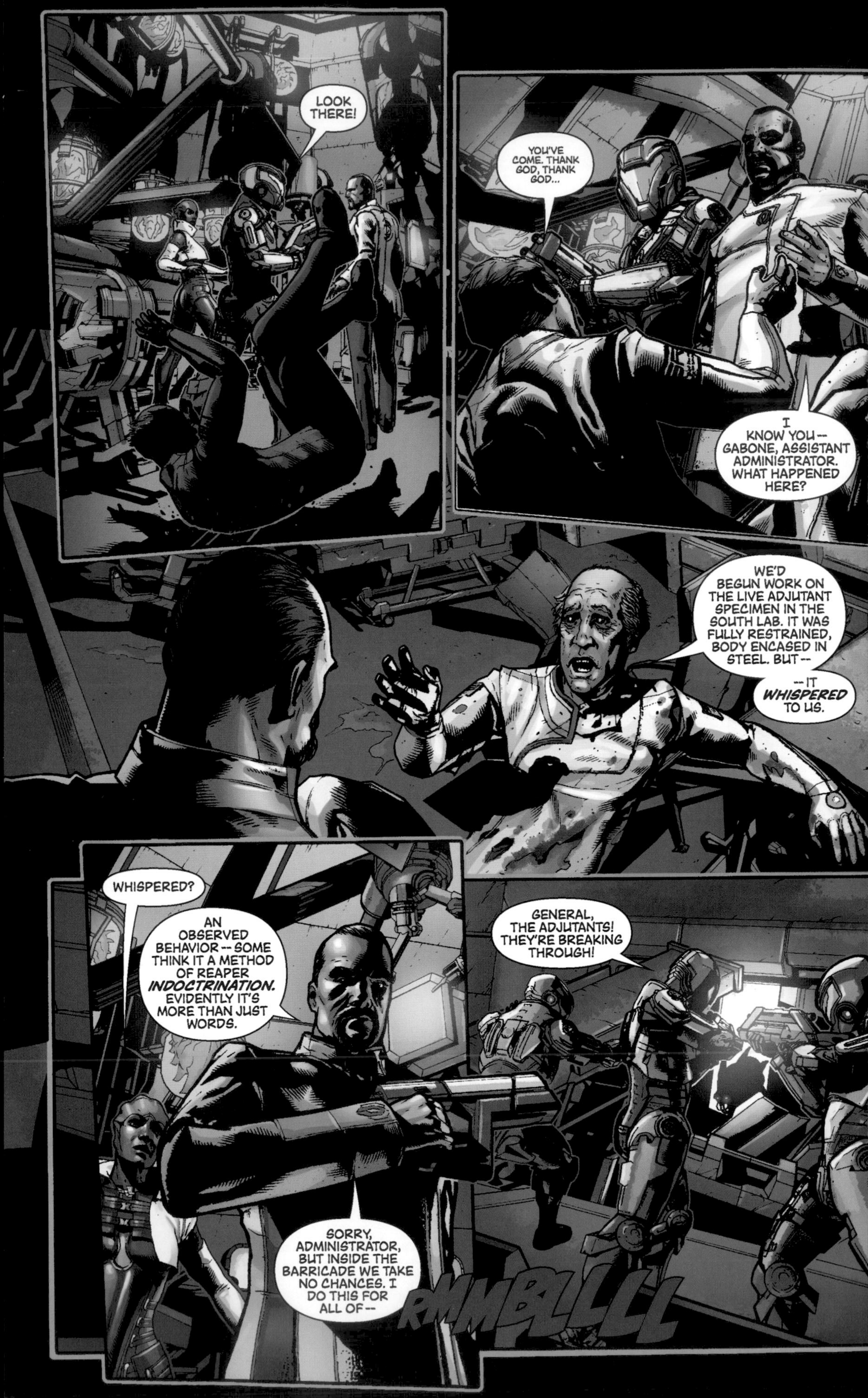
LOOK THERE!
YOU'VE COME. THANK GOD, THANK GOD...
I KNOW YOU -- GABONE, ASSISTANT ADMINISTRATOR. WHAT HAPPENED HERE?
WE'D BEGUN WORK ON THE LIVE ADJUTANT SPECIMEN IN THE SOUTH LAB. IT WAS FULLY RESTRAINED, BODY ENCASED IN STEEL. BUT --
-- IT *WHISPERED* TO US.
WHISPERED?
AN OBSERVED BEHAVIOR -- SOME THINK IT A METHOD OF REAPER *INDOCTRINATION.* EVIDENTLY IT'S MORE THAN JUST WORDS.
GENERAL, THE ADJUTANTS! THEY'RE BREAKING THROUGH!
SORRY, ADMINISTRATOR, BUT INSIDE THE BARRICADE WE TAKE NO CHANCES. I DO THIS FOR ALL OF --
RMMBLLLL

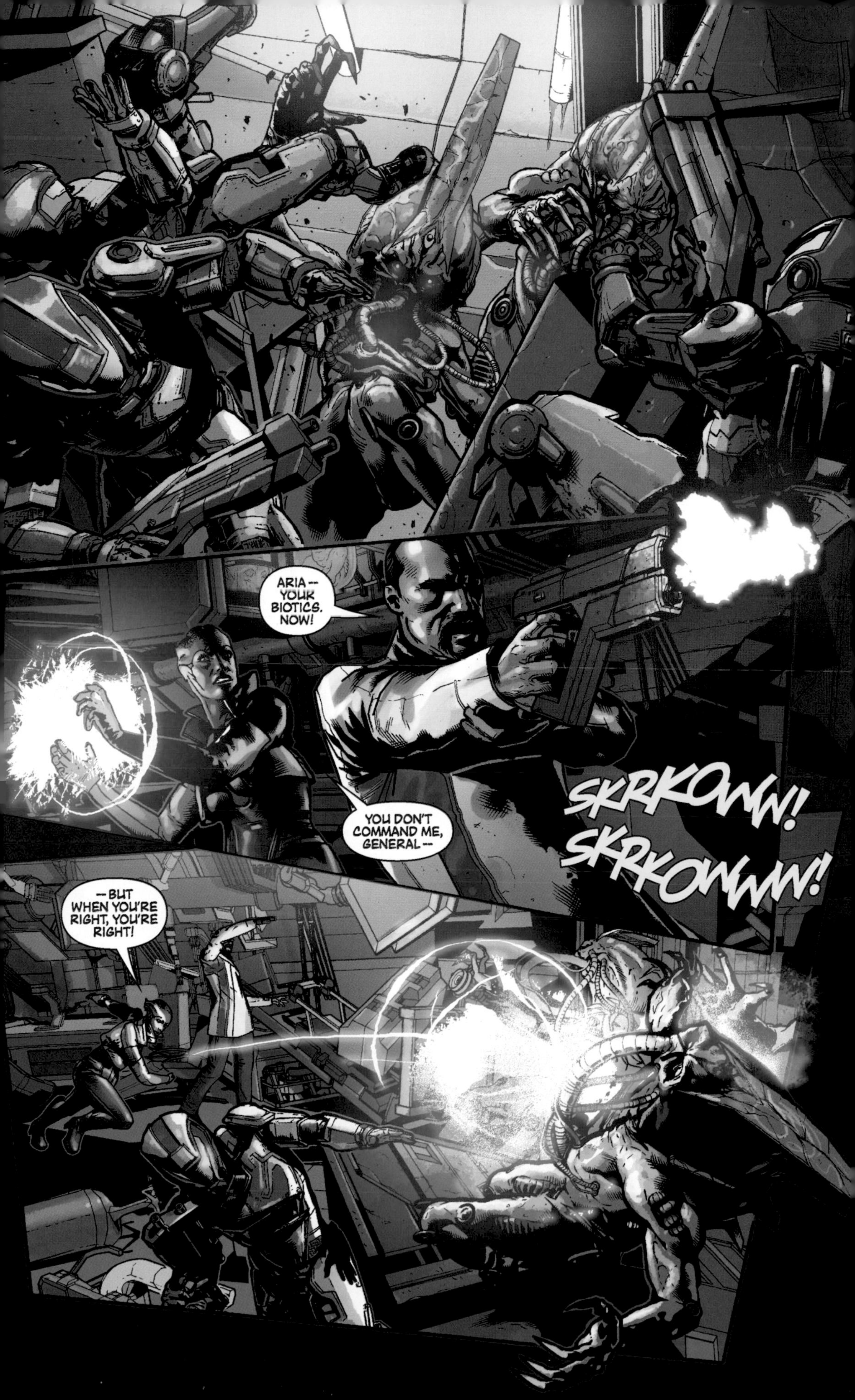

ARIA -- YOUR BIOTICS. NOW!
YOU DON'T COMMAND ME, GENERAL --
SKRKOWW! SKRKOWWW!
-- BUT WHEN YOU'RE RIGHT, YOU'RE RIGHT!

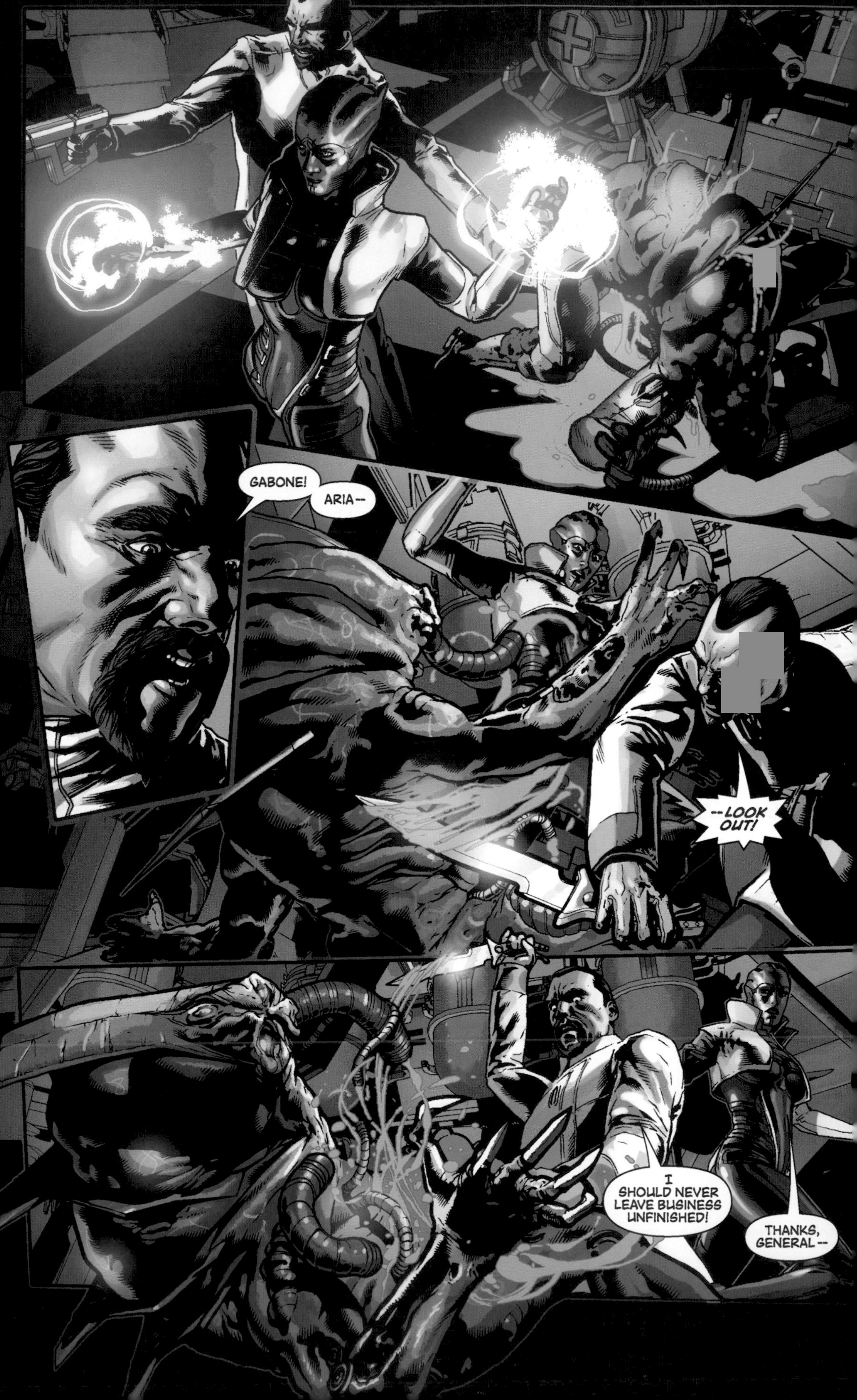
GABONE!
ARIA--
--LOOK OUT!
I SHOULD NEVER LEAVE BUSINESS UNFINISHED!
THANKS, GENERAL--

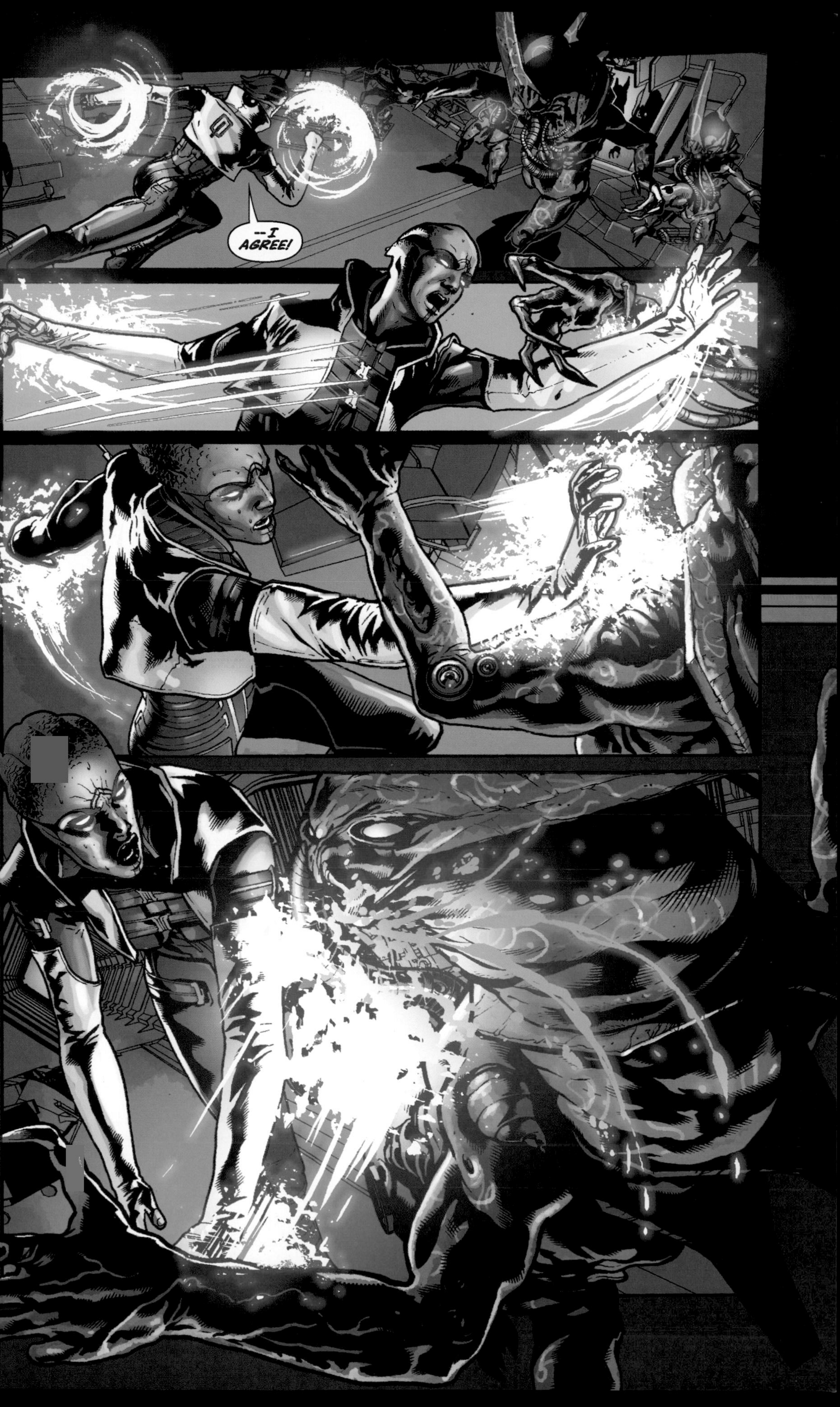
--I AGREE!

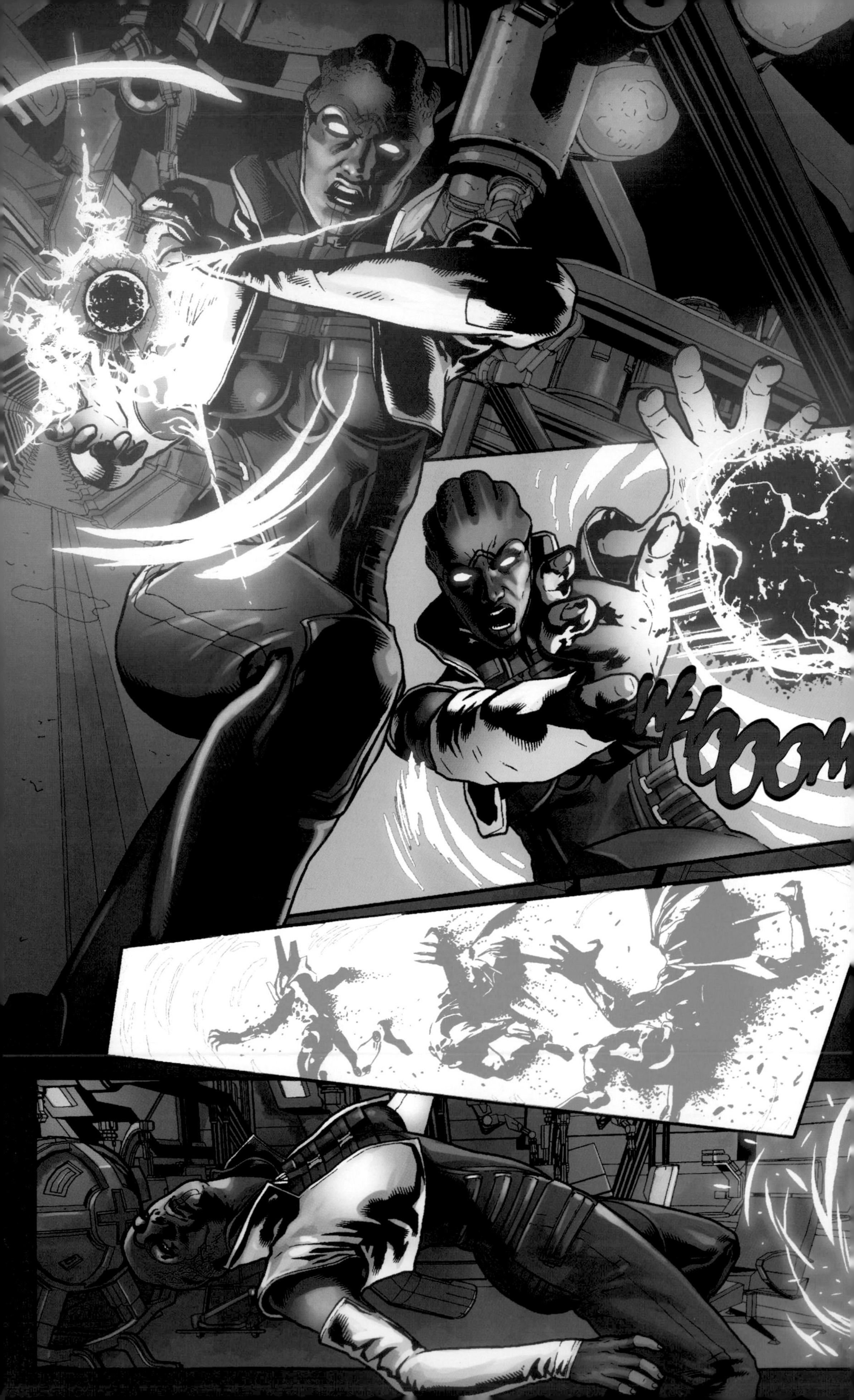
WHOOOM

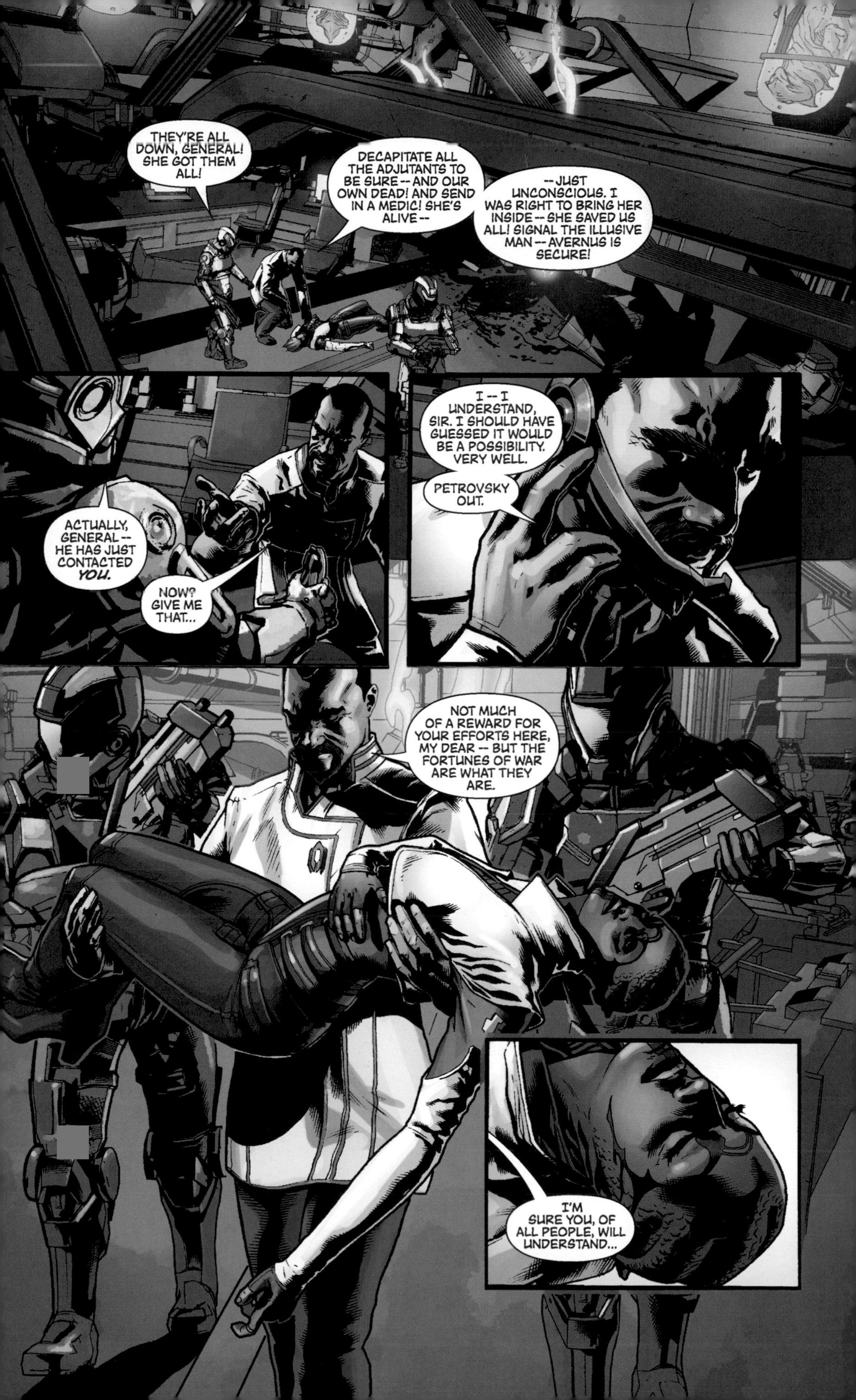
THEY'RE ALL DOWN, GENERAL! SHE GOT THEM ALL!
DECAPITATE ALL THE ADJUTANTS TO BE SURE -- AND OUR OWN DEAD! AND SEND IN A MEDIC! SHE'S ALIVE --
-- JUST UNCONSCIOUS. I WAS RIGHT TO BRING HER INSIDE -- SHE SAVED US ALL! SIGNAL THE ILLUSIVE MAN -- AVERNUS IS SECURE!
ACTUALLY, GENERAL -- HE HAS JUST CONTACTED *YOU.*
NOW? GIVE ME THAT...
I -- I UNDERSTAND, SIR. I SHOULD HAVE GUESSED IT WOULD BE A POSSIBILITY. VERY WELL.
PETROVSKY OUT.
NOT MUCH OF A REWARD FOR YOUR EFFORTS HERE, MY DEAR -- BUT THE FORTUNES OF WAR ARE WHAT THEY ARE.
I'M SURE YOU, OF ALL PEOPLE, WILL UNDERSTAND...

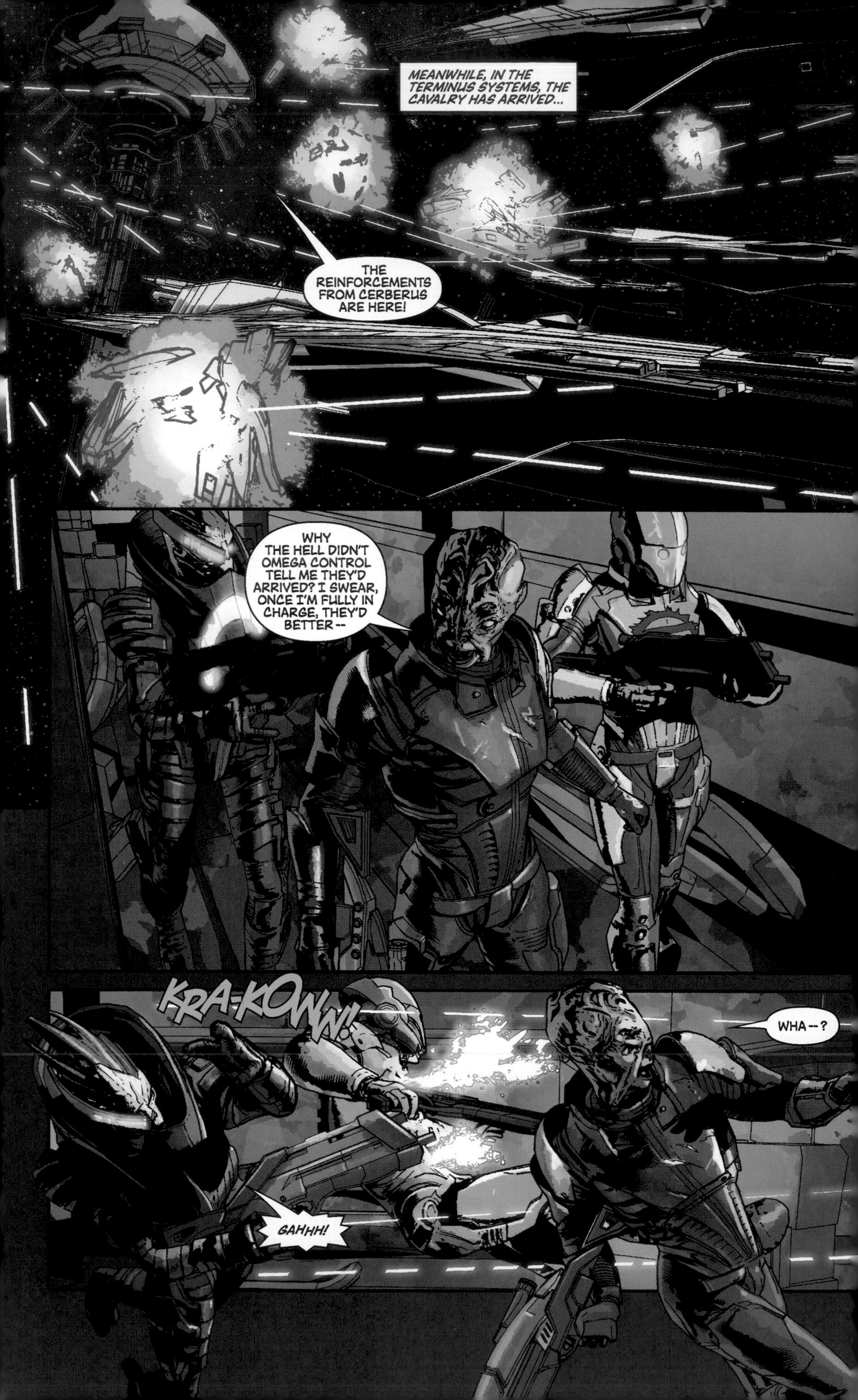
MEANWHILE, IN THE TERMINUS SYSTEMS, THE CAVALRY HAS ARRIVED...
THE REINFORCEMENTS FROM CERBERUS ARE HERE!
WHY THE HELL DIDN'T OMEGA CONTROL TELL ME THEY'D ARRIVED? I SWEAR, ONCE I'M FULLY IN CHARGE, THEY'D BETTER --
KRA-KOWW!
WHA--?
GAHHH!

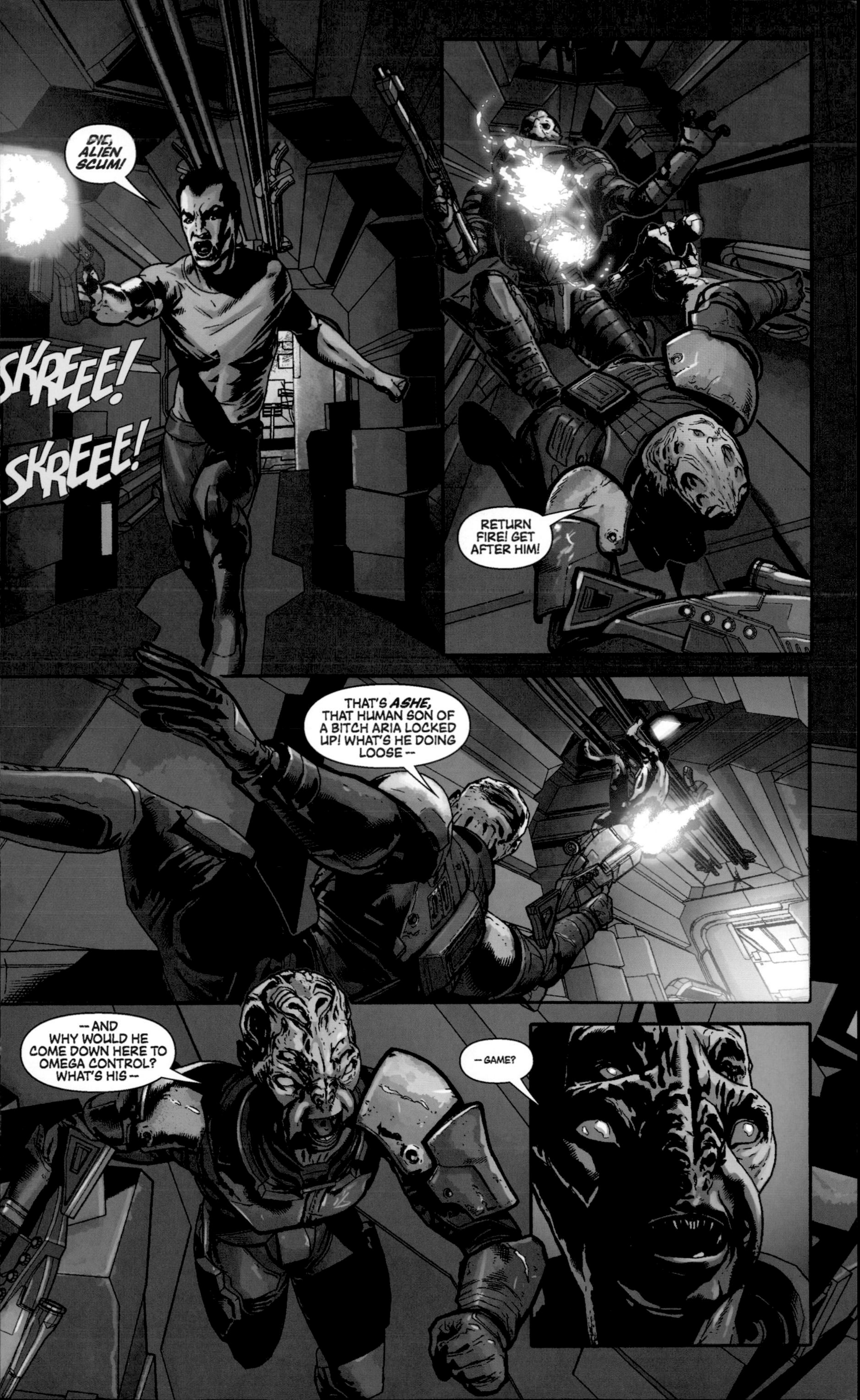
DIE, ALIEN SCUM!
SKREEE!
SKREEE!
RETURN FIRE! GET AFTER HIM!
THAT'S ASHE, THAT HUMAN SON OF A BITCH ARIA LOCKED UP! WHAT'S HE DOING LOOSE --
-- AND WHY WOULD HE COME DOWN HERE TO OMEGA CONTROL? WHAT'S HIS --
-- GAME?

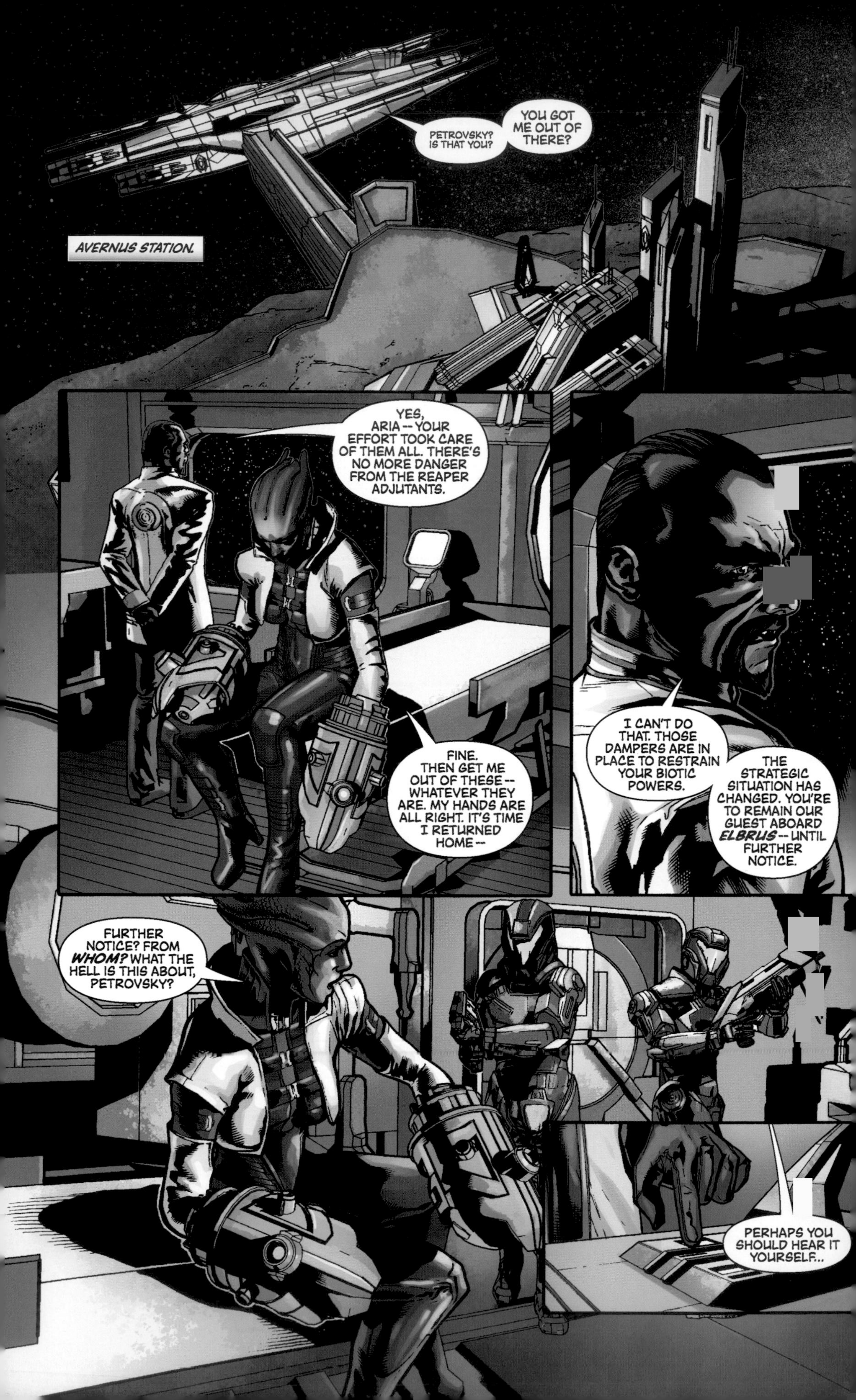
AVERNUS STATION.
PETROVSKY? IS THAT YOU?
YOU GOT ME OUT OF THERE?
YES, ARIA -- YOUR EFFORT TOOK CARE OF THEM ALL. THERE'S NO MORE DANGER FROM THE REAPER ADJUTANTS.
FINE. THEN GET ME OUT OF THESE -- WHATEVER THEY ARE. MY HANDS ARE ALL RIGHT. IT'S TIME I RETURNED HOME --
I CAN'T DO THAT. THOSE DAMPERS ARE IN PLACE TO RESTRAIN YOUR BIOTIC POWERS.
THE STRATEGIC SITUATION HAS CHANGED. YOU'RE TO REMAIN OUR GUEST ABOARD ELBRUS -- UNTIL FURTHER NOTICE.
FURTHER NOTICE? FROM WHOM? WHAT THE HELL IS THIS ABOUT, PETROVSKY?
PERHAPS YOU SHOULD HEAR IT YOURSELF...

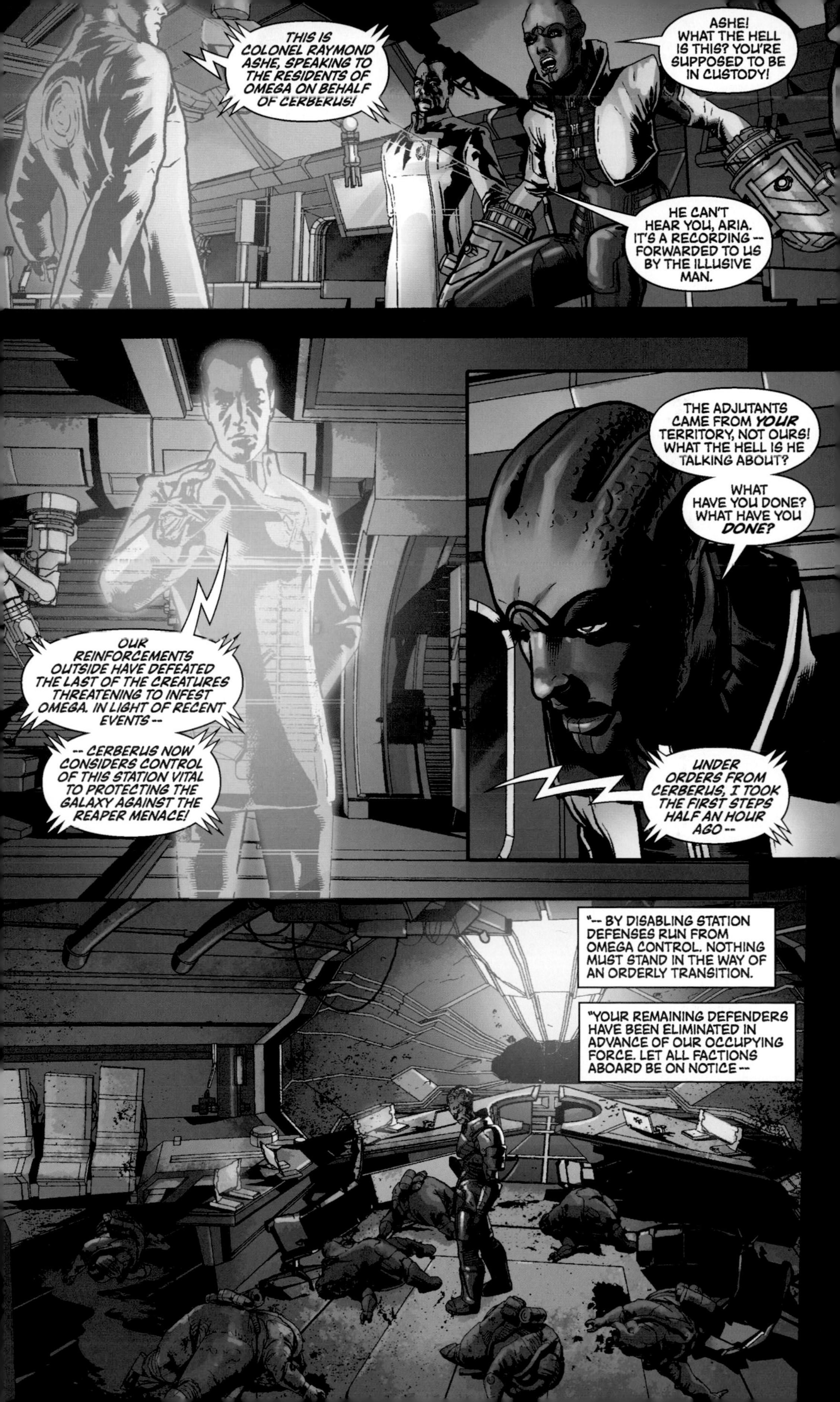

THIS IS COLONEL RAYMOND ASHE, SPEAKING TO THE RESIDENTS OF OMEGA ON BEHALF OF CERBERUS!
ASHE! WHAT THE HELL IS THIS? YOU'RE SUPPOSED TO BE IN CUSTODY!
HE CAN'T HEAR YOU, ARIA. IT'S A RECORDING -- FORWARDED TO US BY THE ILLUSIVE MAN.
OUR REINFORCEMENTS OUTSIDE HAVE DEFEATED THE LAST OF THE CREATURES THREATENING TO INFEST OMEGA. IN LIGHT OF RECENT EVENTS --
-- CERBERUS NOW CONSIDERS CONTROL OF THIS STATION VITAL TO PROTECTING THE GALAXY AGAINST THE REAPER MENACE!
THE ADJUTANTS CAME FROM YOUR TERRITORY, NOT OURS! WHAT THE HELL IS HE TALKING ABOUT?
WHAT HAVE YOU DONE? WHAT HAVE YOU DONE?
UNDER ORDERS FROM CERBERUS, I TOOK THE FIRST STEPS HALF AN HOUR AGO --
"-- BY DISABLING STATION DEFENSES RUN FROM OMEGA CONTROL. NOTHING MUST STAND IN THE WAY OF AN ORDERLY TRANSITION.
"YOUR REMAINING DEFENDERS HAVE BEEN ELIMINATED IN ADVANCE OF OUR OCCUPYING FORCE. LET ALL FACTIONS ABOARD BE ON NOTICE --

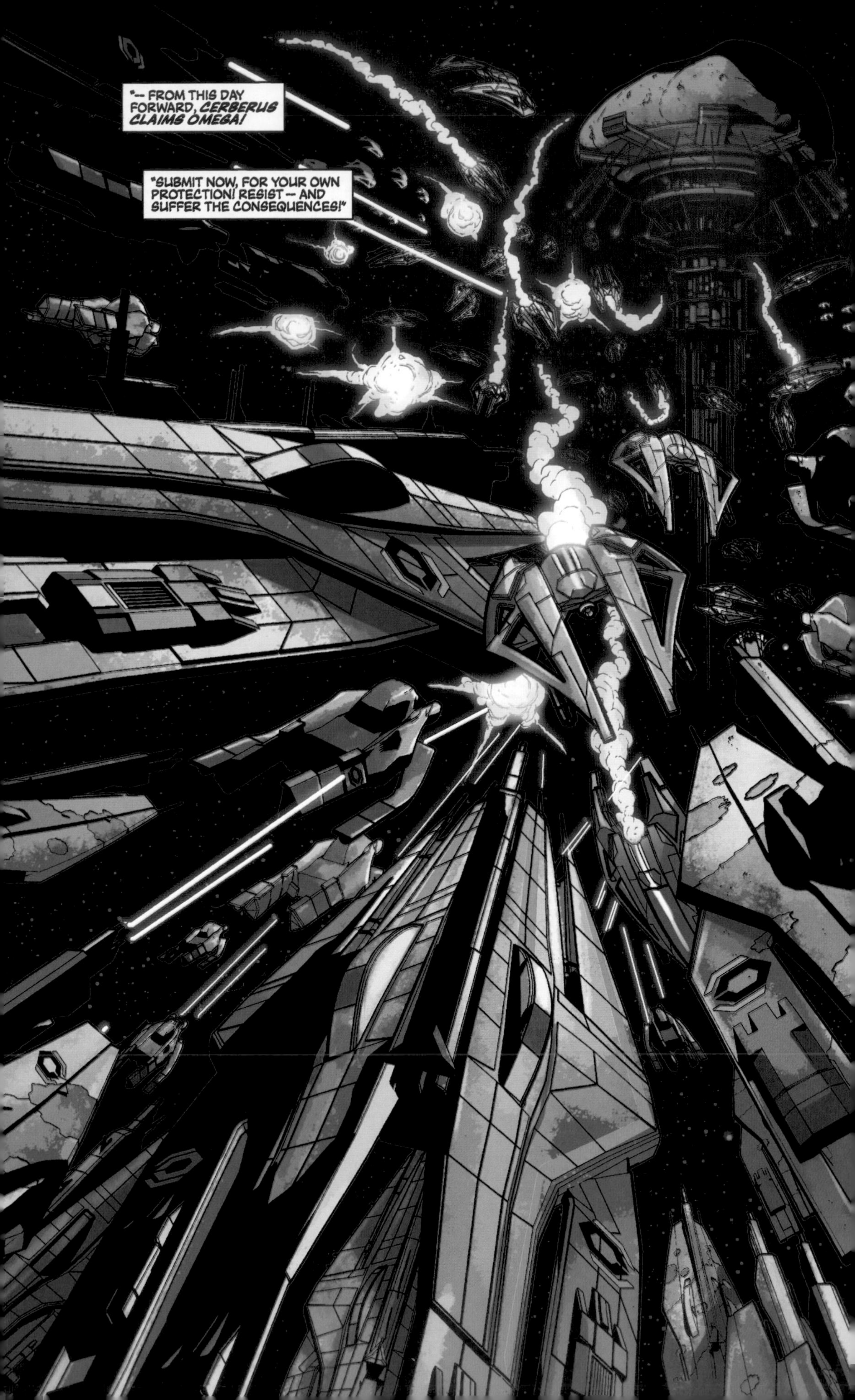
"-- FROM THIS DAY FORWARD, *CERBERUS CLAIMS OMEGA!*
"SUBMIT NOW, FOR YOUR OWN PROTECTION! RESIST -- AND SUFFER THE CONSEQUENCES!"

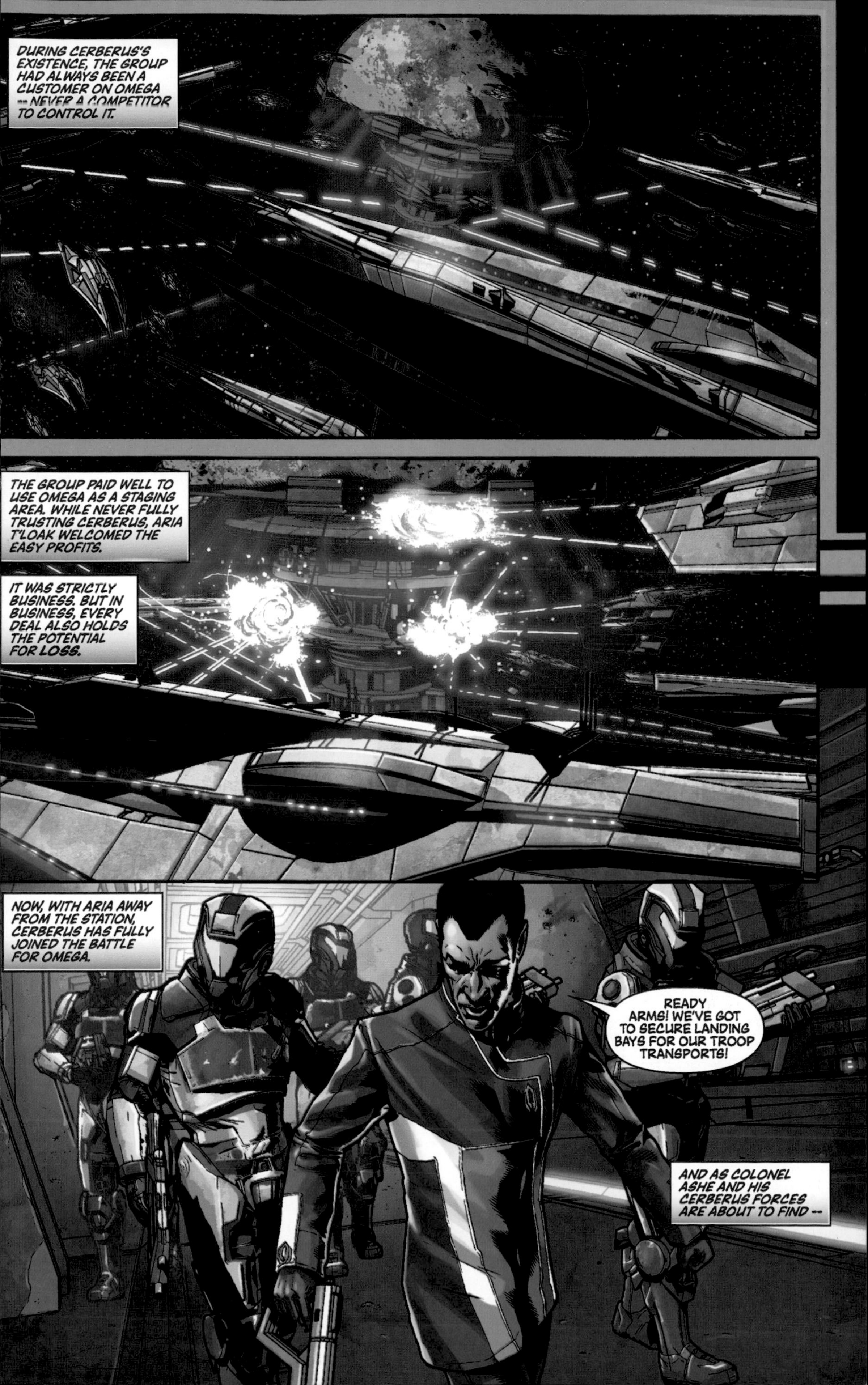
DURING CERBERUS'S EXISTENCE, THE GROUP HAD ALWAYS BEEN A CUSTOMER ON OMEGA -- NEVER A COMPETITOR TO CONTROL IT.
THE GROUP PAID WELL TO USE OMEGA AS A STAGING AREA. WHILE NEVER FULLY TRUSTING CERBERUS, ARIA T'LOAK WELCOMED THE EASY PROFITS.
IT WAS STRICTLY BUSINESS. BUT IN BUSINESS, EVERY DEAL ALSO HOLDS THE POTENTIAL FOR LOSS.
NOW, WITH ARIA AWAY FROM THE STATION, CERBERUS HAS FULLY JOINED THE BATTLE FOR OMEGA.
READY ARMS! WE'VE GOT TO SECURE LANDING BAYS FOR OUR TROOP TRANSPORTS!
AND AS COLONEL ASHE AND HIS CERBERUS FORCES ARE ABOUT TO FIND --

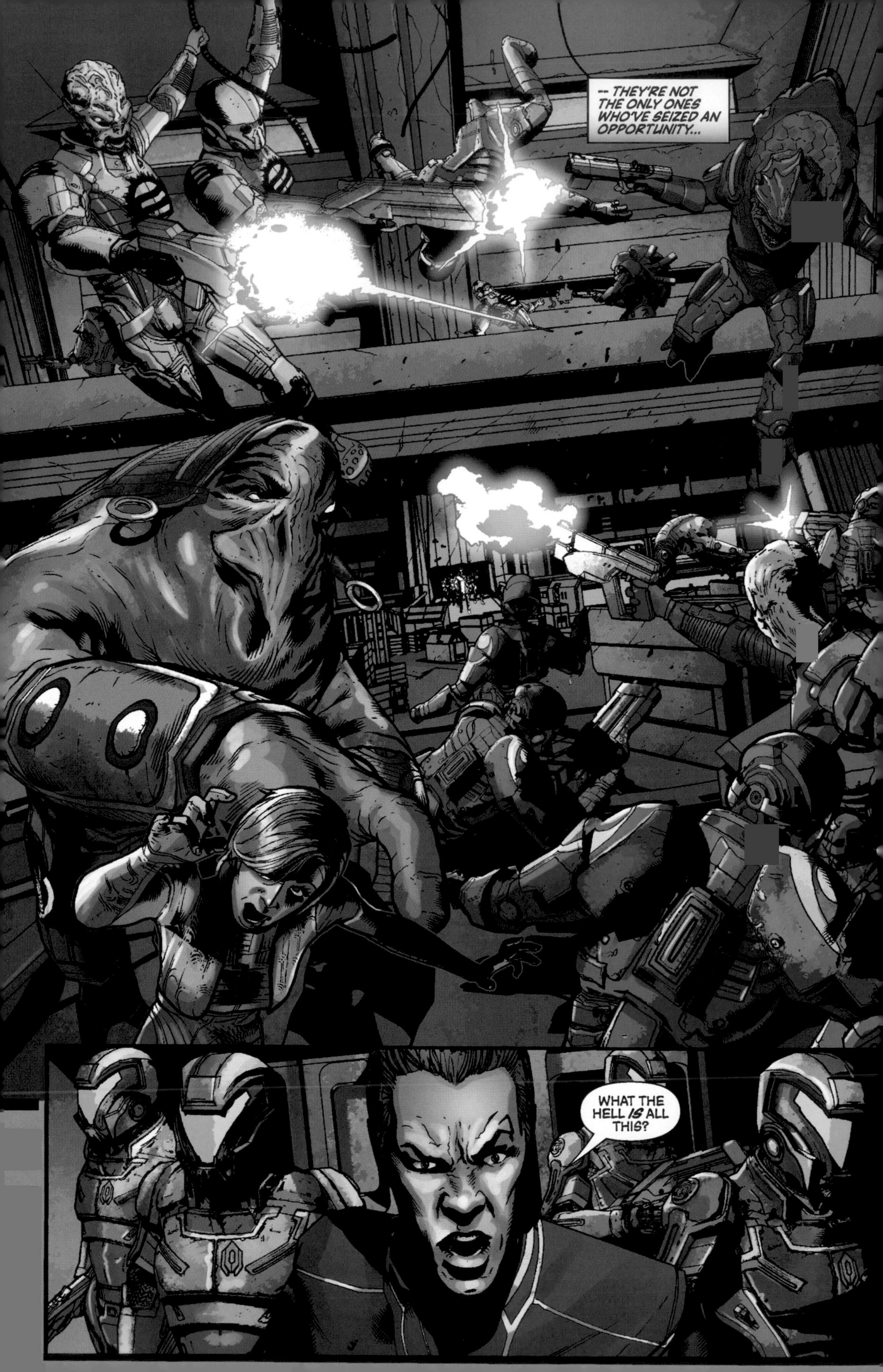
-- THEY'RE NOT THE ONLY ONES WHO'VE SEIZED AN OPPORTUNITY...
WHAT THE HELL IS ALL THIS?

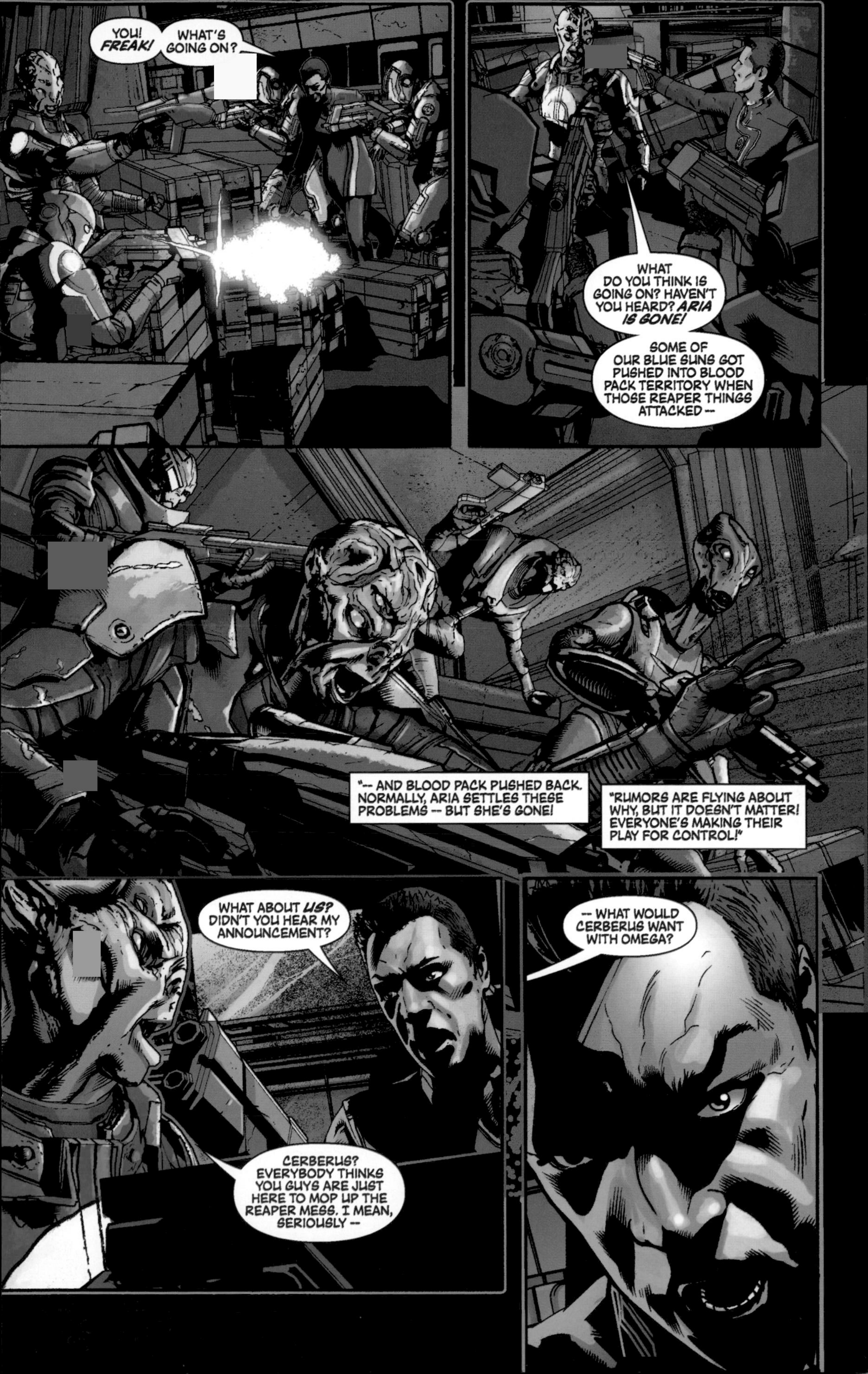
YOU! FREAK!
WHAT'S GOING ON?
WHAT DO YOU THINK IS GOING ON? HAVEN'T YOU HEARD? ARIA IS GONE!
SOME OF OUR BLUE SUNS GOT PUSHED INTO BLOOD PACK TERRITORY WHEN THOSE REAPER THINGS ATTACKED --
"-- AND BLOOD PACK PUSHED BACK. NORMALLY, ARIA SETTLES THESE PROBLEMS -- BUT SHE'S GONE!
"RUMORS ARE FLYING ABOUT WHY, BUT IT DOESN'T MATTER! EVERYONE'S MAKING THEIR PLAY FOR CONTROL!"
WHAT ABOUT US? DIDN'T YOU HEAR MY ANNOUNCEMENT?
CERBERUS? EVERYBODY THINKS YOU GUYS ARE JUST HERE TO MOP UP THE REAPER MESS. I MEAN, SERIOUSLY --
-- WHAT WOULD CERBERUS WANT WITH OMEGA?

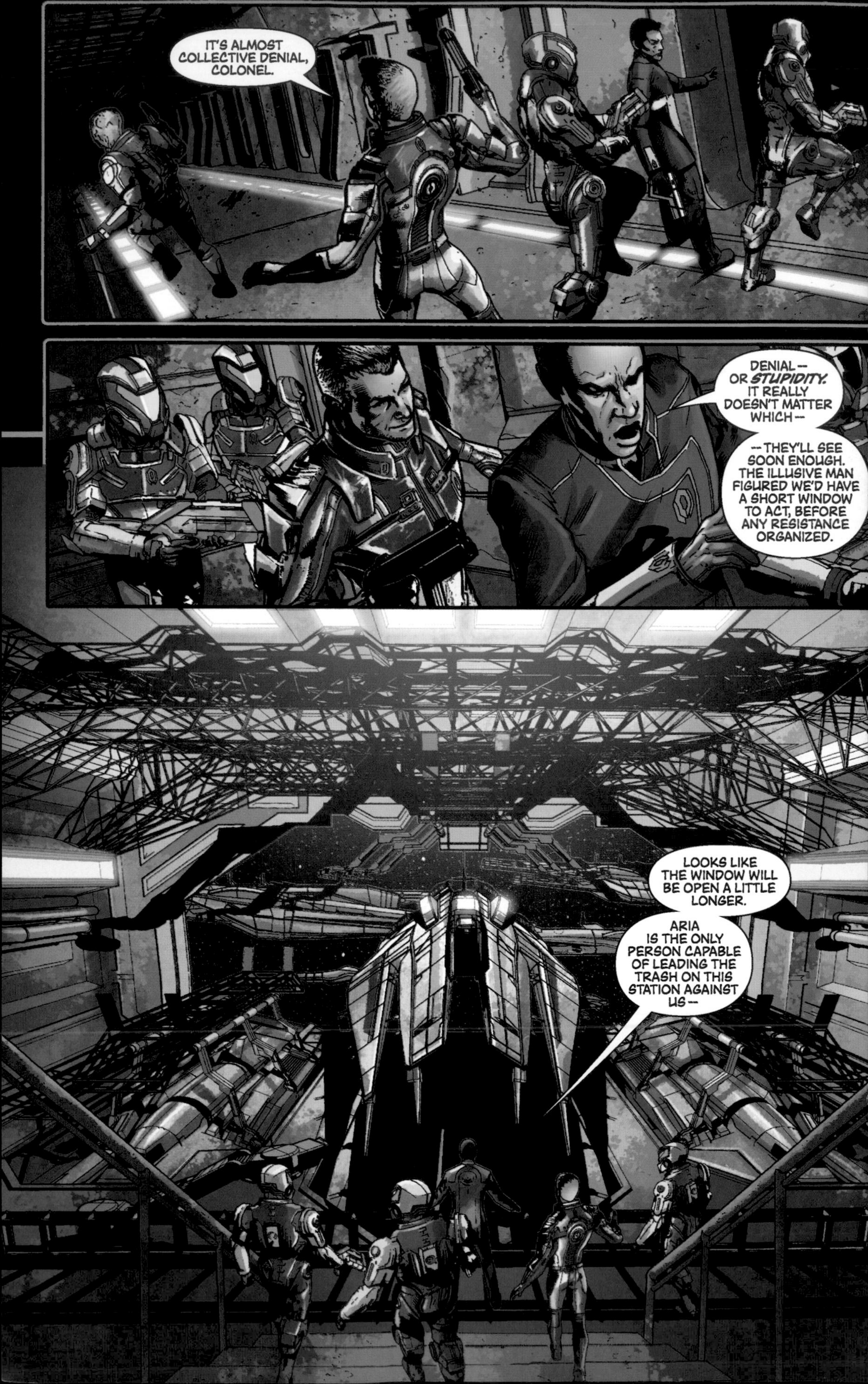
IT'S ALMOST COLLECTIVE DENIAL, COLONEL.
DENIAL -- OR *STUPIDITY.* IT REALLY DOESN'T MATTER WHICH --
-- THEY'LL SEE SOON ENOUGH. THE ILLUSIVE MAN FIGURED WE'D HAVE A SHORT WINDOW TO ACT, BEFORE ANY RESISTANCE ORGANIZED.
LOOKS LIKE THE WINDOW WILL BE OPEN A LITTLE LONGER.
ARIA IS THE ONLY PERSON CAPABLE OF LEADING THE TRASH ON THIS STATION AGAINST US --

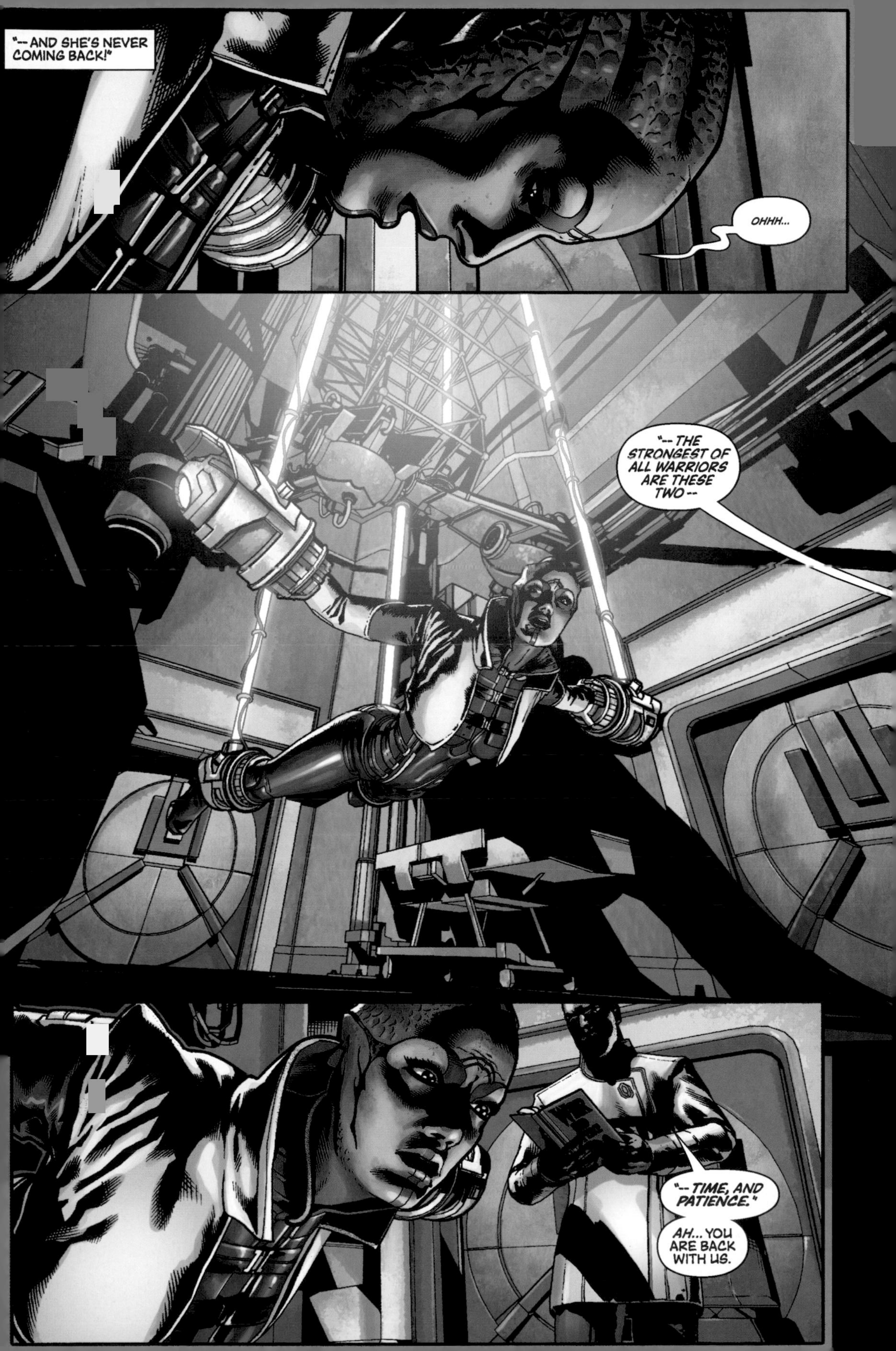
"-- AND SHE'S NEVER COMING BACK!"
OHHH...
"-- THE STRONGEST OF ALL WARRIORS ARE THESE TWO --
"-- TIME, AND PATIENCE."
AH... YOU ARE BACK WITH US.

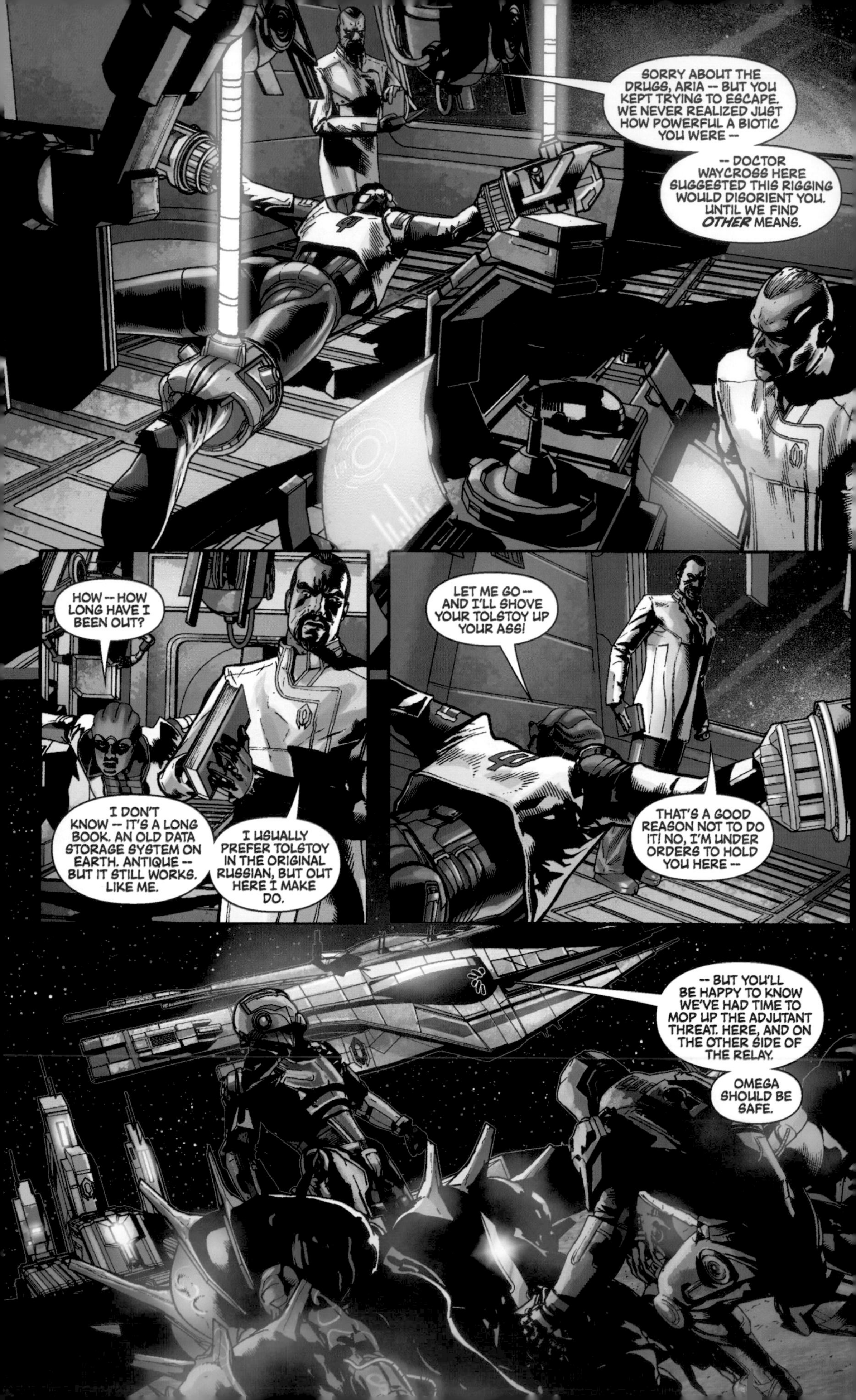

SORRY ABOUT THE DRUGS, ARIA -- BUT YOU KEPT TRYING TO ESCAPE. WE NEVER REALIZED JUST HOW POWERFUL A BIOTIC YOU WERE --
-- DOCTOR WAYCROSS HERE SUGGESTED THIS RIGGING WOULD DISORIENT YOU. UNTIL WE FIND *OTHER* MEANS.
HOW -- HOW LONG HAVE I BEEN OUT?
I DON'T KNOW -- IT'S A LONG BOOK. AN OLD DATA STORAGE SYSTEM ON EARTH. ANTIQUE -- BUT IT STILL WORKS. LIKE ME.
I USUALLY PREFER TOLSTOY IN THE ORIGINAL RUSSIAN, BUT OUT HERE I MAKE DO.
LET ME GO -- AND I'LL SHOVE YOUR TOLSTOY UP YOUR ASS!
THAT'S A GOOD REASON NOT TO DO IT! NO, I'M UNDER ORDERS TO HOLD YOU HERE --
-- BUT YOU'LL BE HAPPY TO KNOW WE'VE HAD TIME TO MOP UP THE ADJUTANT THREAT. HERE, AND ON THE OTHER SIDE OF THE RELAY.
OMEGA SHOULD BE SAFE.

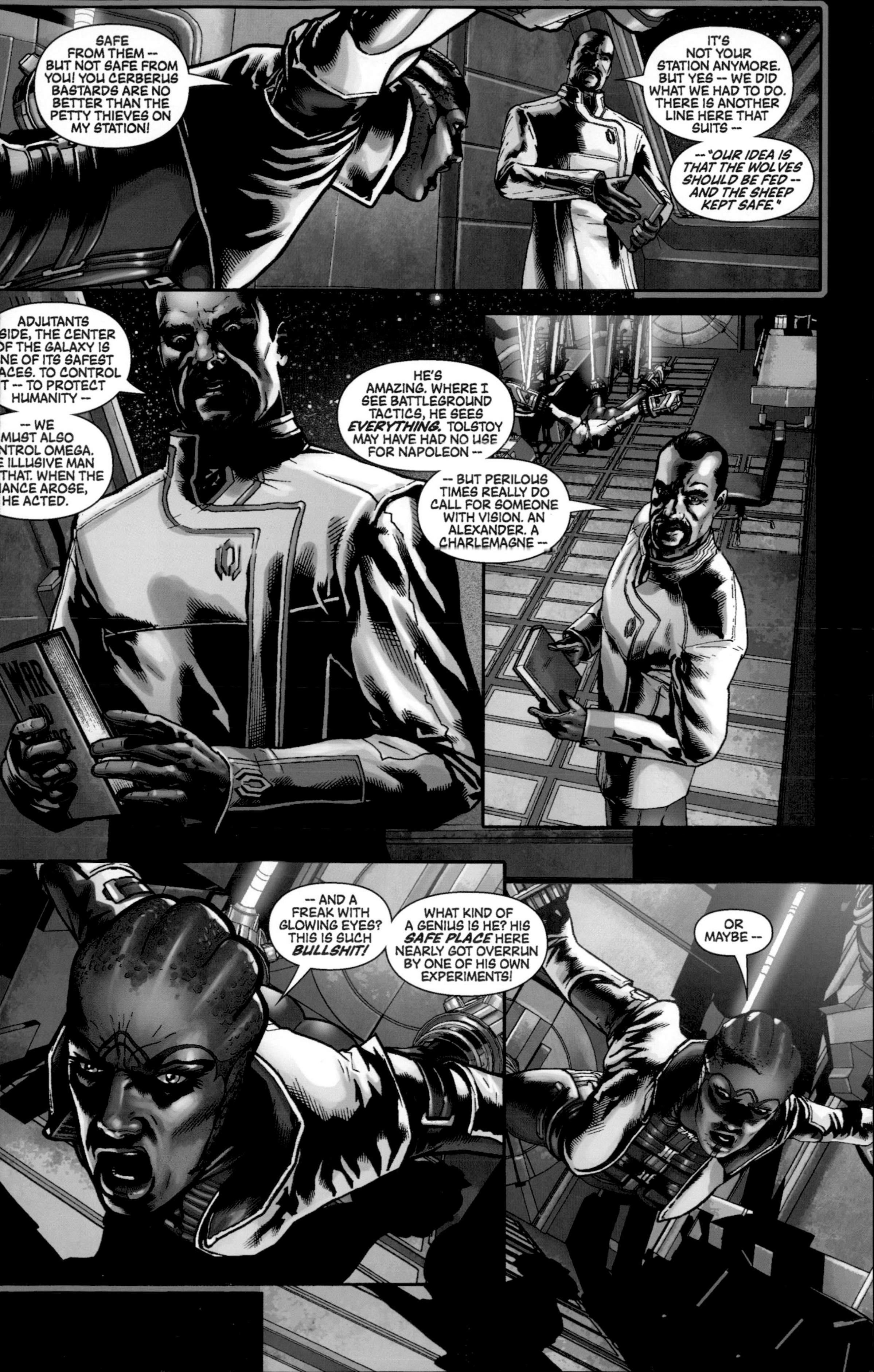
SAFE FROM THEM -- BUT NOT SAFE FROM YOU! YOU CERBERUS BASTARDS ARE NO BETTER THAN THE PETTY THIEVES ON MY STATION!
IT'S NOT YOUR STATION ANYMORE. BUT YES -- WE DID WHAT WE HAD TO DO. THERE IS ANOTHER LINE HERE THAT SUITS --
-- "OUR IDEA IS THAT THE WOLVES SHOULD BE FED -- AND THE SHEEP KEPT SAFE."
ADJUTANTS SIDE, THE CENTER F THE GALAXY IS NE OF ITS SAFEST ACES. TO CONTROL T -- TO PROTECT HUMANITY --
-- WE MUST ALSO NTROL OMEGA. E ILLUSIVE MAN THAT. WHEN THE HANCE AROSE, HE ACTED.
HE'S AMAZING. WHERE I SEE BATTLEGROUND TACTICS, HE SEES EVERYTHING. TOLSTOY MAY HAVE HAD NO USE FOR NAPOLEON --
-- BUT PERILOUS TIMES REALLY DO CALL FOR SOMEONE WITH VISION. AN ALEXANDER. A CHARLEMAGNE --
-- AND A FREAK WITH GLOWING EYES? THIS IS SUCH BULLSHIT!
WHAT KIND OF A GENIUS IS HE? HIS SAFE PLACE HERE NEARLY GOT OVERRUN BY ONE OF HIS OWN EXPERIMENTS!
OR MAYBE --

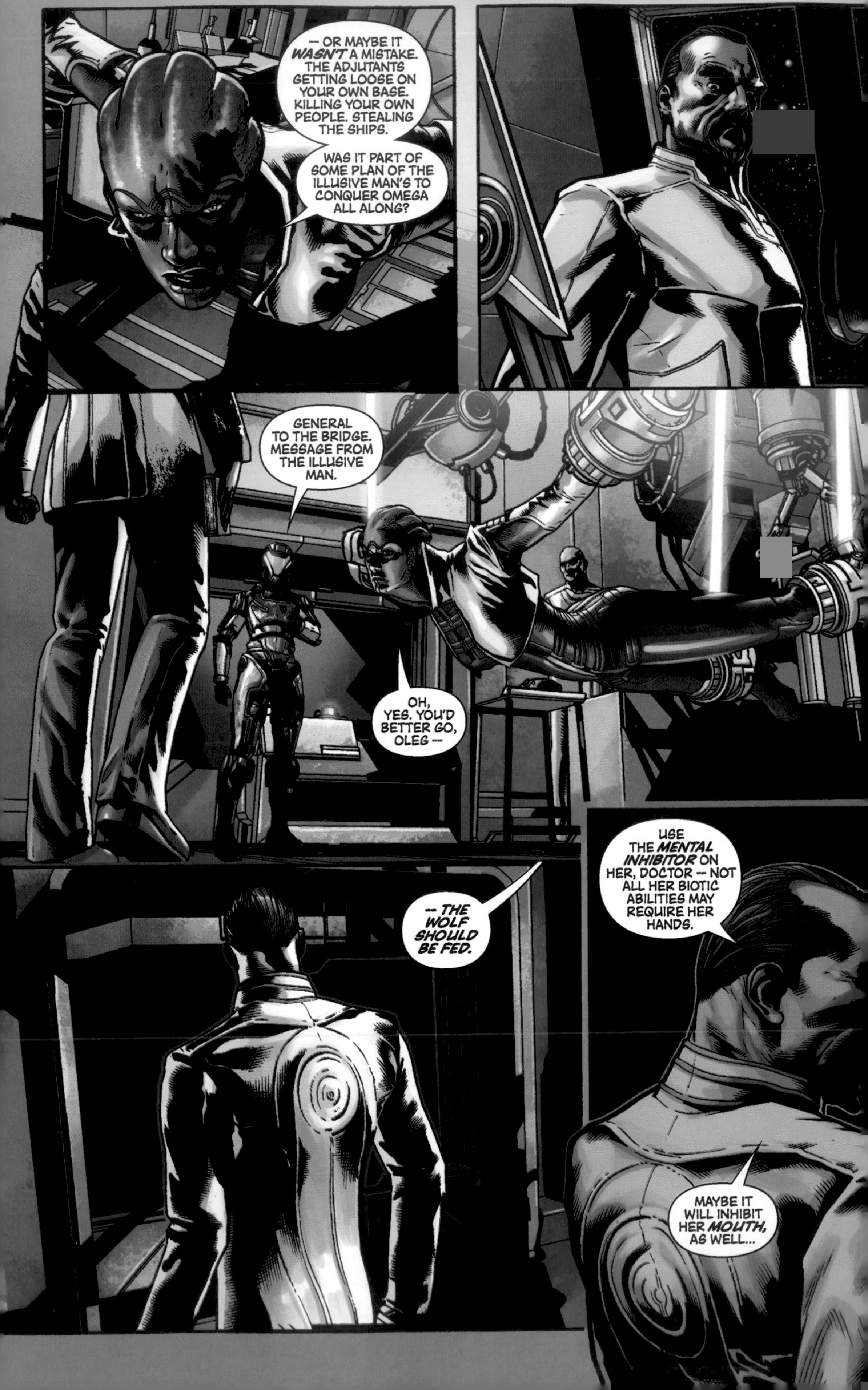
-- OR MAYBE IT WASN'T A MISTAKE. THE ADJUTANTS GETTING LOOSE ON YOUR OWN BASE. KILLING YOUR OWN PEOPLE. STEALING THE SHIPS.
WAS IT PART OF SOME PLAN OF THE ILLUSIVE MAN'S TO CONQUER OMEGA ALL ALONG?
GENERAL TO THE BRIDGE. MESSAGE FROM THE ILLUSIVE MAN.
OH, YES. YOU'D BETTER GO, OLEG --
-- THE WOLF SHOULD BE FED.
USE THE MENTAL INHIBITOR ON HER, DOCTOR -- NOT ALL HER BIOTIC ABILITIES MAY REQUIRE HER HANDS.
MAYBE IT WILL INHIBIT HER MOUTH, AS WELL...

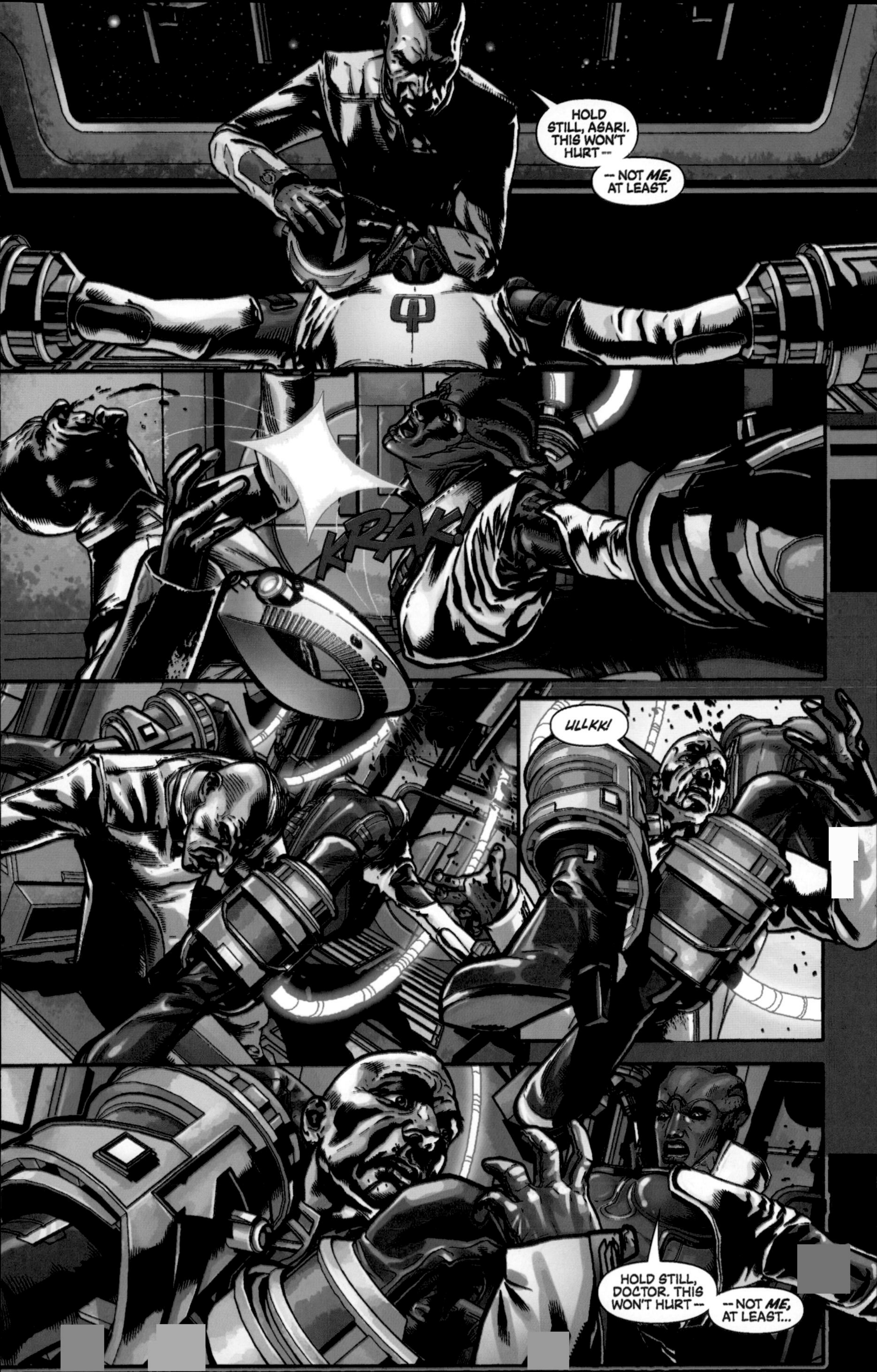
HOLD STILL, ASARI. THIS WON'T HURT --
-- NOT *ME,* AT LEAST.
KRAK!
ULLKK!
HOLD STILL, DOCTOR. THIS WON'T HURT --
-- NOT *ME,* AT LEAST...

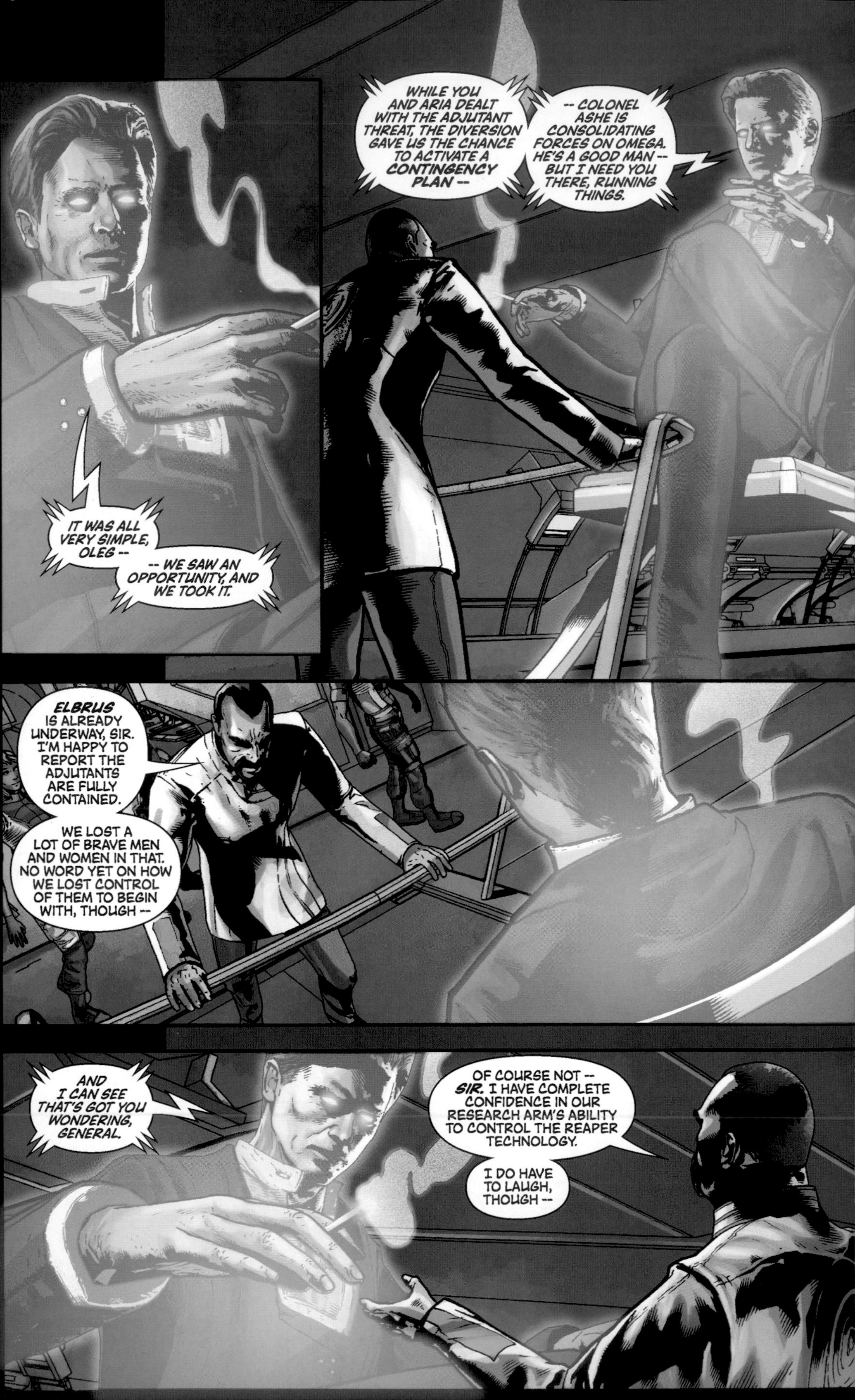

WHILE YOU AND ARIA DEALT WITH THE ADJUTANT THREAT, THE DIVERSION GAVE US THE CHANCE TO ACTIVATE A CONTINGENCY PLAN --
-- COLONEL ASHE IS CONSOLIDATING FORCES ON OMEGA. HE'S A GOOD MAN -- BUT I NEED YOU THERE, RUNNING THINGS.
IT WAS ALL VERY SIMPLE, OLEG --
-- WE SAW AN OPPORTUNITY, AND WE TOOK IT.
ELBRUS IS ALREADY UNDERWAY, SIR. I'M HAPPY TO REPORT THE ADJUTANTS ARE FULLY CONTAINED.
WE LOST A LOT OF BRAVE MEN AND WOMEN IN THAT. NO WORD YET ON HOW WE LOST CONTROL OF THEM TO BEGIN WITH, THOUGH --
AND I CAN SEE THAT'S GOT YOU WONDERING, GENERAL.
OF COURSE NOT -- SIR. I HAVE COMPLETE CONFIDENCE IN OUR RESEARCH ARM'S ABILITY TO CONTROL THE REAPER TECHNOLOGY.
I DO HAVE TO LAUGH, THOUGH --

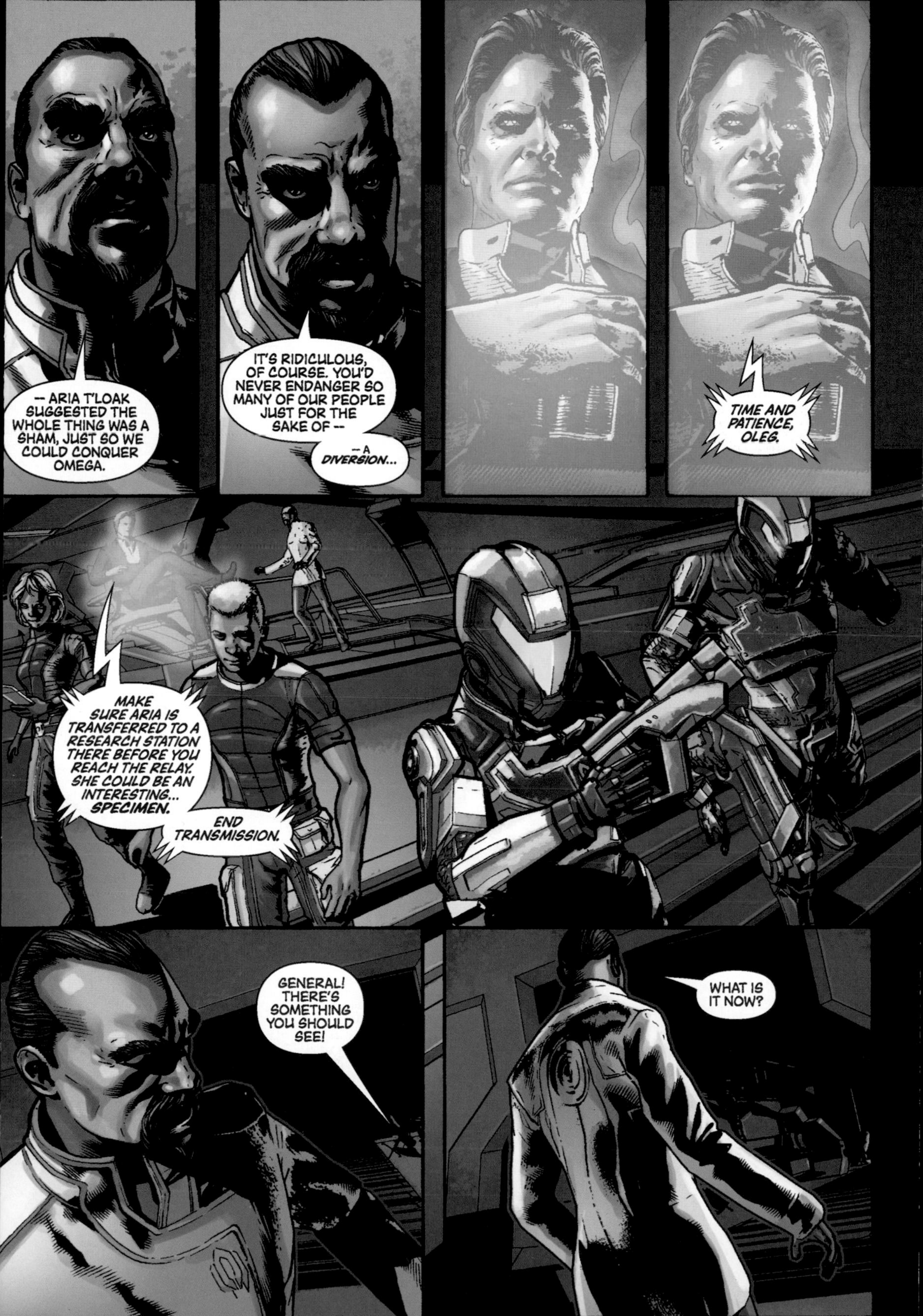
-- ARIA T'LOAK SUGGESTED THE WHOLE THING WAS A SHAM, JUST SO WE COULD CONQUER OMEGA.
IT'S RIDICULOUS, OF COURSE. YOU'D NEVER ENDANGER SO MANY OF OUR PEOPLE JUST FOR THE SAKE OF --
-- A *DIVERSION...*
TIME AND PATIENCE, OLEG.
MAKE SURE ARIA IS TRANSFERRED TO A RESEARCH STATION THERE BEFORE YOU REACH THE RELAY. SHE COULD BE AN INTERESTING... ***SPECIMEN.***
END TRANSMISSION.
GENERAL! THERE'S SOMETHING YOU SHOULD SEE!
WHAT IS IT NOW?

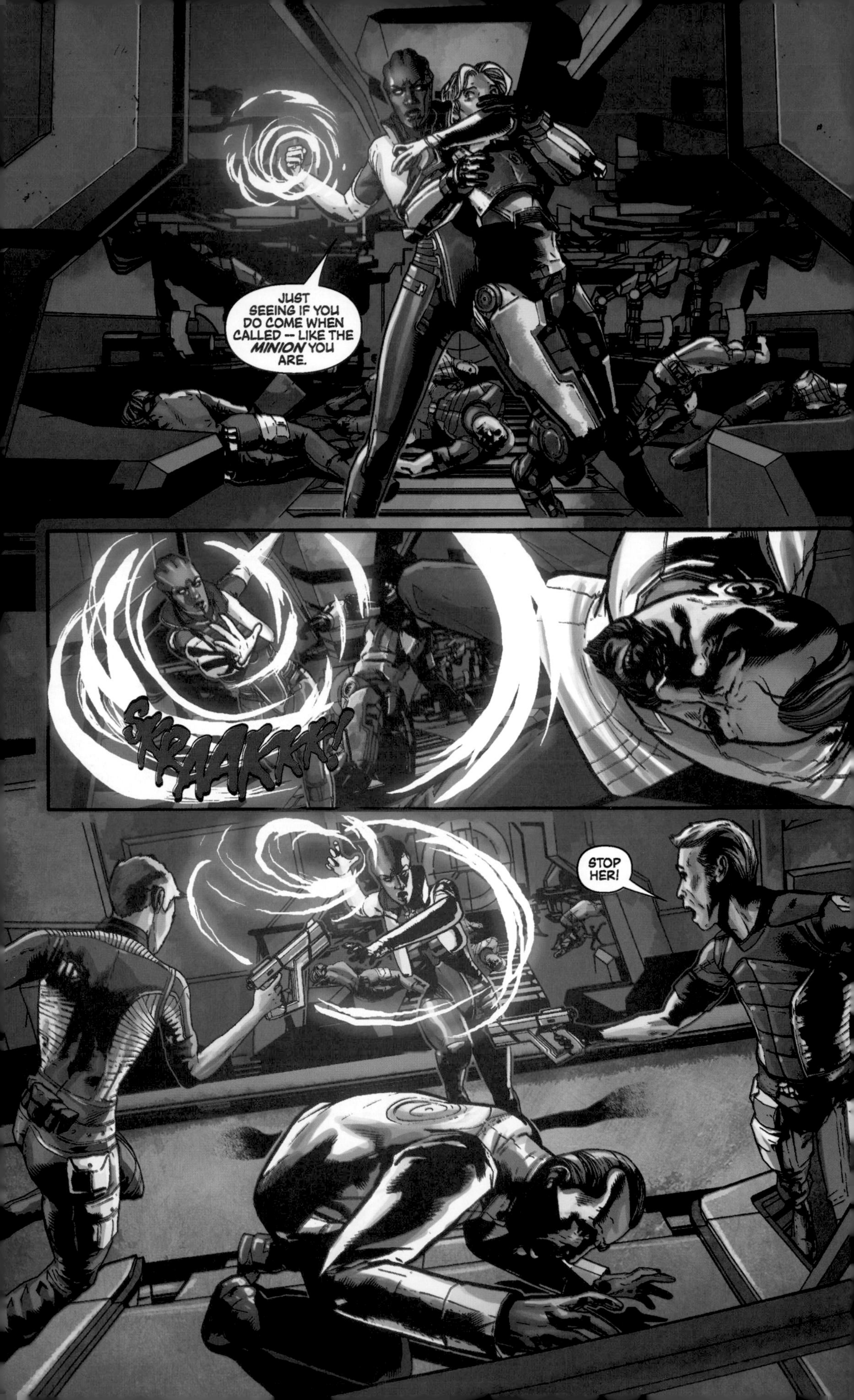
JUST SEEING IF YOU DO COME WHEN CALLED -- LIKE THE MINION YOU ARE.
SKRAAKKK!
STOP HER!

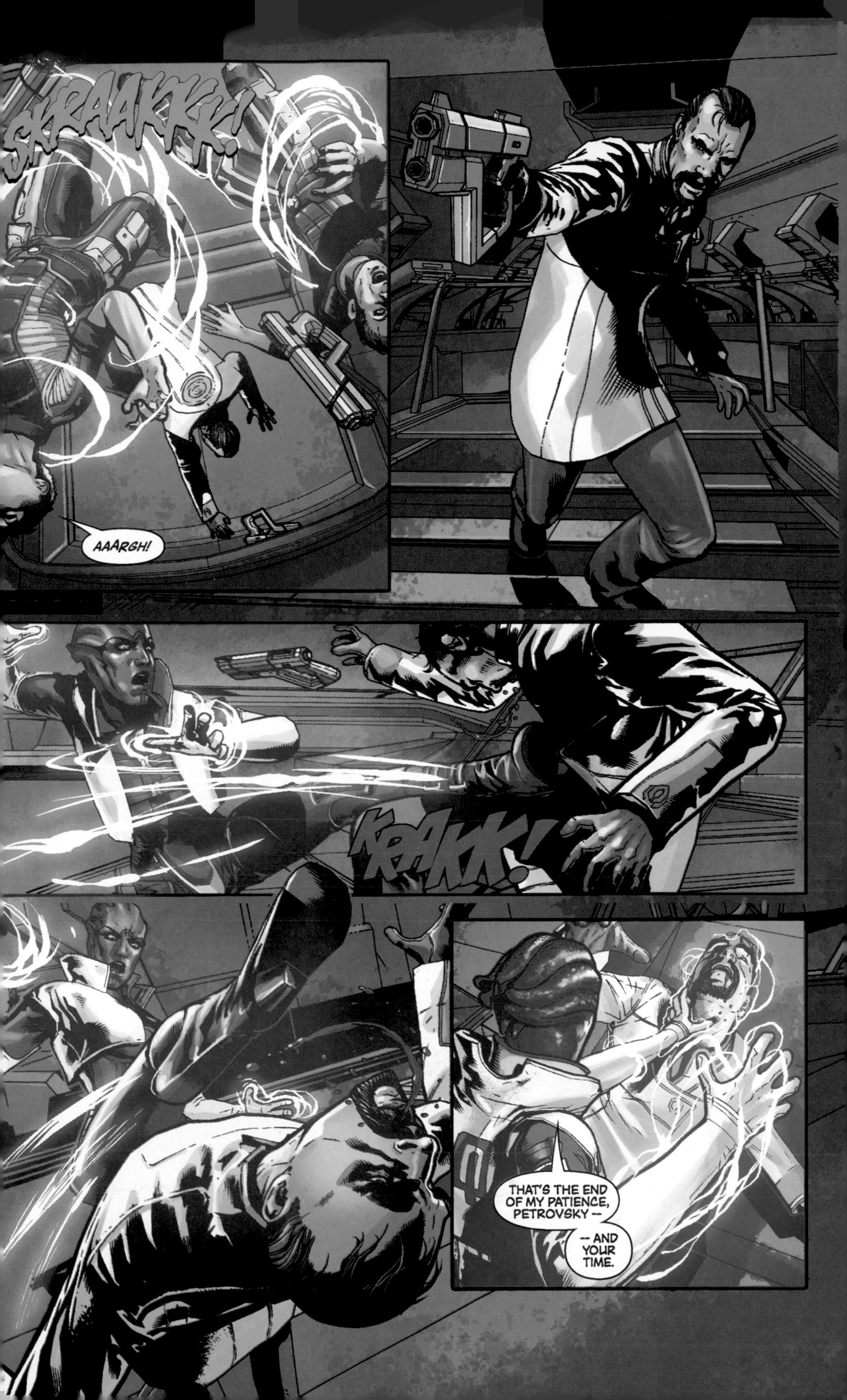
SKRAAKKK!
AAARGH!
KRAKK!
THAT'S THE END OF MY PATIENCE, PETROVSKY --
-- AND YOUR TIME.

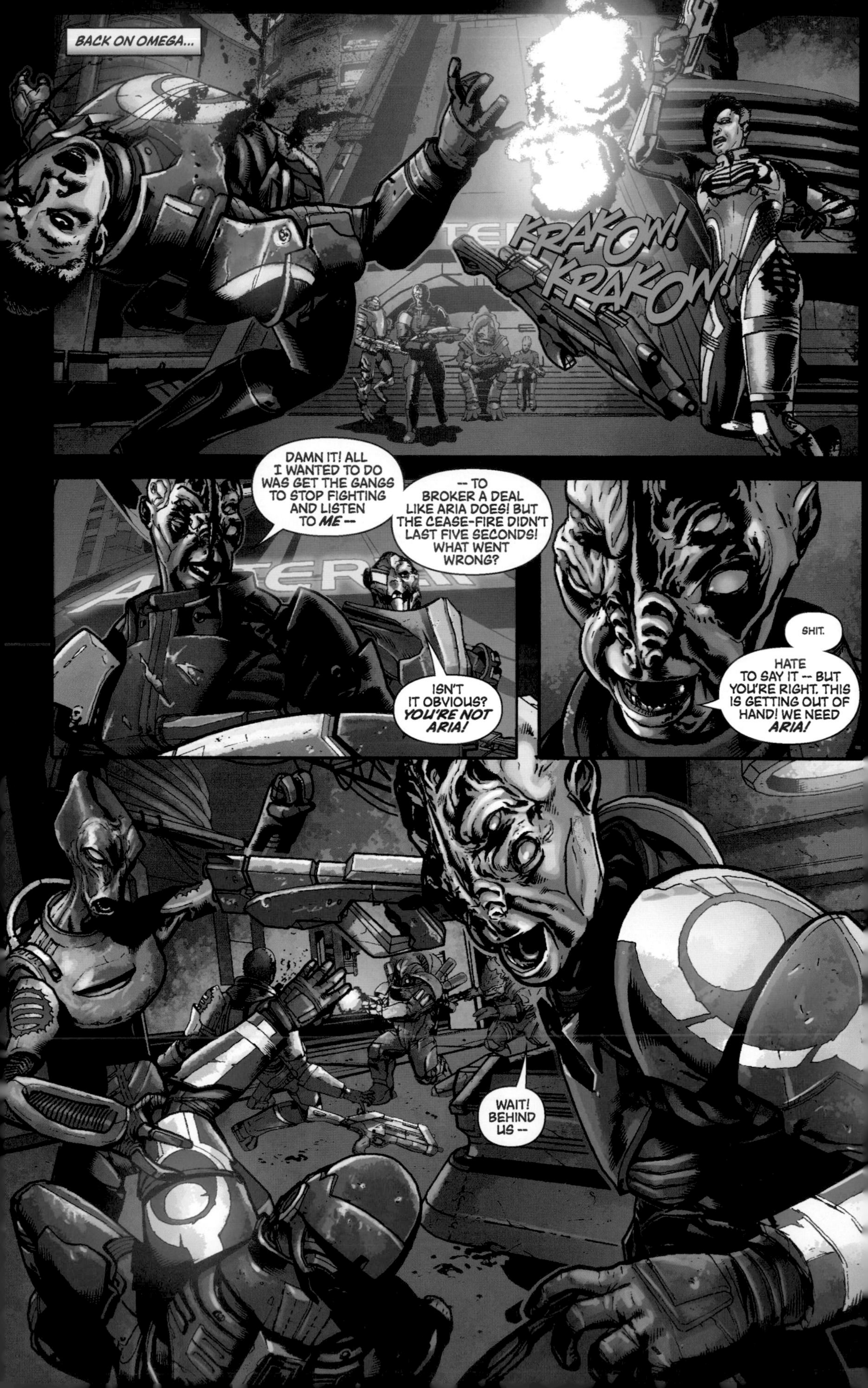
BACK ON OMEGA...
KRAKOW! KRAKOW!
DAMN IT! ALL I WANTED TO DO WAS GET THE GANGS TO STOP FIGHTING AND LISTEN TO *ME* --
-- TO BROKER A DEAL LIKE ARIA DOES! BUT THE CEASE-FIRE DIDN'T LAST FIVE SECONDS! WHAT WENT WRONG?
ISN'T IT OBVIOUS? ***YOU'RE NOT ARIA!***
SHIT.
HATE TO SAY IT -- BUT YOU'RE RIGHT. THIS IS GETTING OUT OF HAND! WE NEED ***ARIA!***
WAIT! BEHIND US --

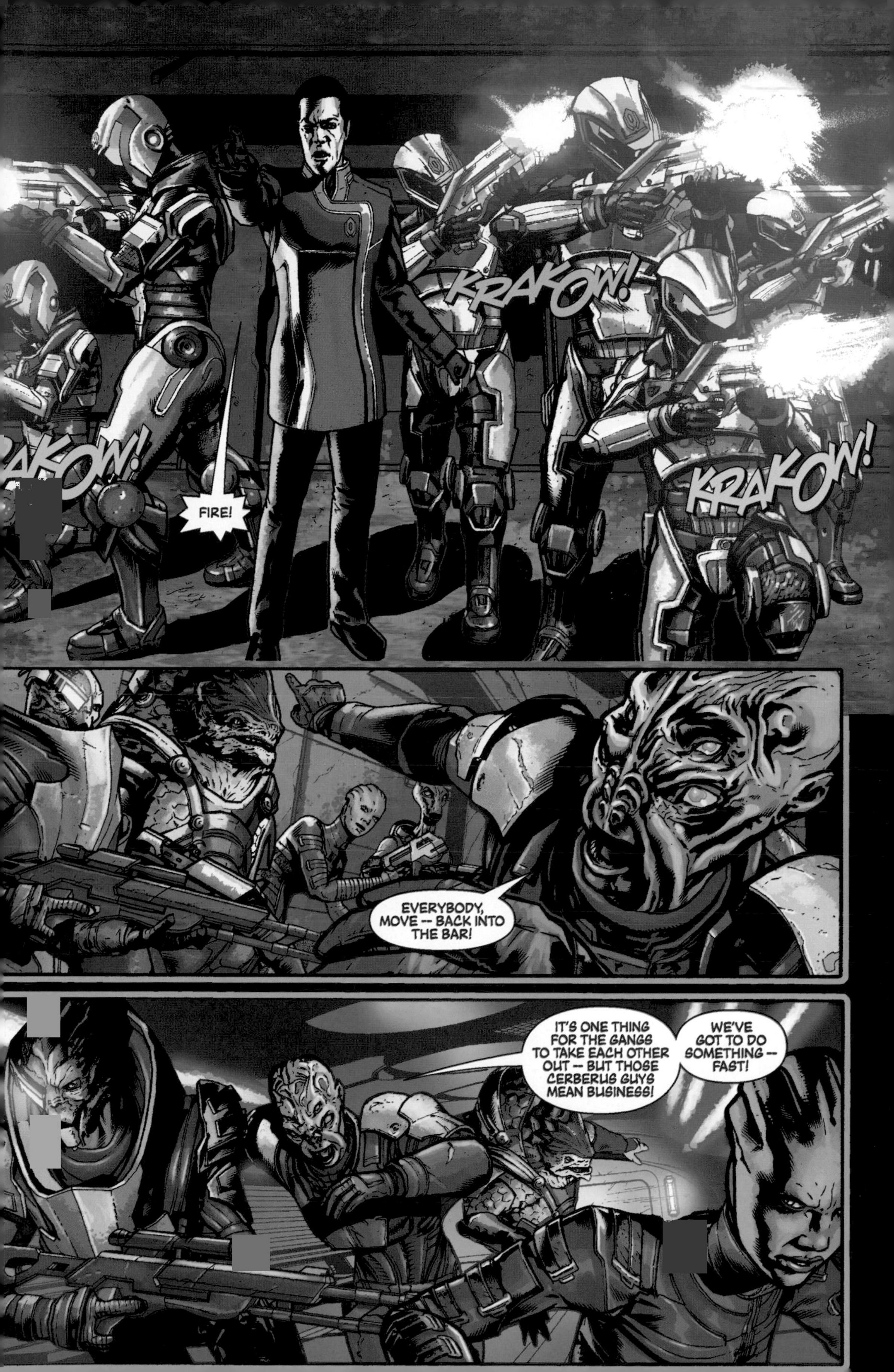
AKOW!
FIRE!
KRAKOW!
KRAKOW!
EVERYBODY, MOVE -- BACK INTO THE BAR!
IT'S ONE THING FOR THE GANGS TO TAKE EACH OTHER OUT -- BUT THOSE CERBERUS GUYS MEAN BUSINESS!
WE'VE GOT TO DO SOMETHING -- FAST!

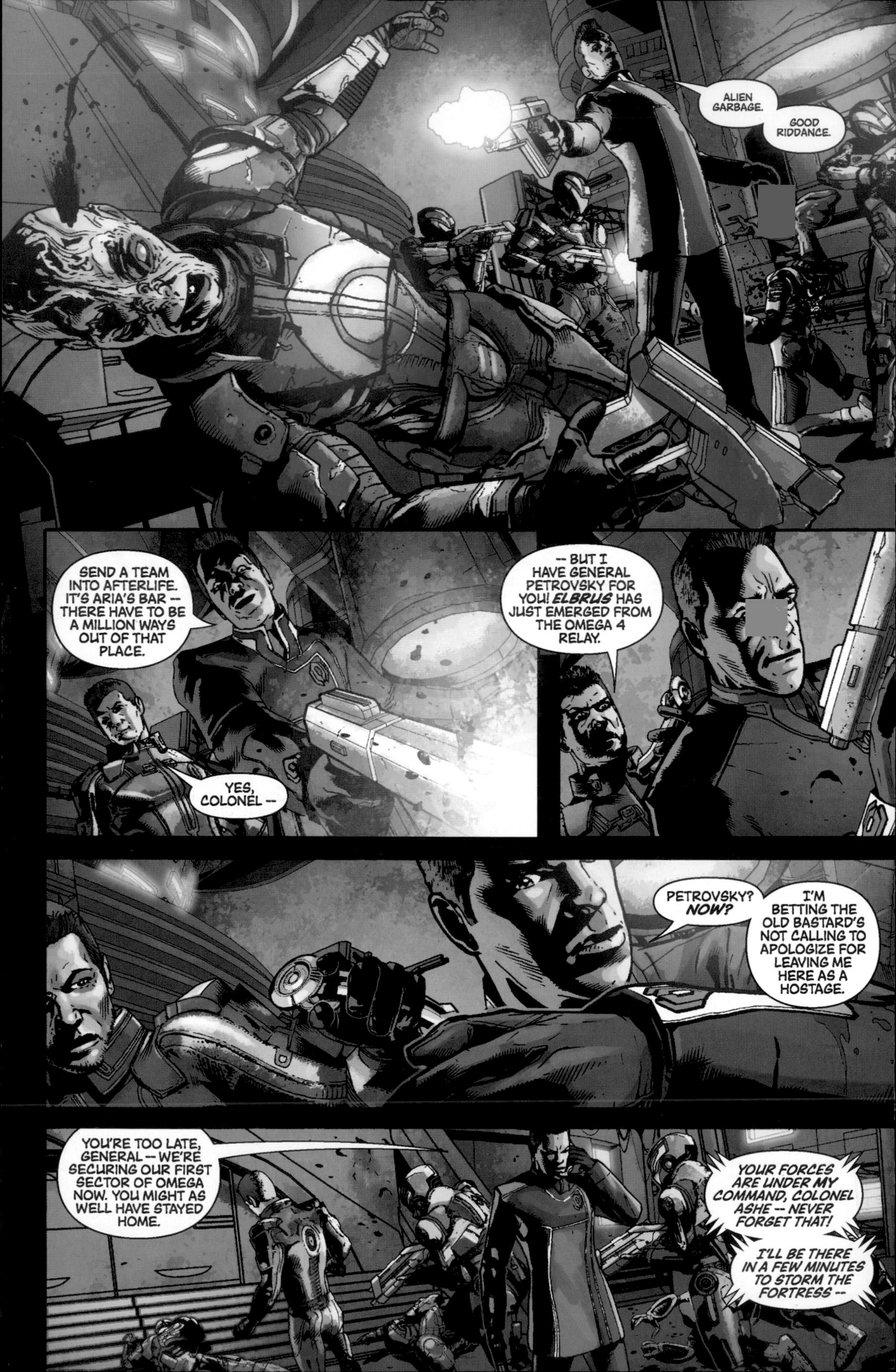
ALIEN GARBAGE.
GOOD RIDDANCE.
SEND A TEAM INTO AFTERLIFE. IT'S ARIA'S BAR -- THERE HAVE TO BE A MILLION WAYS OUT OF THAT PLACE.
YES, COLONEL --
-- BUT I HAVE GENERAL PETROVSKY FOR YOU! *ELBRUS* HAS JUST EMERGED FROM THE OMEGA 4 RELAY.
PETROVSKY? *NOW?*
I'M BETTING THE OLD BASTARD'S NOT CALLING TO APOLOGIZE FOR LEAVING ME HERE AS A HOSTAGE.
YOU'RE TOO LATE, GENERAL -- WE'RE SECURING OUR FIRST SECTOR OF OMEGA NOW. YOU MIGHT AS WELL HAVE STAYED HOME.
YOUR FORCES ARE UNDER MY COMMAND, COLONEL ASHE -- NEVER FORGET THAT!
I'LL BE THERE IN A FEW MINUTES TO STORM THE FORTRESS --

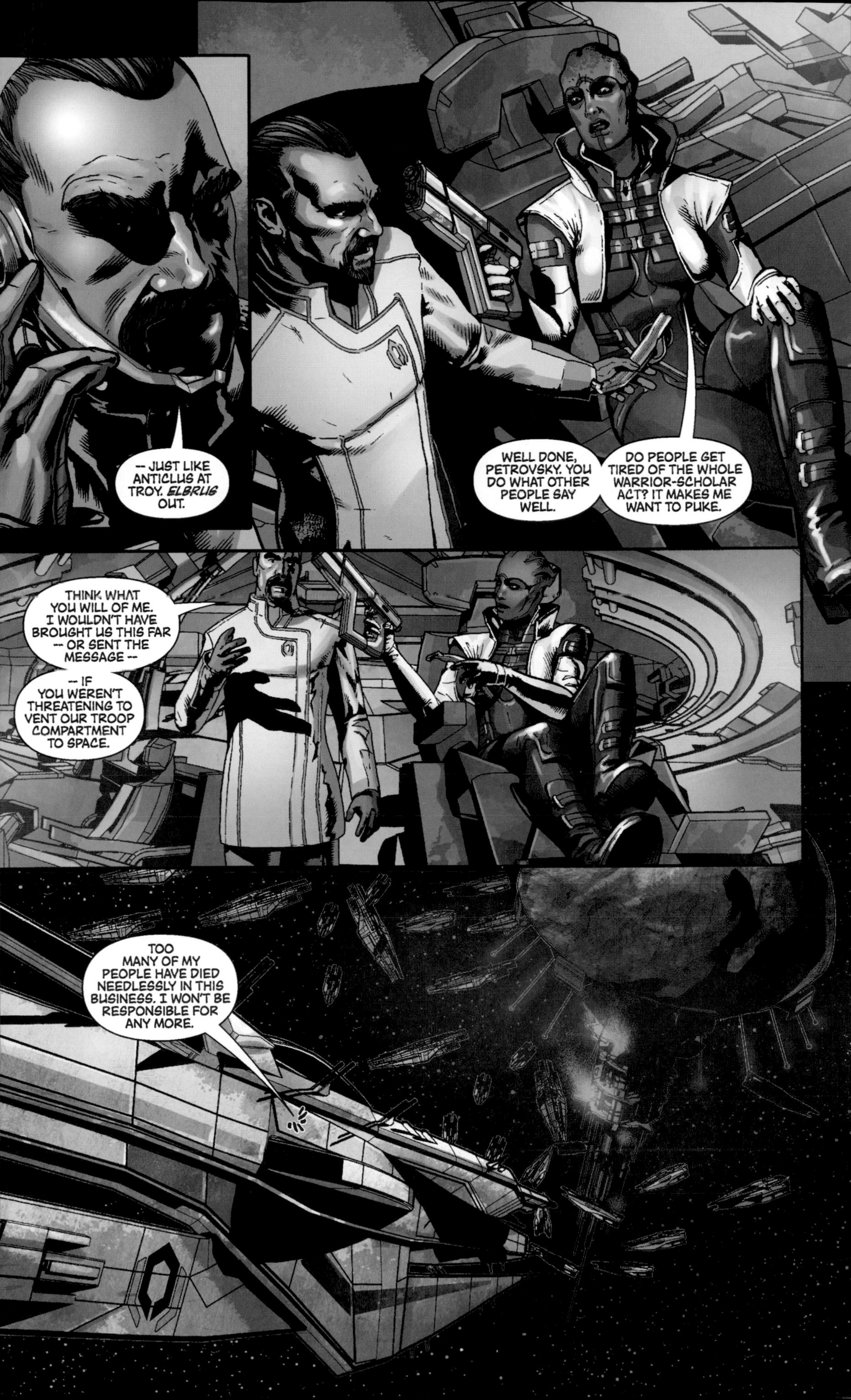
-- JUST LIKE ANTICLUS AT TROY. ELBRUS OUT.
WELL DONE, PETROVSKY. YOU DO WHAT OTHER PEOPLE SAY WELL.
DO PEOPLE GET TIRED OF THE WHOLE WARRIOR-SCHOLAR ACT? IT MAKES ME WANT TO PUKE.
THINK WHAT YOU WILL OF ME. I WOULDN'T HAVE BROUGHT US THIS FAR -- OR SENT THE MESSAGE --
-- IF YOU WEREN'T THREATENING TO VENT OUR TROOP COMPARTMENT TO SPACE.
TOO MANY OF MY PEOPLE HAVE DIED NEEDLESSLY IN THIS BUSINESS. I WON'T BE RESPONSIBLE FOR ANY MORE.

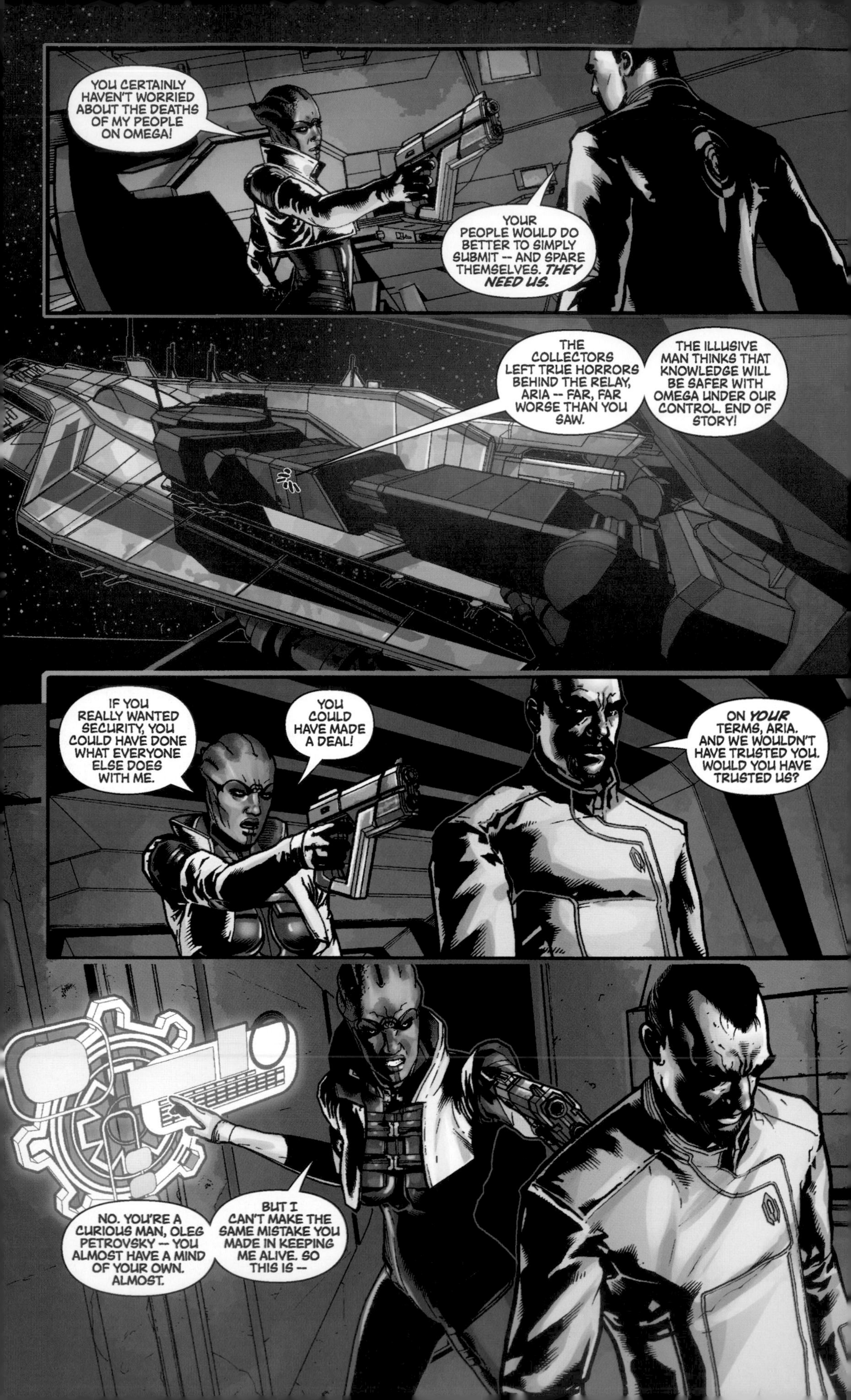
YOU CERTAINLY HAVEN'T WORRIED ABOUT THE DEATHS OF MY PEOPLE ON OMEGA!
YOUR PEOPLE WOULD DO BETTER TO SIMPLY SUBMIT -- AND SPARE THEMSELVES. THEY NEED US.
THE COLLECTORS LEFT TRUE HORRORS BEHIND THE RELAY, ARIA -- FAR, FAR WORSE THAN YOU SAW.
THE ILLUSIVE MAN THINKS THAT KNOWLEDGE WILL BE SAFER WITH OMEGA UNDER OUR CONTROL. END OF STORY!
IF YOU REALLY WANTED SECURITY, YOU COULD HAVE DONE WHAT EVERYONE ELSE DOES WITH ME.
YOU COULD HAVE MADE A DEAL!
ON YOUR TERMS, ARIA. AND WE WOULDN'T HAVE TRUSTED YOU. WOULD YOU HAVE TRUSTED US?
NO. YOU'RE A CURIOUS MAN, OLEG PETROVSKY -- YOU ALMOST HAVE A MIND OF YOUR OWN. ALMOST.
BUT I CAN'T MAKE THE SAME MISTAKE YOU MADE IN KEEPING ME ALIVE. SO THIS IS --

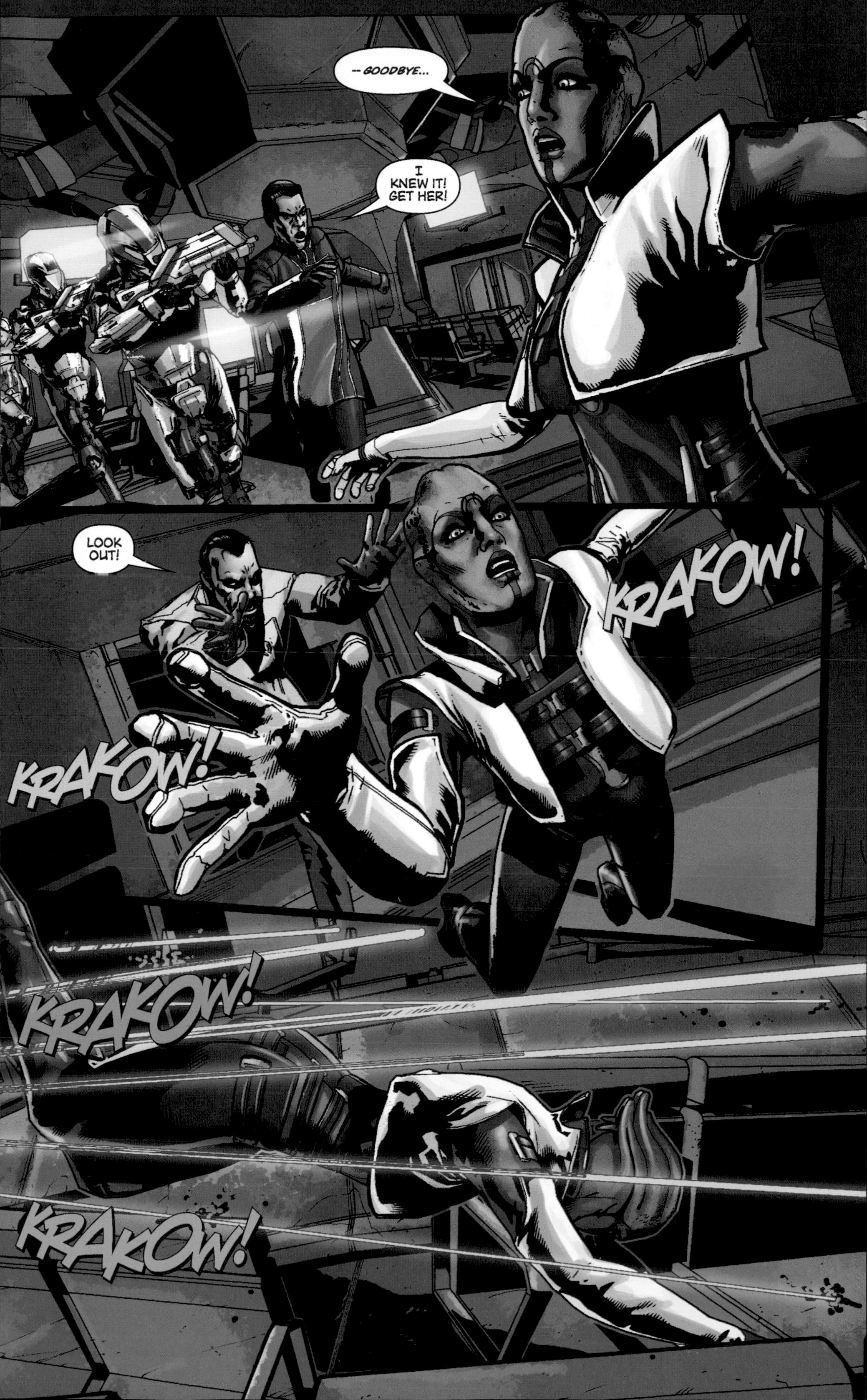
-- GOODBYE...
I KNEW IT! GET HER!
LOOK OUT!
KRAKOW!
KRAKOW!
KRAKOW!
KRAKOW!

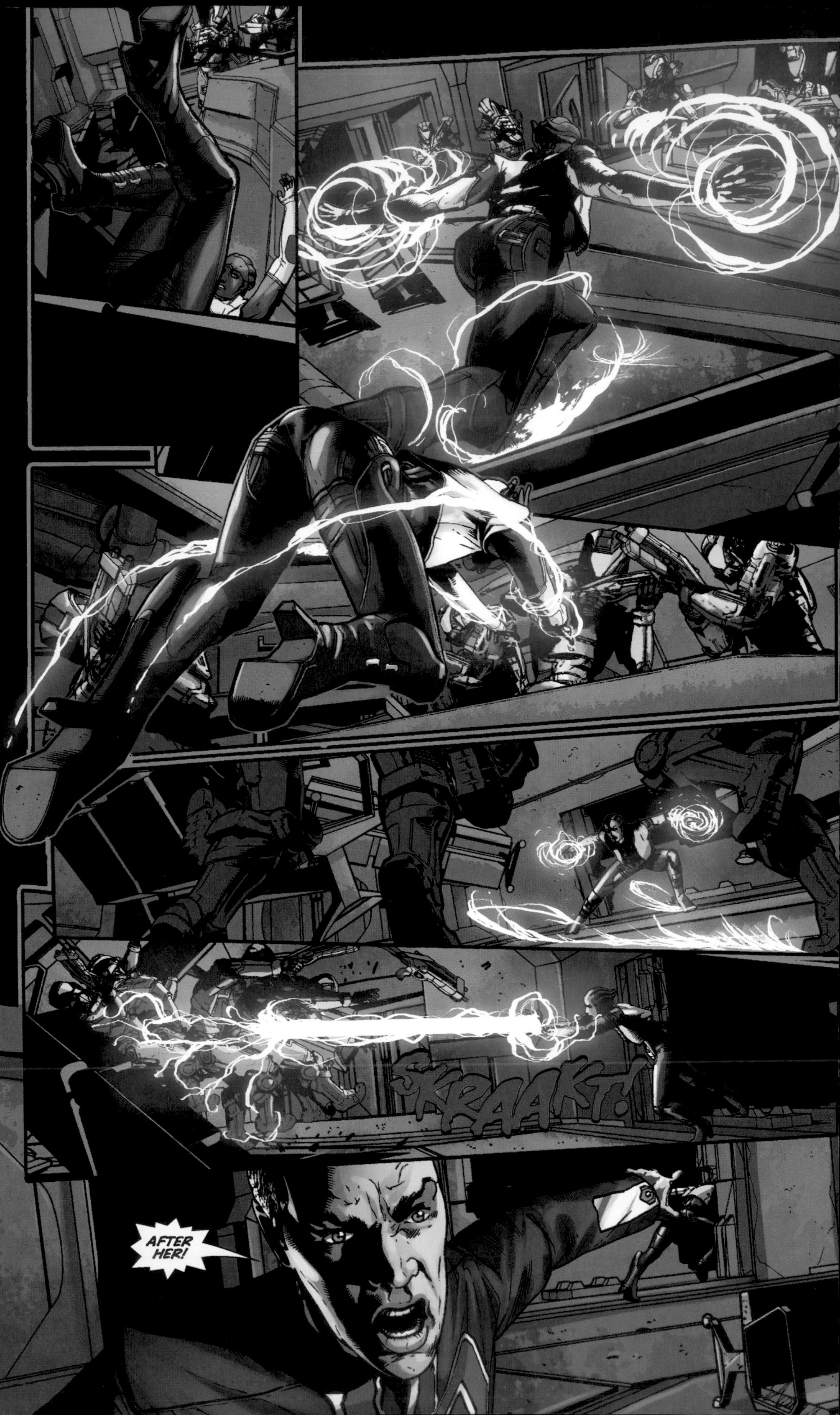
SKRAAKT!
AFTER HER!

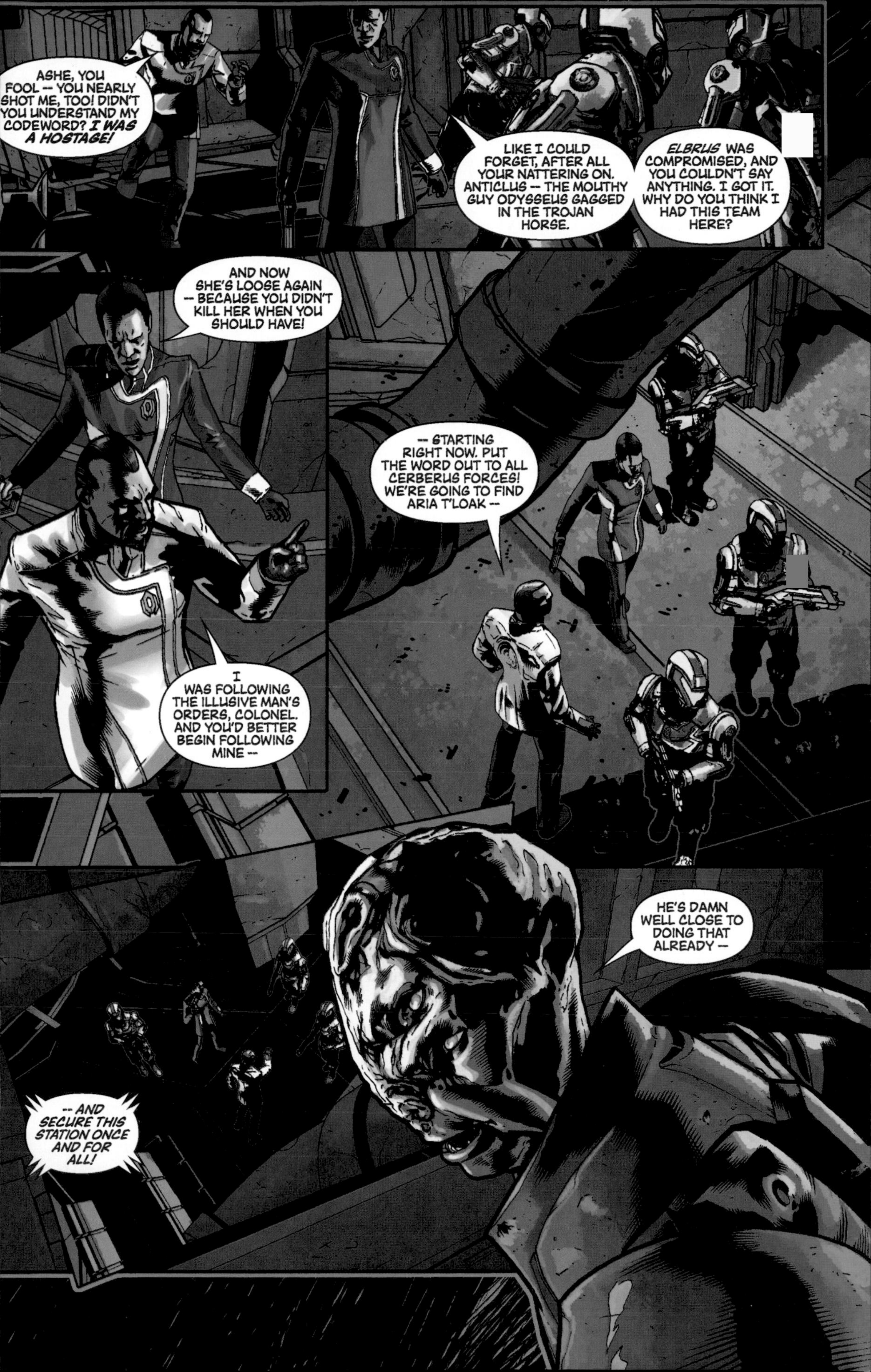
ASHE, YOU FOOL -- YOU NEARLY SHOT ME, TOO! DIDN'T YOU UNDERSTAND MY CODEWORD? I WAS A HOSTAGE!
LIKE I COULD FORGET, AFTER ALL YOUR NATTERING ON. ANTICLUS -- THE MOUTHY GUY ODYSSEUS GAGGED IN THE TROJAN HORSE.
ELBRUS WAS COMPROMISED, AND YOU COULDN'T SAY ANYTHING. I GOT IT. WHY DO YOU THINK I HAD THIS TEAM HERE?
AND NOW SHE'S LOOSE AGAIN -- BECAUSE YOU DIDN'T KILL HER WHEN YOU SHOULD HAVE!
I WAS FOLLOWING THE ILLUSIVE MAN'S ORDERS, COLONEL. AND YOU'D BETTER BEGIN FOLLOWING MINE --
-- STARTING RIGHT NOW. PUT THE WORD OUT TO ALL CERBERUS FORCES! WE'RE GOING TO FIND ARIA T'LOAK --
-- AND SECURE THIS STATION ONCE AND FOR ALL!
HE'S DAMN WELL CLOSE TO DOING THAT ALREADY --

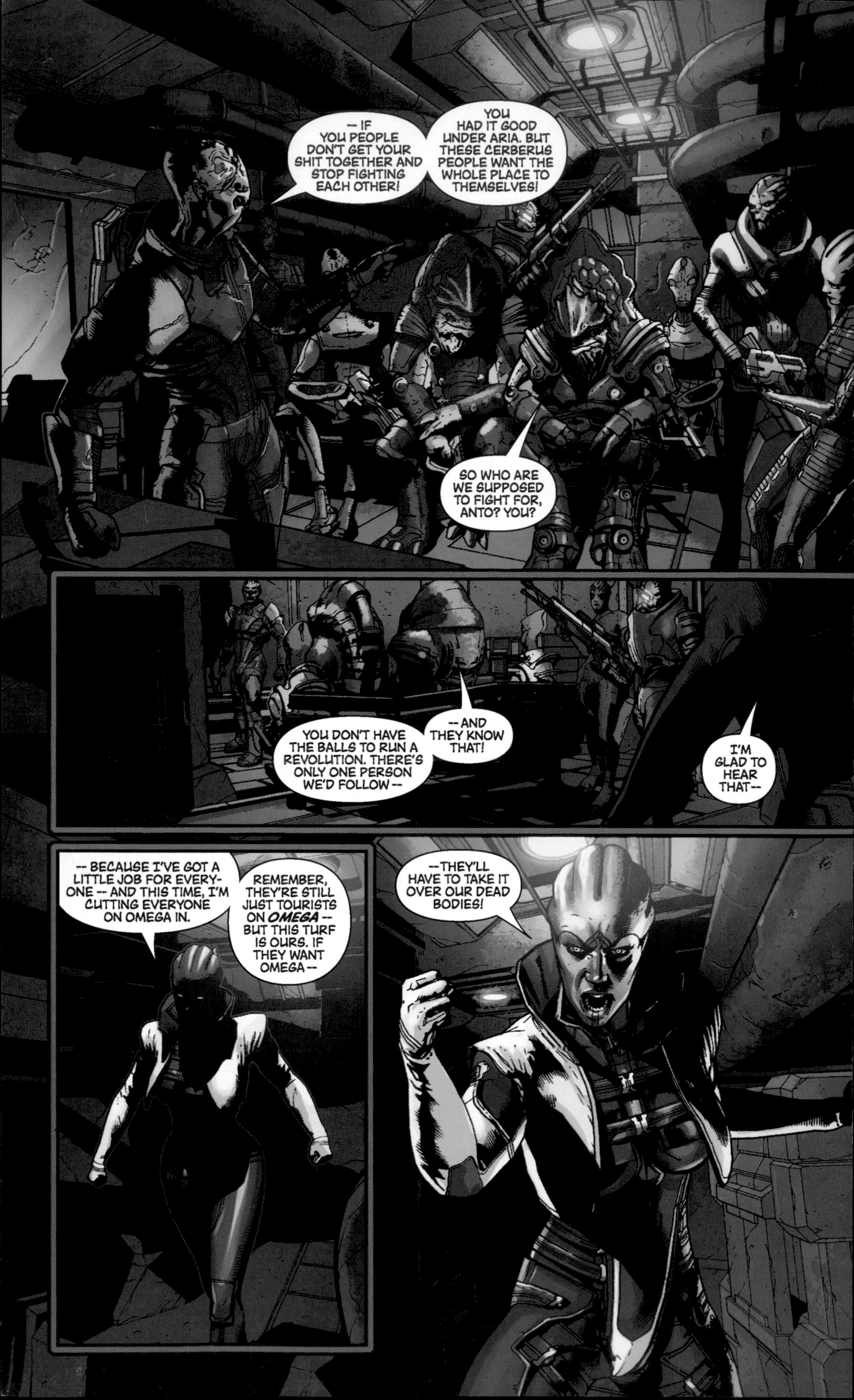
-- IF YOU PEOPLE DON'T GET YOUR SHIT TOGETHER AND STOP FIGHTING EACH OTHER!
YOU HAD IT GOOD UNDER ARIA. BUT THESE CERBERUS PEOPLE WANT THE WHOLE PLACE TO THEMSELVES!
SO WHO ARE WE SUPPOSED TO FIGHT FOR, ANTO? YOU?
YOU DON'T HAVE THE BALLS TO RUN A REVOLUTION. THERE'S ONLY ONE PERSON WE'D FOLLOW --
-- AND THEY KNOW THAT!
I'M GLAD TO HEAR THAT--
-- BECAUSE I'VE GOT A LITTLE JOB FOR EVERY-ONE -- AND THIS TIME, I'M CUTTING EVERYONE ON OMEGA IN.
REMEMBER, THEY'RE STILL JUST TOURISTS ON *OMEGA* -- BUT THIS TURF IS OURS. IF THEY WANT OMEGA --
-- THEY'LL HAVE TO TAKE IT OVER OUR DEAD BODIES!

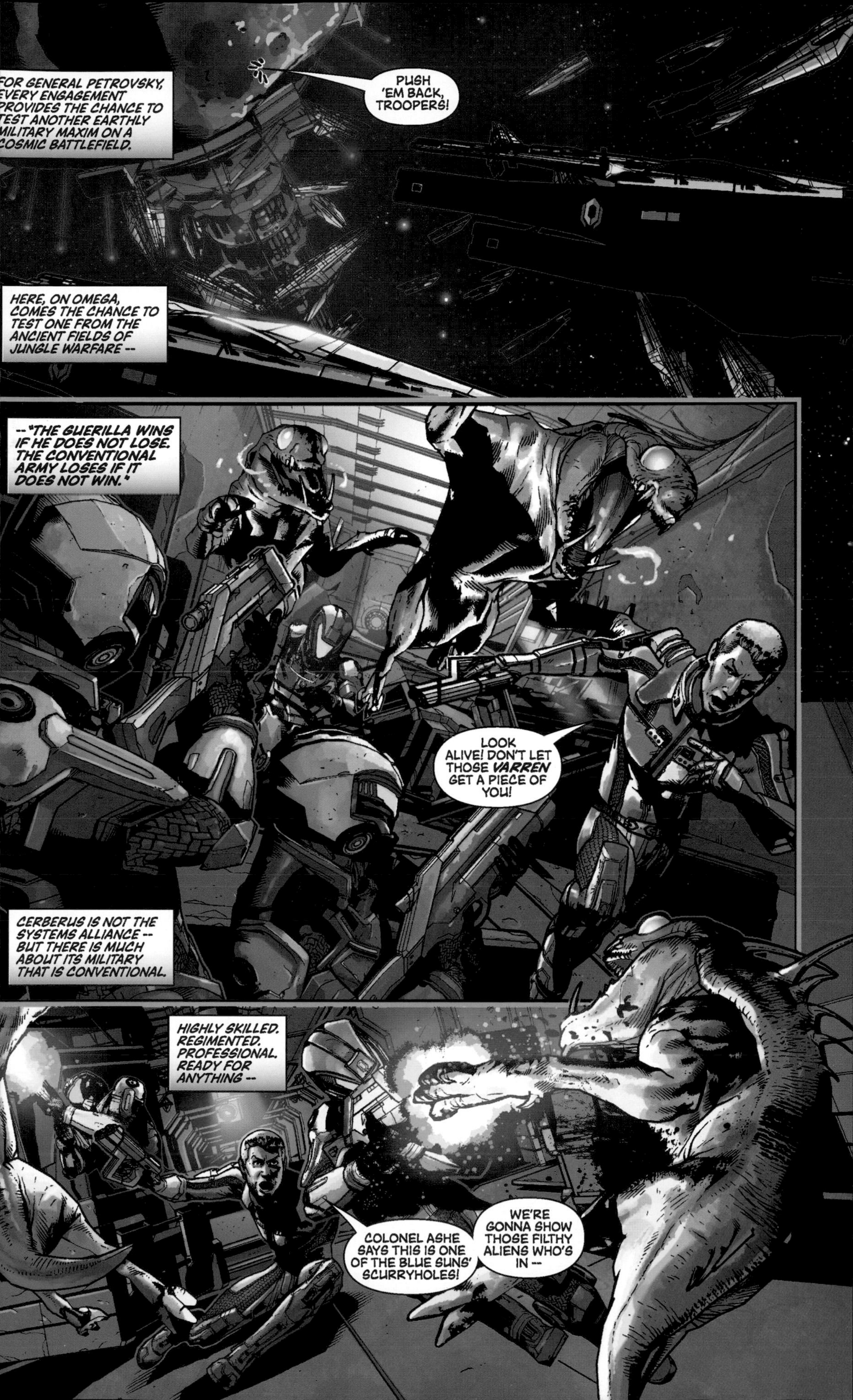
FOR GENERAL PETROVSKY, EVERY ENGAGEMENT PROVIDES THE CHANCE TO TEST ANOTHER EARTHLY MILITARY MAXIM ON A COSMIC BATTLEFIELD.
PUSH 'EM BACK, TROOPERS!
HERE, ON OMEGA, COMES THE CHANCE TO TEST ONE FROM THE ANCIENT FIELDS OF JUNGLE WARFARE --
--"THE GUERILLA WINS IF HE DOES NOT LOSE. THE CONVENTIONAL ARMY LOSES IF IT DOES NOT WIN."
LOOK ALIVE! DON'T LET THOSE VARREN GET A PIECE OF YOU!
CERBERUS IS NOT THE SYSTEMS ALLIANCE -- BUT THERE IS MUCH ABOUT ITS MILITARY THAT IS CONVENTIONAL.
HIGHLY SKILLED. REGIMENTED. PROFESSIONAL. READY FOR ANYTHING --
COLONEL ASHE SAYS THIS IS ONE OF THE BLUE SUNS' SCURRYHOLES!
WE'RE GONNA SHOW THOSE FILTHY ALIENS WHO'S IN --

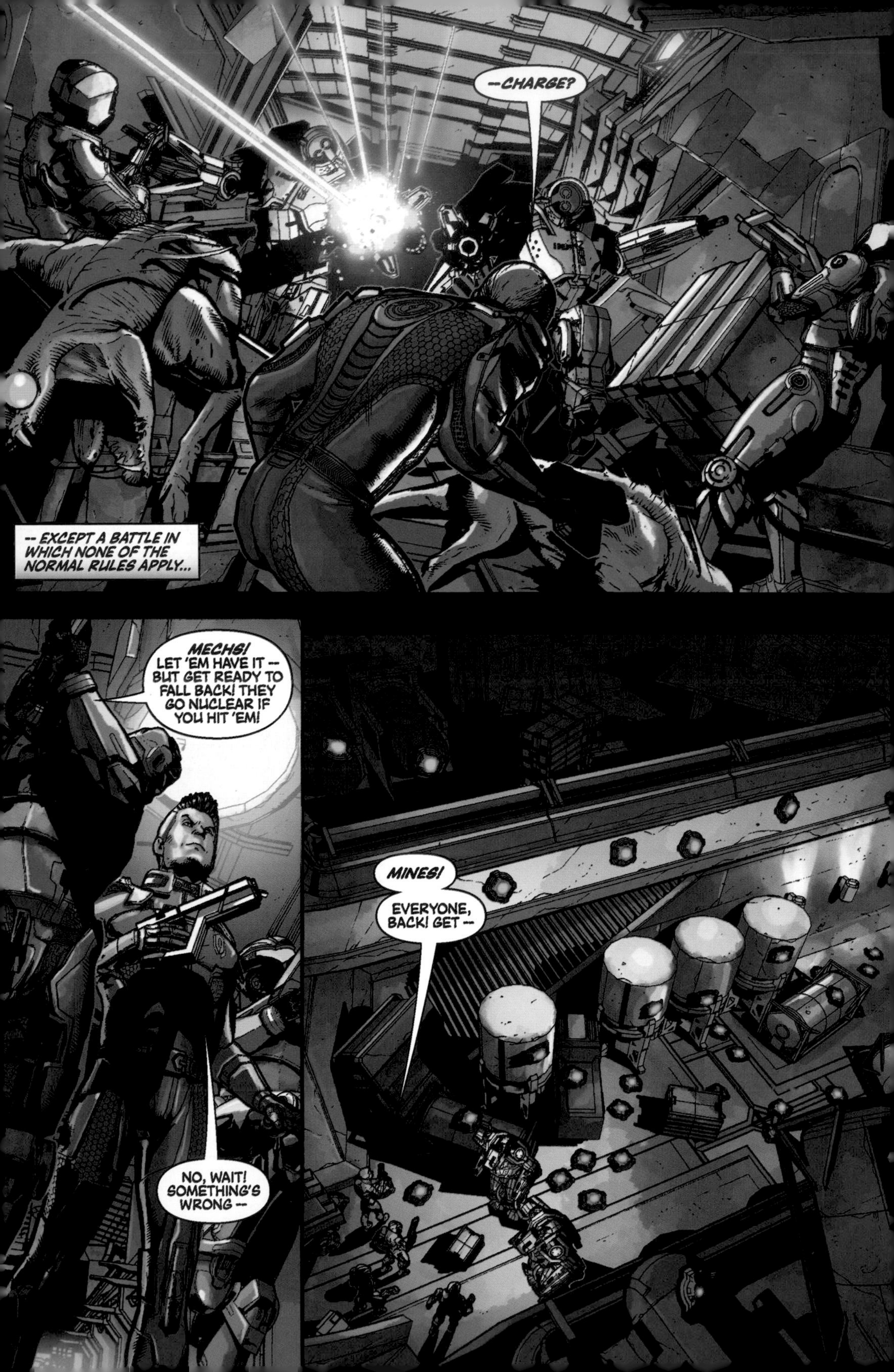
--CHARGE?
-- EXCEPT A BATTLE IN WHICH NONE OF THE NORMAL RULES APPLY...
MECHS! LET 'EM HAVE IT -- BUT GET READY TO FALL BACK! THEY GO NUCLEAR IF YOU HIT 'EM!
NO, WAIT! SOMETHING'S WRONG --
MINES!
EVERYONE, BACK! GET --

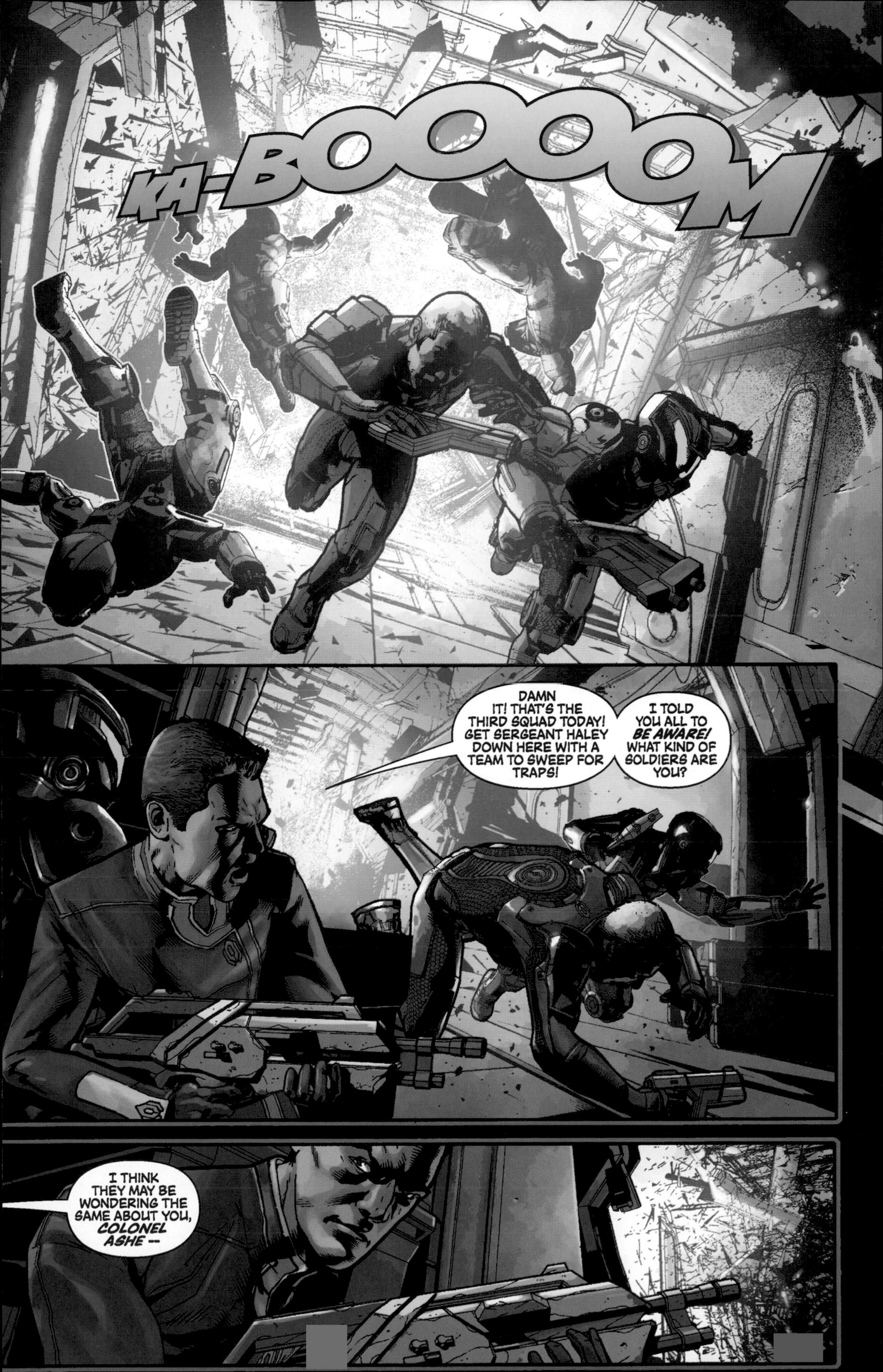
KA-BOOOOM
DAMN IT! THAT'S THE THIRD SQUAD TODAY! GET SERGEANT HALEY DOWN HERE WITH A TEAM TO SWEEP FOR TRAPS!
I TOLD YOU ALL TO *BE AWARE!* WHAT KIND OF SOLDIERS ARE YOU?
I THINK THEY MAY BE WONDERING THE SAME ABOUT YOU, *COLONEL ASHE* --

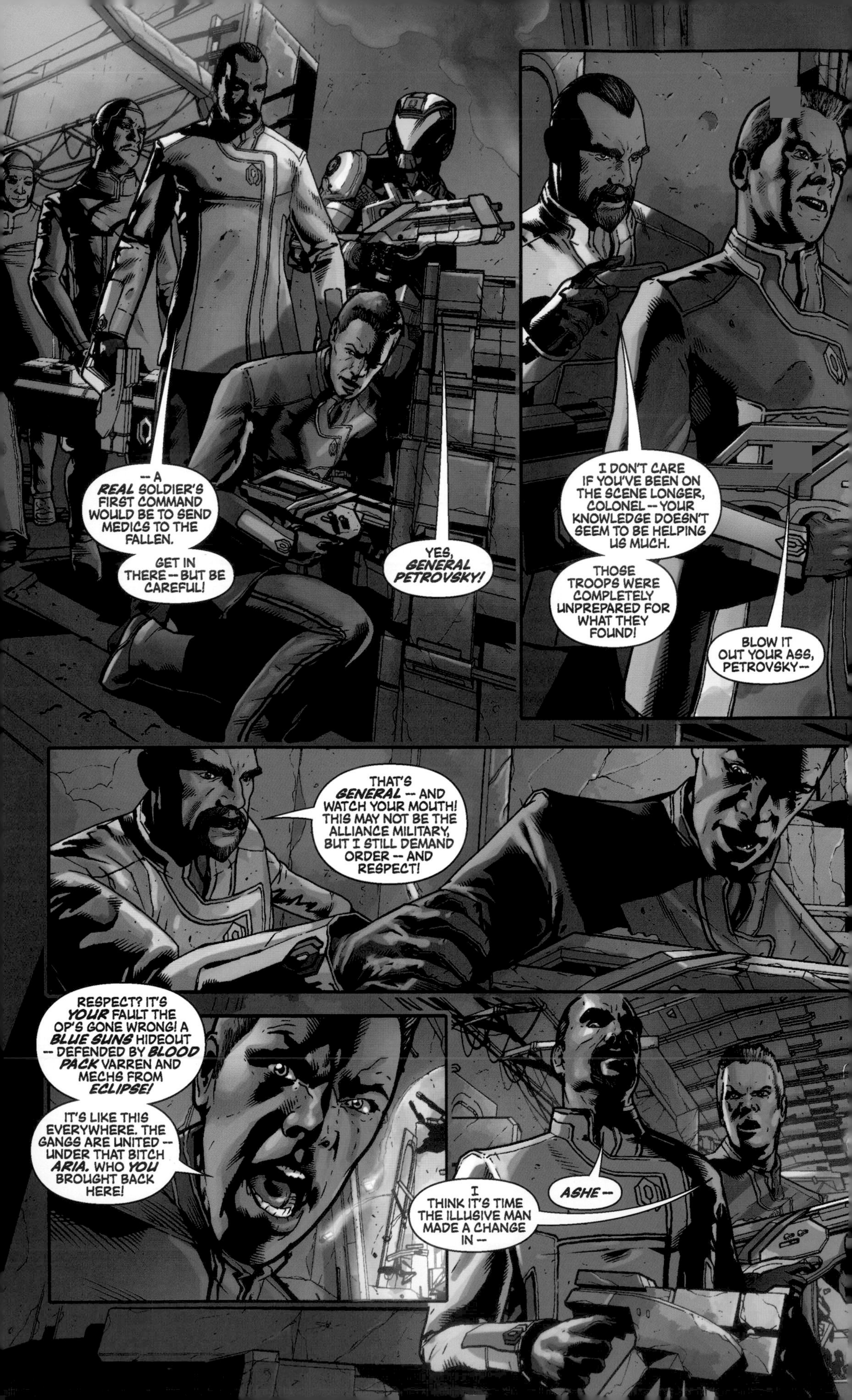
-- A REAL SOLDIER'S FIRST COMMAND WOULD BE TO SEND MEDICS TO THE FALLEN.
GET IN THERE -- BUT BE CAREFUL!
YES, GENERAL PETROVSKY!
I DON'T CARE IF YOU'VE BEEN ON THE SCENE LONGER, COLONEL -- YOUR KNOWLEDGE DOESN'T SEEM TO BE HELPING US MUCH.
THOSE TROOPS WERE COMPLETELY UNPREPARED FOR WHAT THEY FOUND!
BLOW IT OUT YOUR ASS, PETROVSKY--
THAT'S GENERAL -- AND WATCH YOUR MOUTH! THIS MAY NOT BE THE ALLIANCE MILITARY, BUT I STILL DEMAND ORDER -- AND RESPECT!
RESPECT? IT'S YOUR FAULT THE OP'S GONE WRONG! A BLUE SUNS HIDEOUT -- DEFENDED BY BLOOD PACK VARREN AND MECHS FROM ECLIPSE!
IT'S LIKE THIS EVERYWHERE. THE GANGS ARE UNITED -- UNDER THAT BITCH ARIA. WHO YOU BROUGHT BACK HERE!
ASHE --
I THINK IT'S TIME THE ILLUSIVE MAN MADE A CHANGE IN --

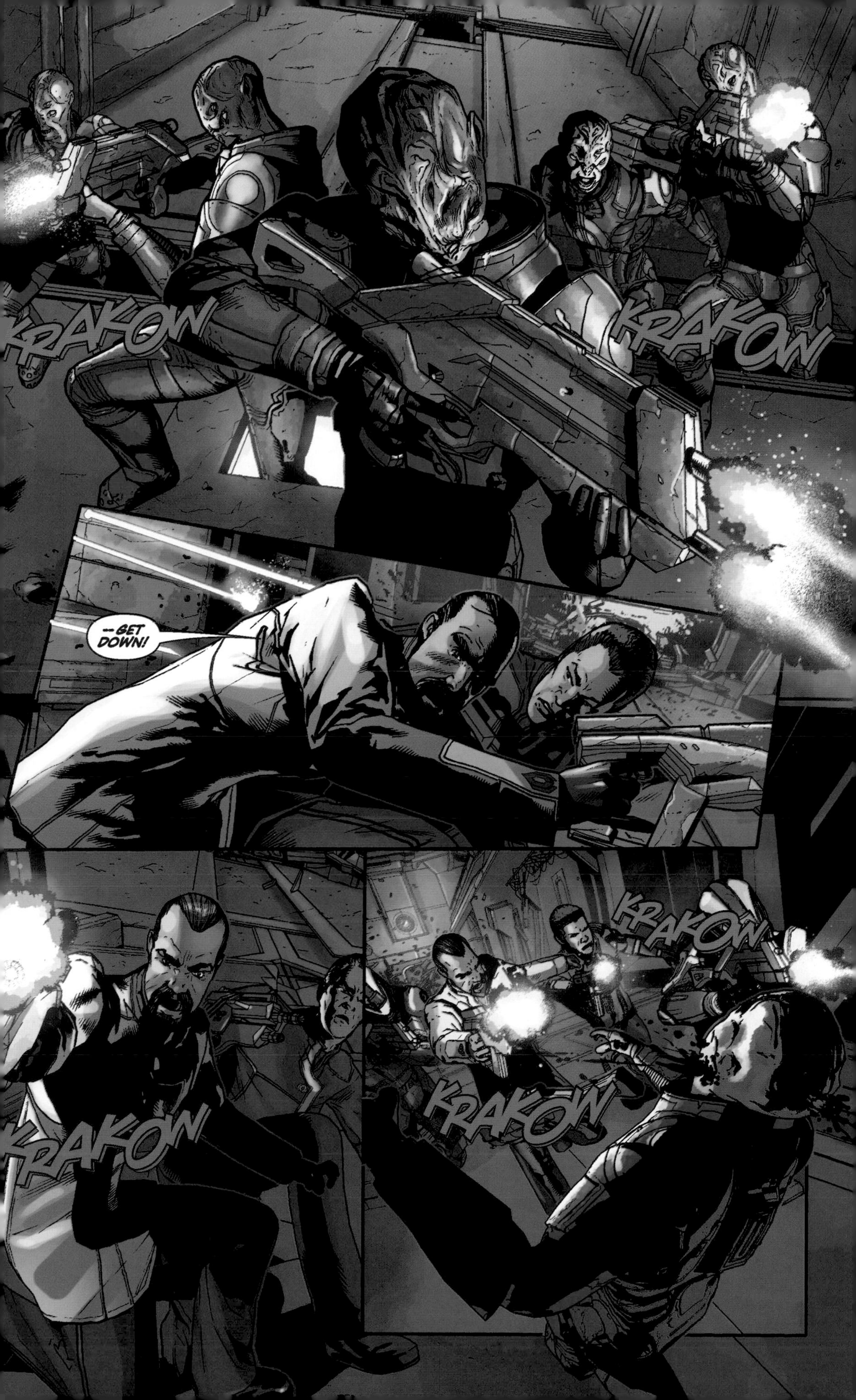
KRAKOW
KRAKOW
--GET DOWN!
KRAKOW
KRAKOW
KRAKOW

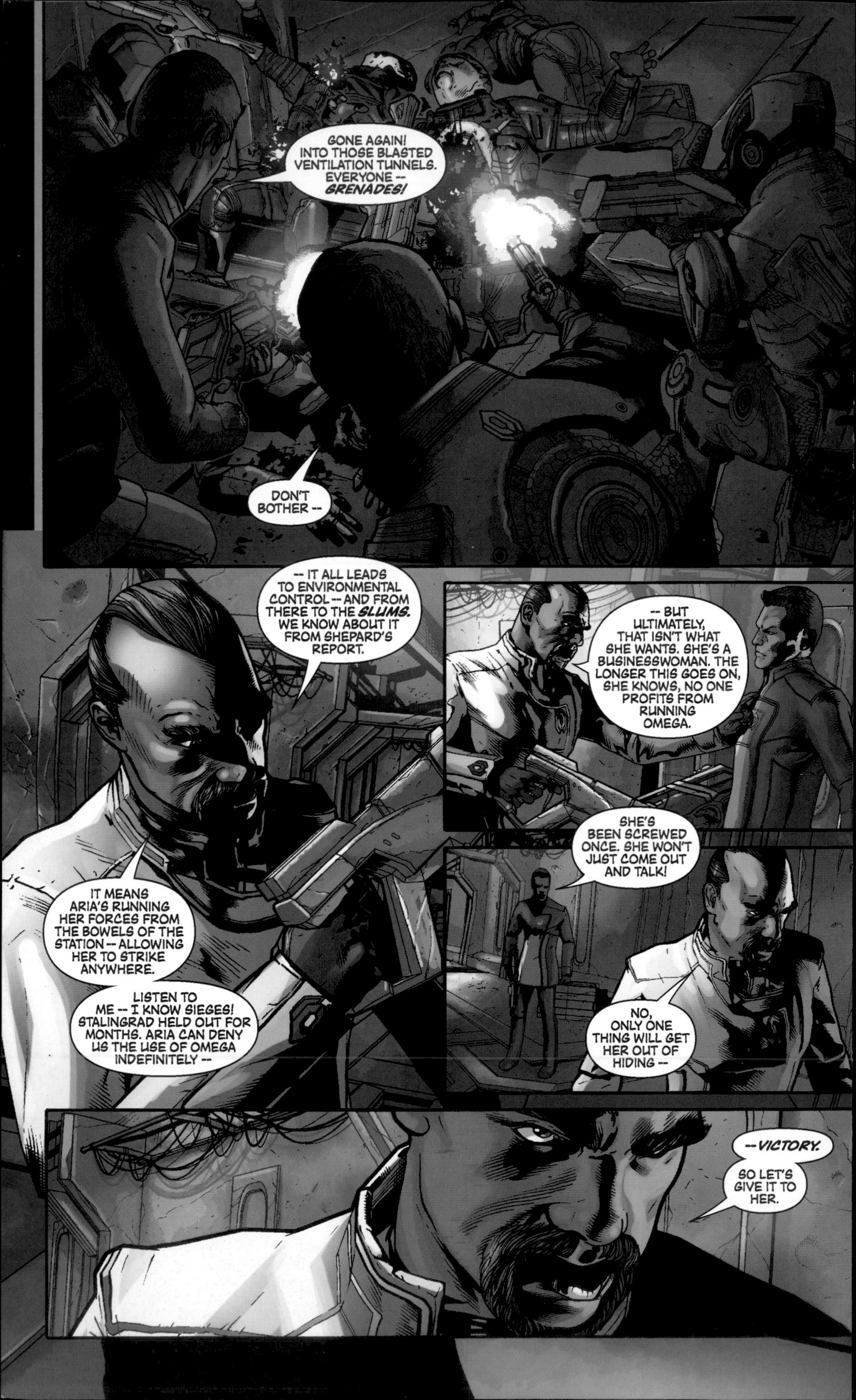
GONE AGAIN! INTO THOSE BLASTED VENTILATION TUNNELS. EVERYONE -- GRENADES!
DON'T BOTHER --
-- IT ALL LEADS TO ENVIRONMENTAL CONTROL -- AND FROM THERE TO THE SLUMS. WE KNOW ABOUT IT FROM SHEPARD'S REPORT.
IT MEANS ARIA'S RUNNING HER FORCES FROM THE BOWELS OF THE STATION -- ALLOWING HER TO STRIKE ANYWHERE.
LISTEN TO ME -- I KNOW SIEGES! STALINGRAD HELD OUT FOR MONTHS. ARIA CAN DENY US THE USE OF OMEGA INDEFINITELY --
-- BUT ULTIMATELY, THAT ISN'T WHAT SHE WANTS. SHE'S A BUSINESSWOMAN. THE LONGER THIS GOES ON, SHE KNOWS, NO ONE PROFITS FROM RUNNING OMEGA.
SHE'S BEEN SCREWED ONCE. SHE WON'T JUST COME OUT AND TALK!
NO, ONLY ONE THING WILL GET HER OUT OF HIDING --
--VICTORY.
SO LET'S GIVE IT TO HER.

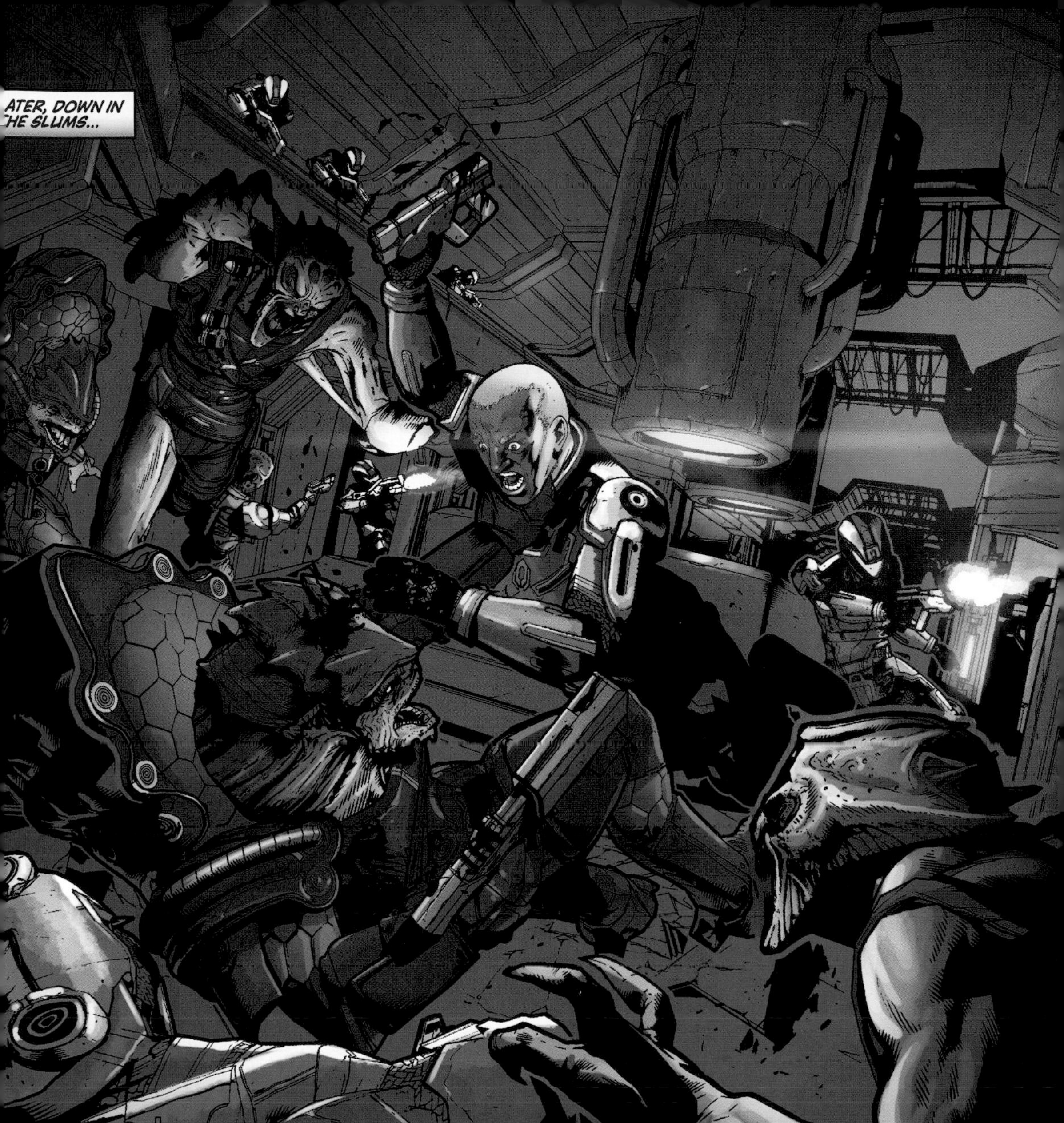
ATER, DOWN IN
HE SLUMS...

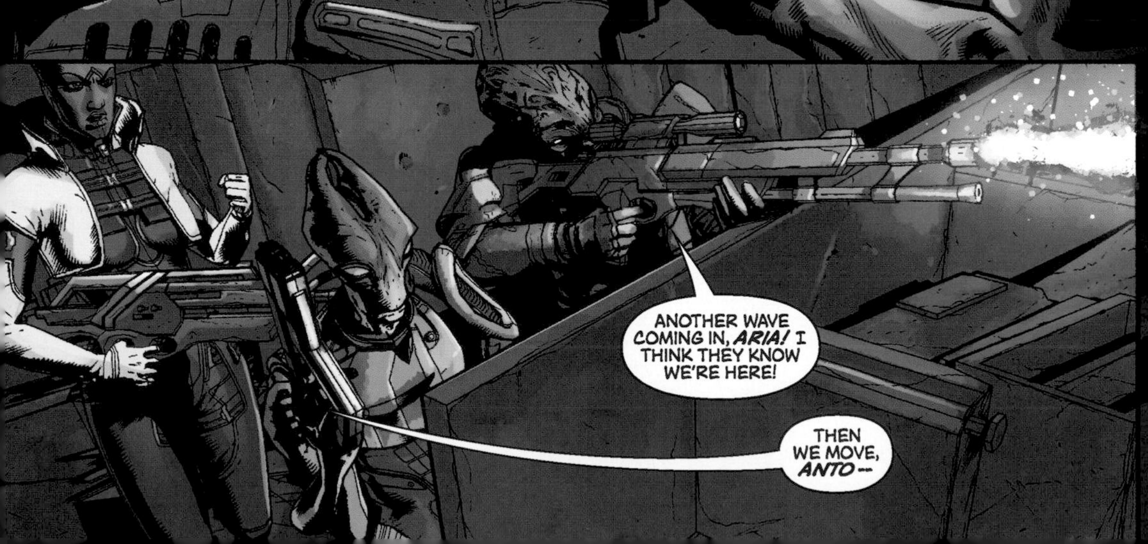
ANOTHER WAVE COMING IN, ARIA! I THINK THEY KNOW WE'RE HERE!
THEN WE MOVE, ANTO--

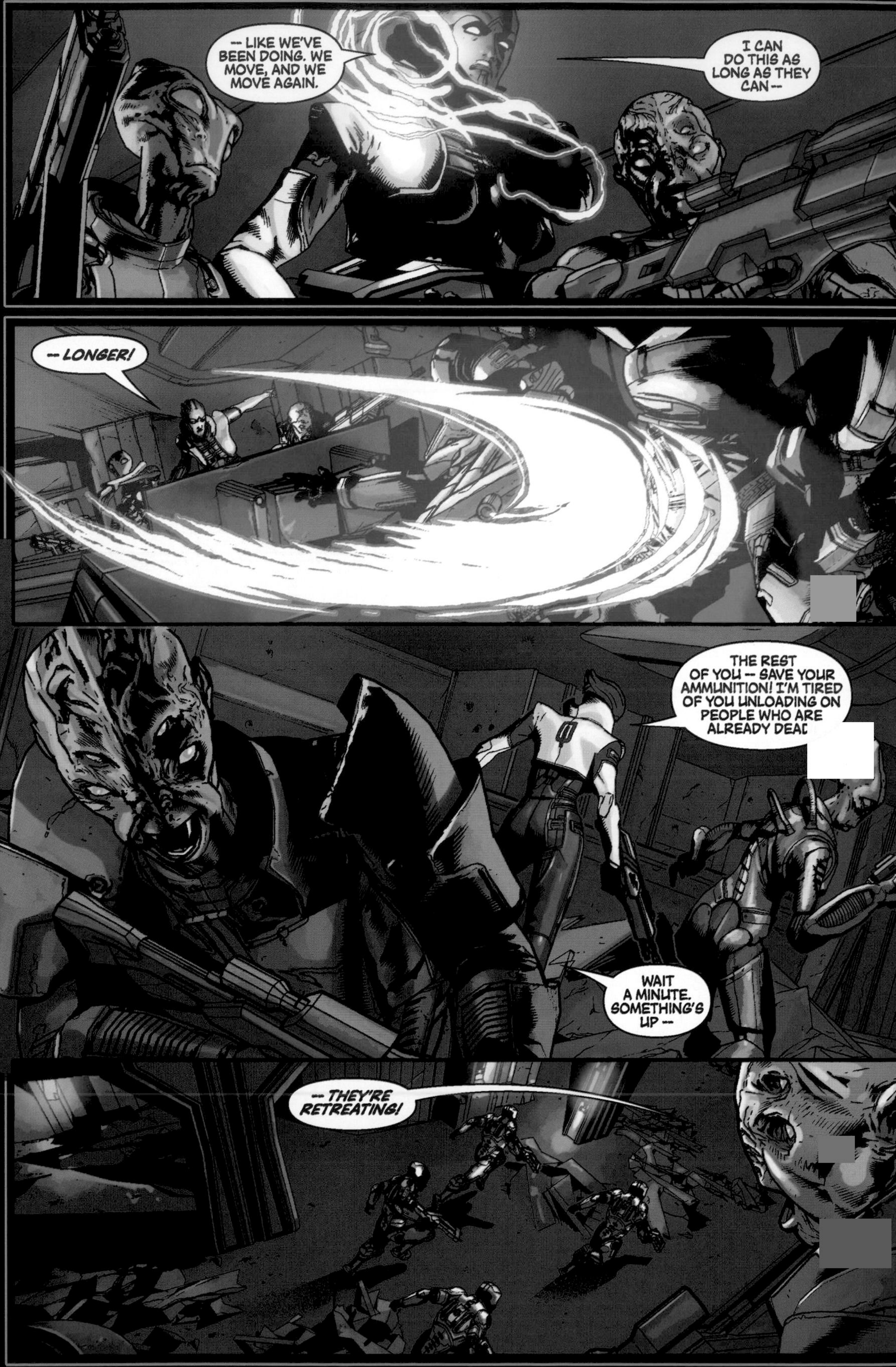
-- LIKE WE'VE BEEN DOING. WE MOVE, AND WE MOVE AGAIN.
I CAN DO THIS AS LONG AS THEY CAN --
-- LONGER!
THE REST OF YOU -- SAVE YOUR AMMUNITION! I'M TIRED OF YOU UNLOADING ON PEOPLE WHO ARE ALREADY DEAD
WAIT A MINUTE. SOMETHING'S UP --
-- THEY'RE RETREATING!

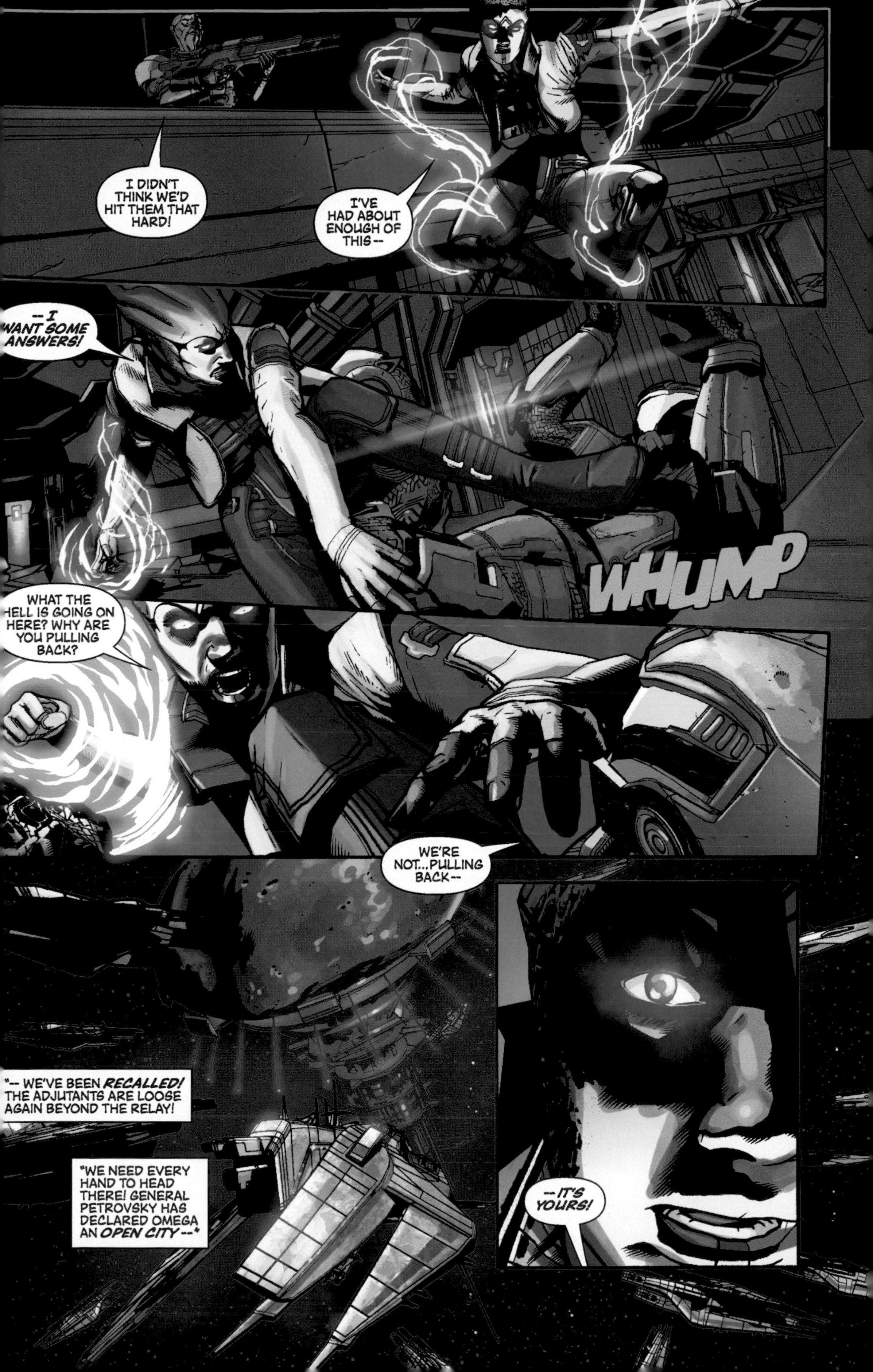
I DIDN'T THINK WE'D HIT THEM THAT HARD!
I'VE HAD ABOUT ENOUGH OF THIS --
-- I WANT SOME ANSWERS!
WHUMP
WHAT THE HELL IS GOING ON HERE? WHY ARE YOU PULLING BACK?
WE'RE NOT...PULLING BACK--
"-- WE'VE BEEN RECALLED! THE ADJUTANTS ARE LOOSE AGAIN BEYOND THE RELAY!
"WE NEED EVERY HAND TO HEAD THERE! GENERAL PETROVSKY HAS DECLARED OMEGA AN OPEN CITY --"
-- IT'S YOURS!

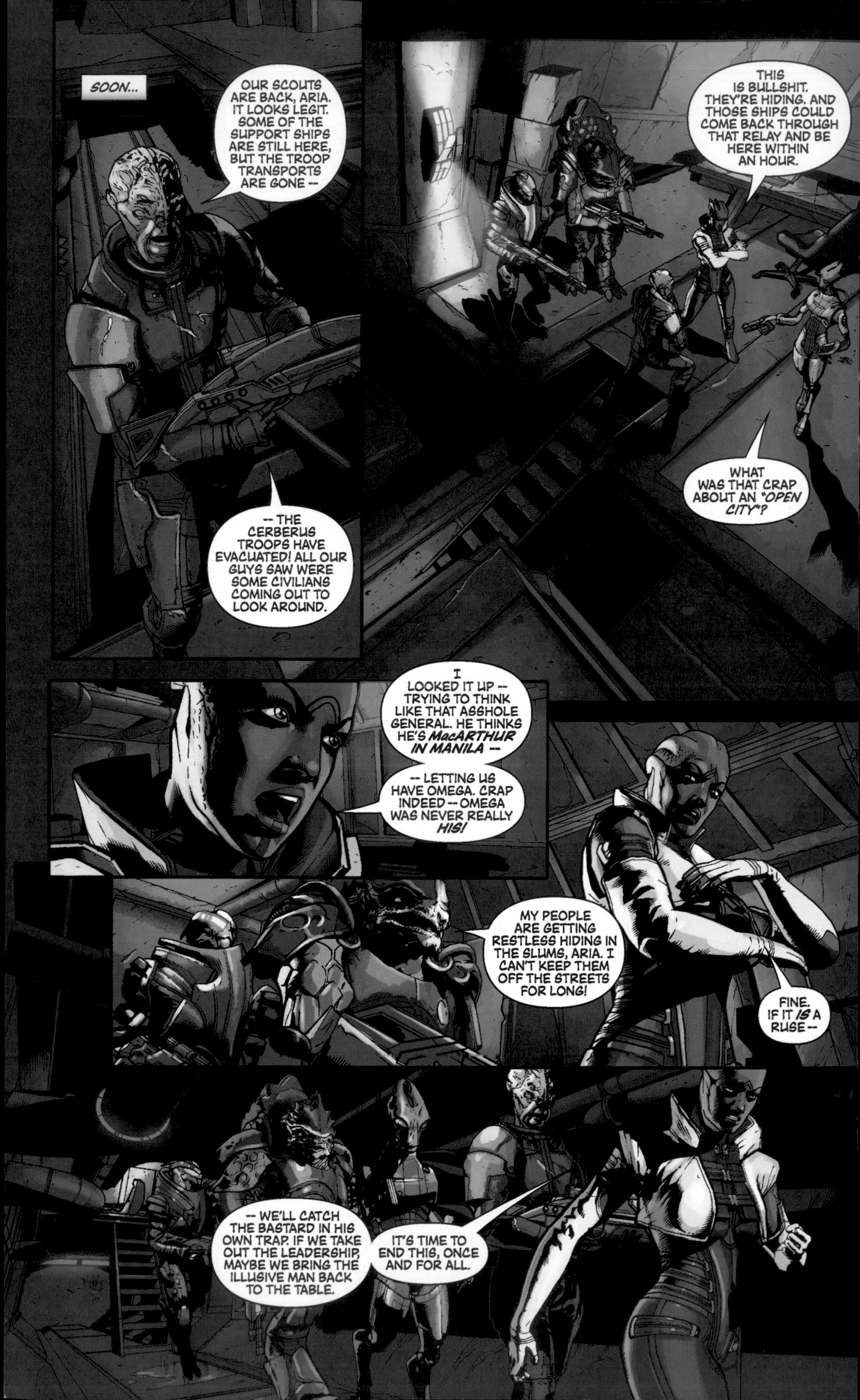
SOON...
OUR SCOUTS ARE BACK, ARIA. IT LOOKS LEGIT. SOME OF THE SUPPORT SHIPS ARE STILL HERE, BUT THE TROOP TRANSPORTS ARE GONE --
-- THE CERBERUS TROOPS HAVE EVACUATED! ALL OUR GUYS SAW WERE SOME CIVILIANS COMING OUT TO LOOK AROUND.
THIS IS BULLSHIT. THEY'RE HIDING. AND THOSE SHIPS COULD COME BACK THROUGH THAT RELAY AND BE HERE WITHIN AN HOUR.
WHAT WAS THAT CRAP ABOUT AN "OPEN CITY"?
I LOOKED IT UP -- TRYING TO THINK LIKE THAT ASSHOLE GENERAL. HE THINKS HE'S MacARTHUR IN MANILA --
-- LETTING US HAVE OMEGA. CRAP INDEED -- OMEGA WAS NEVER REALLY HIS!
MY PEOPLE ARE GETTING RESTLESS HIDING IN THE SLUMS, ARIA. I CAN'T KEEP THEM OFF THE STREETS FOR LONG!
FINE. IF IT IS A RUSE --
-- WE'LL CATCH THE BASTARD IN HIS OWN TRAP. IF WE TAKE OUT THE LEADERSHIP, MAYBE WE BRING THE ILLUSIVE MAN BACK TO THE TABLE.
IT'S TIME TO END THIS, ONCE AND FOR ALL.

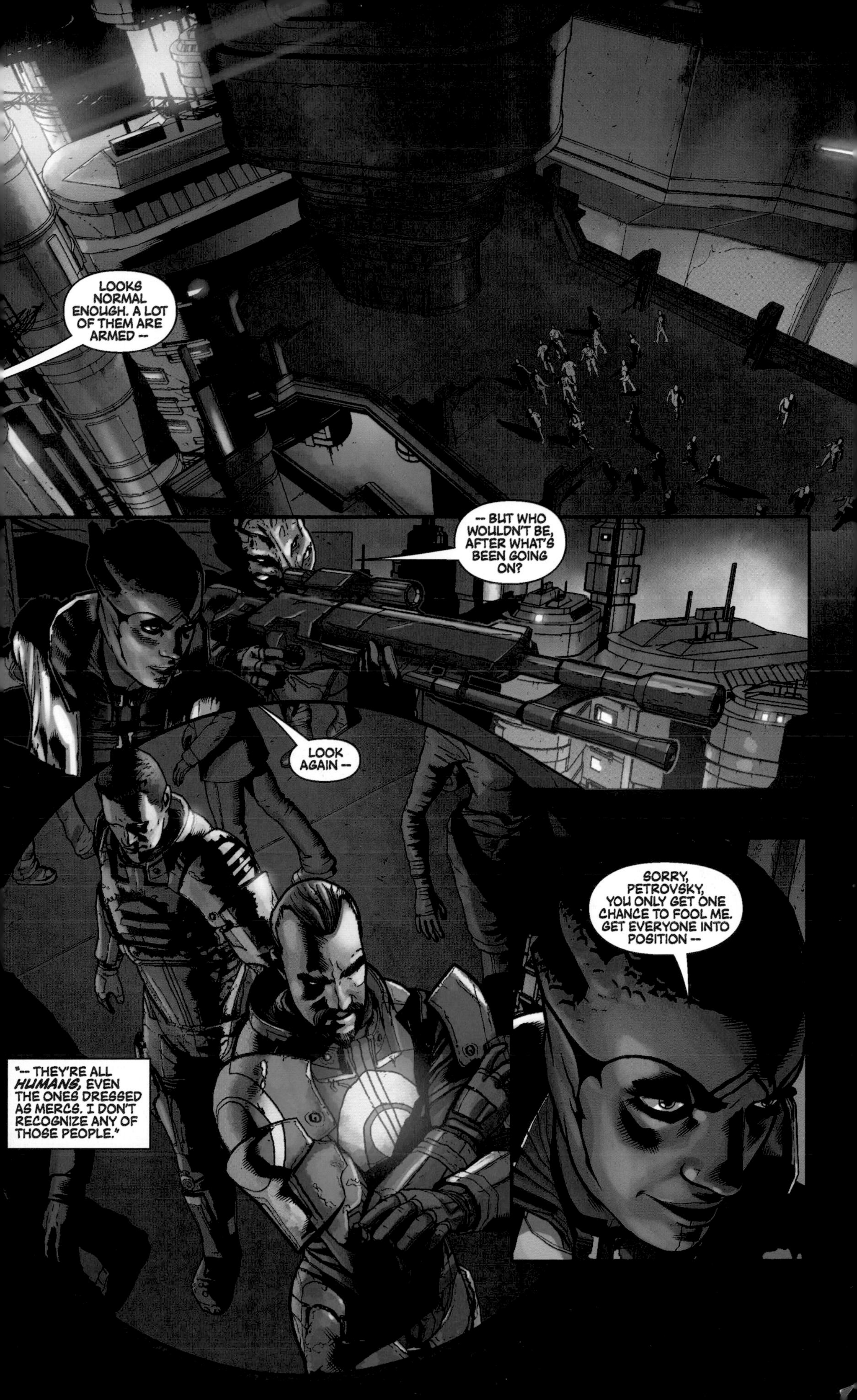
LOOKS NORMAL ENOUGH. A LOT OF THEM ARE ARMED --
-- BUT WHO WOULDN'T BE, AFTER WHAT'S BEEN GOING ON?
LOOK AGAIN --
"-- THEY'RE ALL *HUMANS*, EVEN THE ONES DRESSED AS MERCS. I DON'T RECOGNIZE ANY OF THOSE PEOPLE."
SORRY, PETROVSKY, YOU ONLY GET ONE CHANCE TO FOOL ME. GET EVERYONE INTO POSITION --

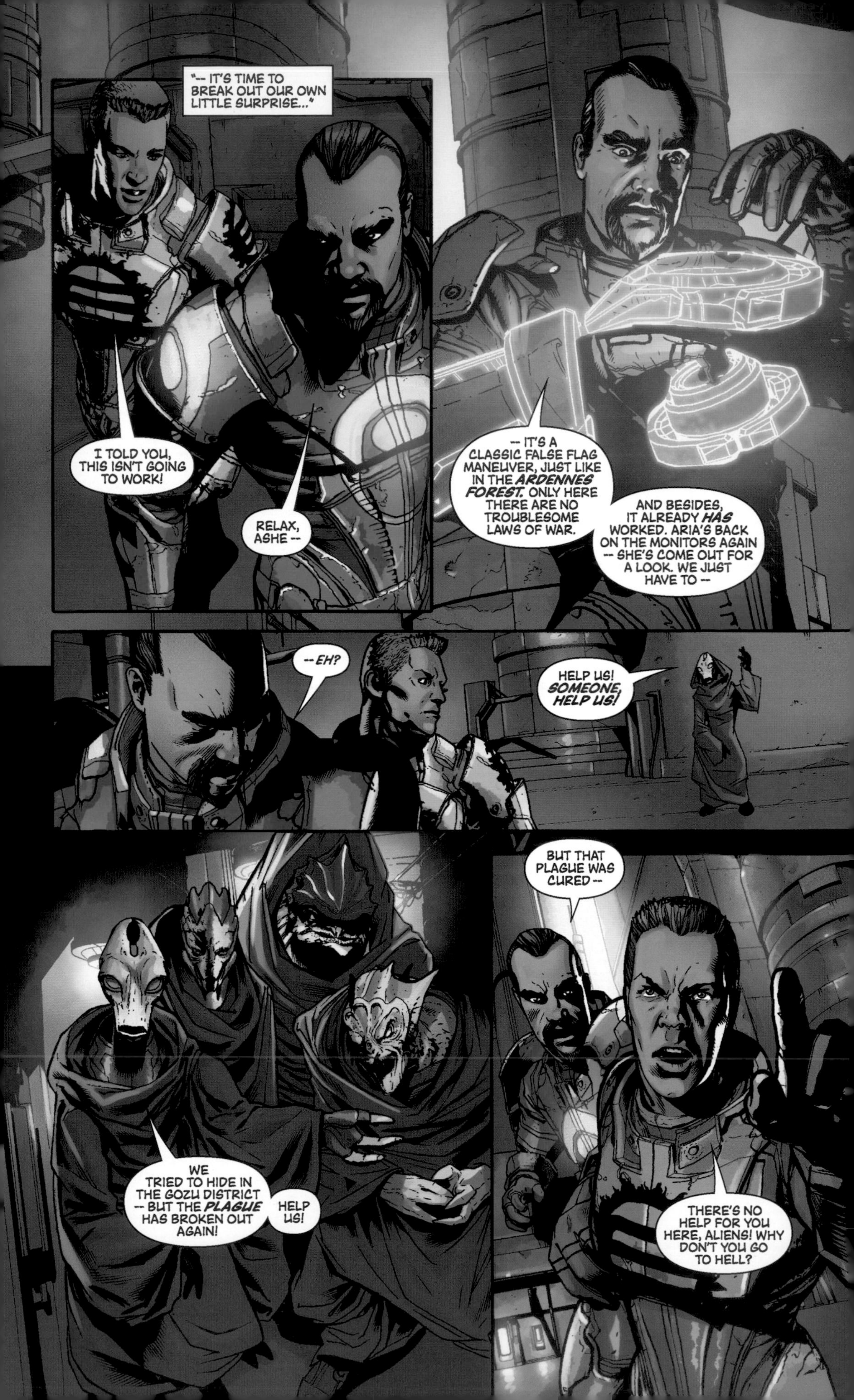
"-- IT'S TIME TO BREAK OUT OUR OWN LITTLE SURPRISE..."
I TOLD YOU, THIS ISN'T GOING TO WORK!
RELAX, ASHE --
-- IT'S A CLASSIC FALSE FLAG MANEUVER, JUST LIKE IN THE ARDENNES FOREST. ONLY HERE THERE ARE NO TROUBLESOME LAWS OF WAR.
AND BESIDES, IT ALREADY HAS WORKED. ARIA'S BACK ON THE MONITORS AGAIN -- SHE'S COME OUT FOR A LOOK. WE JUST HAVE TO --
-- EH?
HELP US! SOMEONE, HELP US!
WE TRIED TO HIDE IN THE GOZU DISTRICT -- BUT THE PLAGUE HAS BROKEN OUT AGAIN!
HELP US!
BUT THAT PLAGUE WAS CURED --
THERE'S NO HELP FOR YOU HERE, ALIENS! WHY DON'T YOU GO TO HELL?

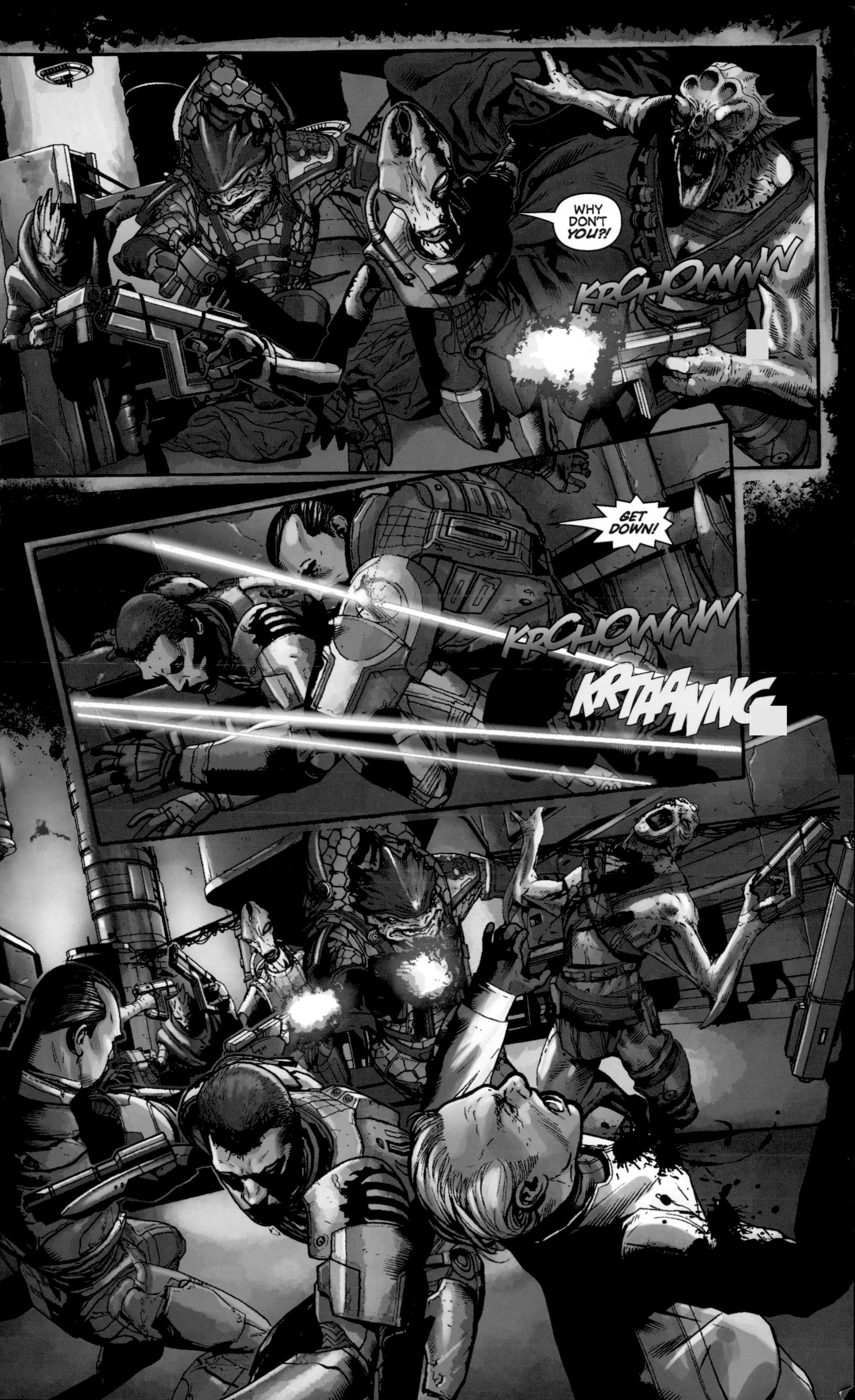
WHY DON'T YOU?!
KRCHOWWW
GET DOWN!
KRCHOWWW
KRTAANNG

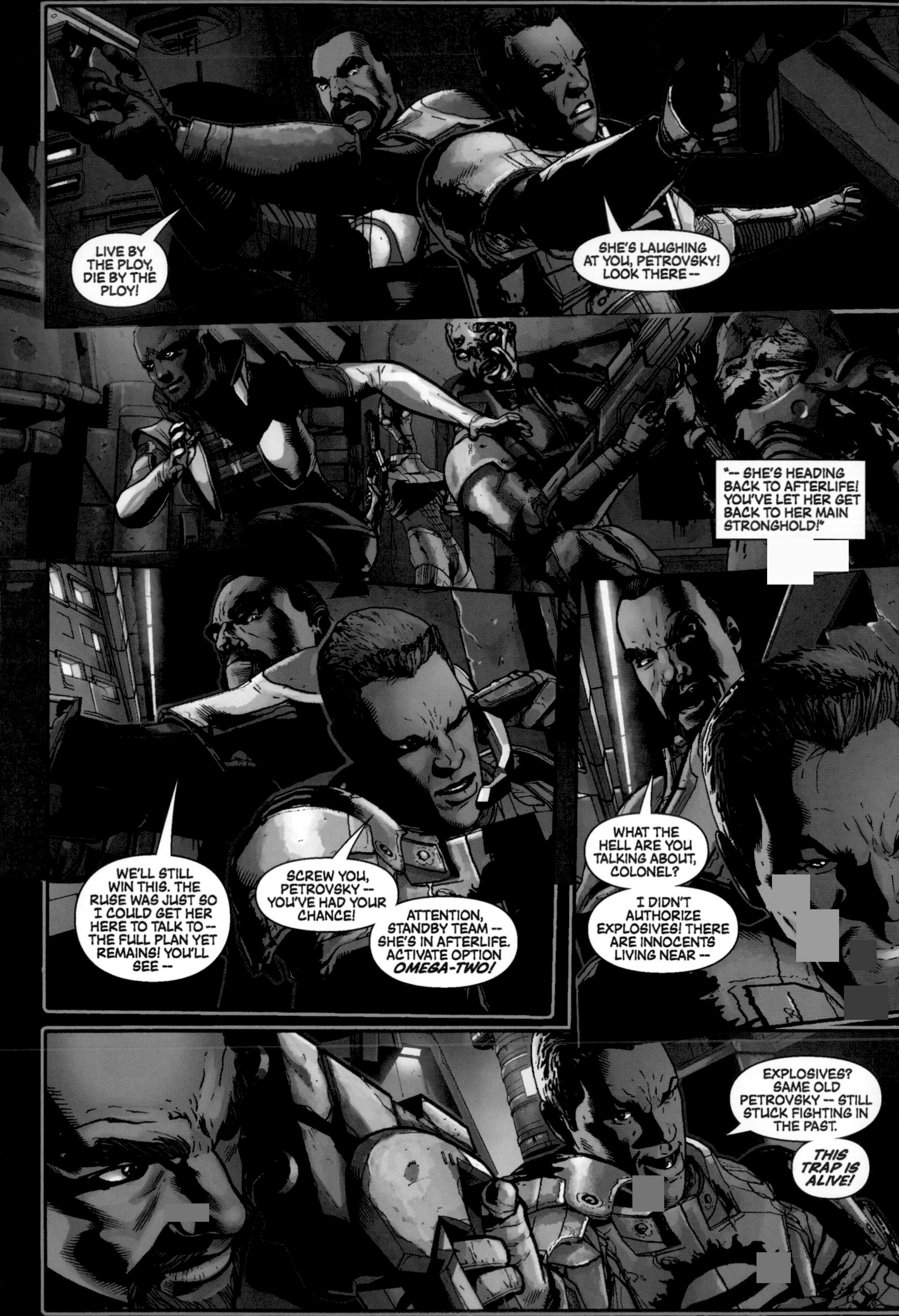
LIVE BY THE PLOY, DIE BY THE PLOY!
SHE'S LAUGHING AT YOU, PETROVSKY! LOOK THERE --
"-- SHE'S HEADING BACK TO AFTERLIFE! YOU'VE LET HER GET BACK TO HER MAIN STRONGHOLD!"
WE'LL STILL WIN THIS. THE RUSE WAS JUST SO I COULD GET HER HERE TO TALK TO -- THE FULL PLAN YET REMAINS! YOU'LL SEE --
SCREW YOU, PETROVSKY -- YOU'VE HAD YOUR CHANCE!
ATTENTION, STANDBY TEAM -- SHE'S IN AFTERLIFE. ACTIVATE OPTION *OMEGA-TWO!*
WHAT THE HELL ARE YOU TALKING ABOUT, COLONEL?
I DIDN'T AUTHORIZE EXPLOSIVES! THERE ARE INNOCENTS LIVING NEAR --
EXPLOSIVES? SAME OLD PETROVSKY -- STILL STUCK FIGHTING IN THE PAST.
THIS TRAP IS ALIVE!

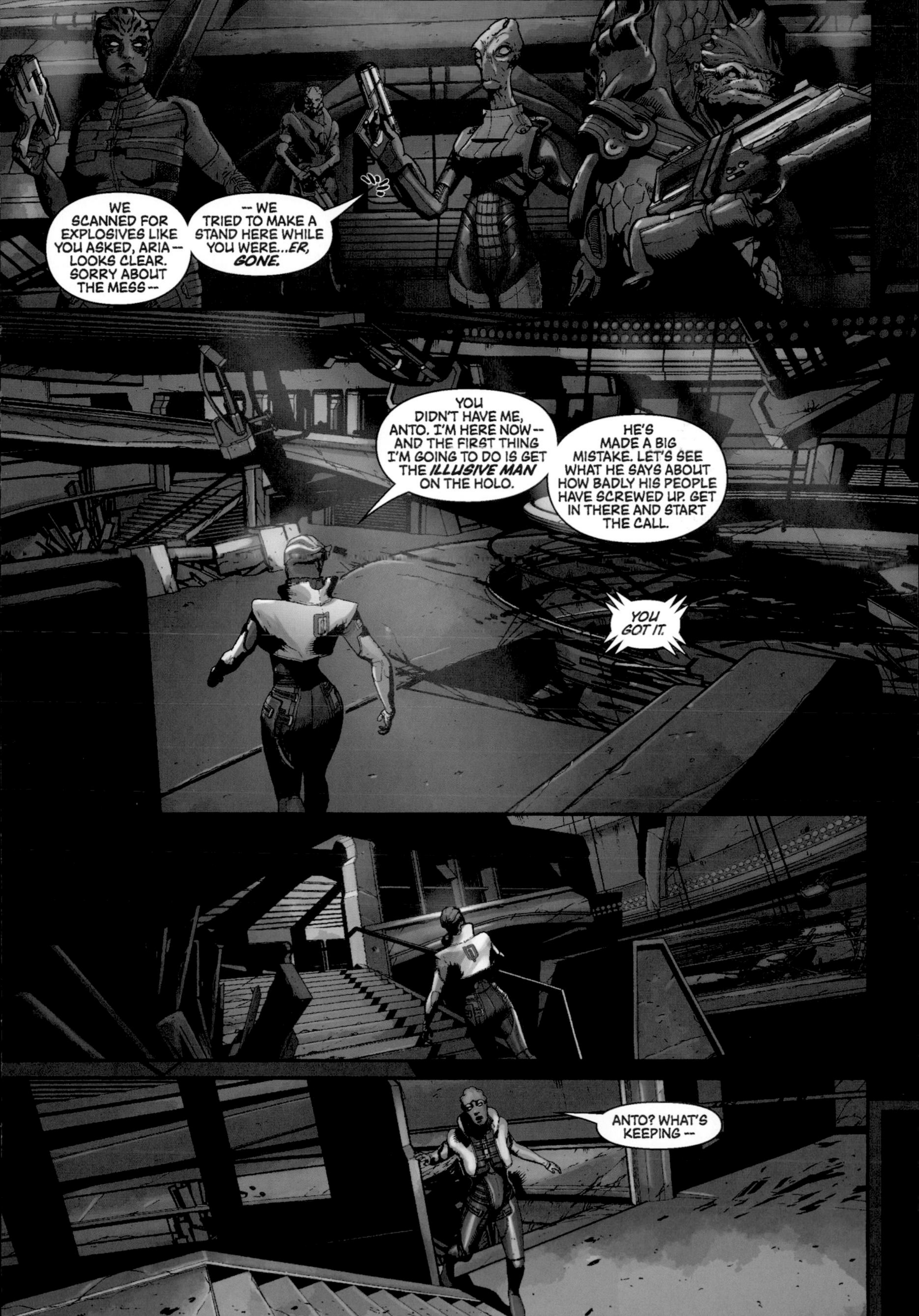
WE SCANNED FOR EXPLOSIVES LIKE YOU ASKED, ARIA -- LOOKS CLEAR. SORRY ABOUT THE MESS --
-- WE TRIED TO MAKE A STAND HERE WHILE YOU WERE... ER, GONE.
YOU DIDN'T HAVE ME, ANTO. I'M HERE NOW -- AND THE FIRST THING I'M GOING TO DO IS GET THE ILLUSIVE MAN ON THE HOLO.
HE'S MADE A BIG MISTAKE. LET'S SEE WHAT HE SAYS ABOUT HOW BADLY HIS PEOPLE HAVE SCREWED UP. GET IN THERE AND START THE CALL.
YOU GOT IT.
ANTO? WHAT'S KEEPING --

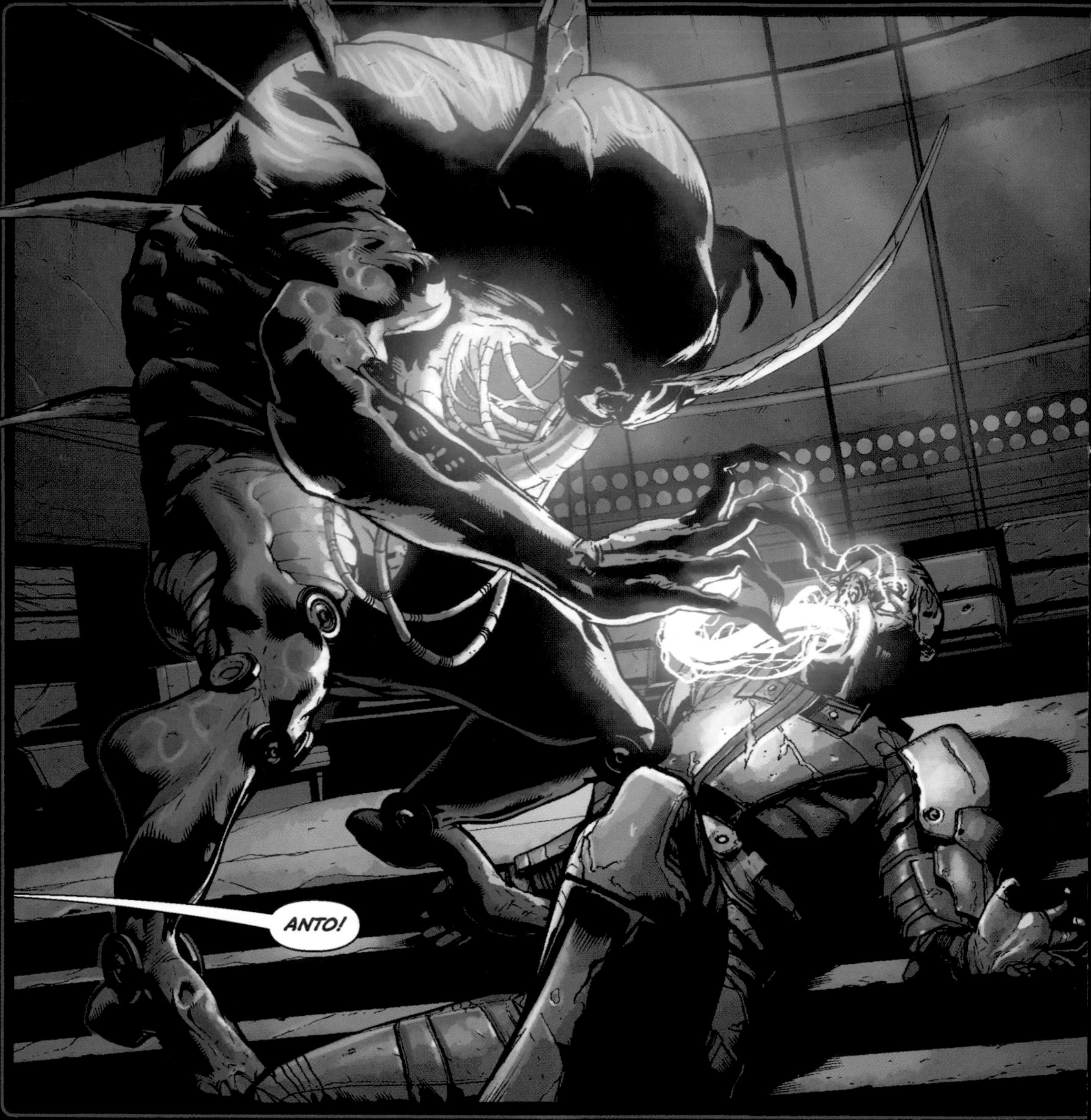
ANTO!

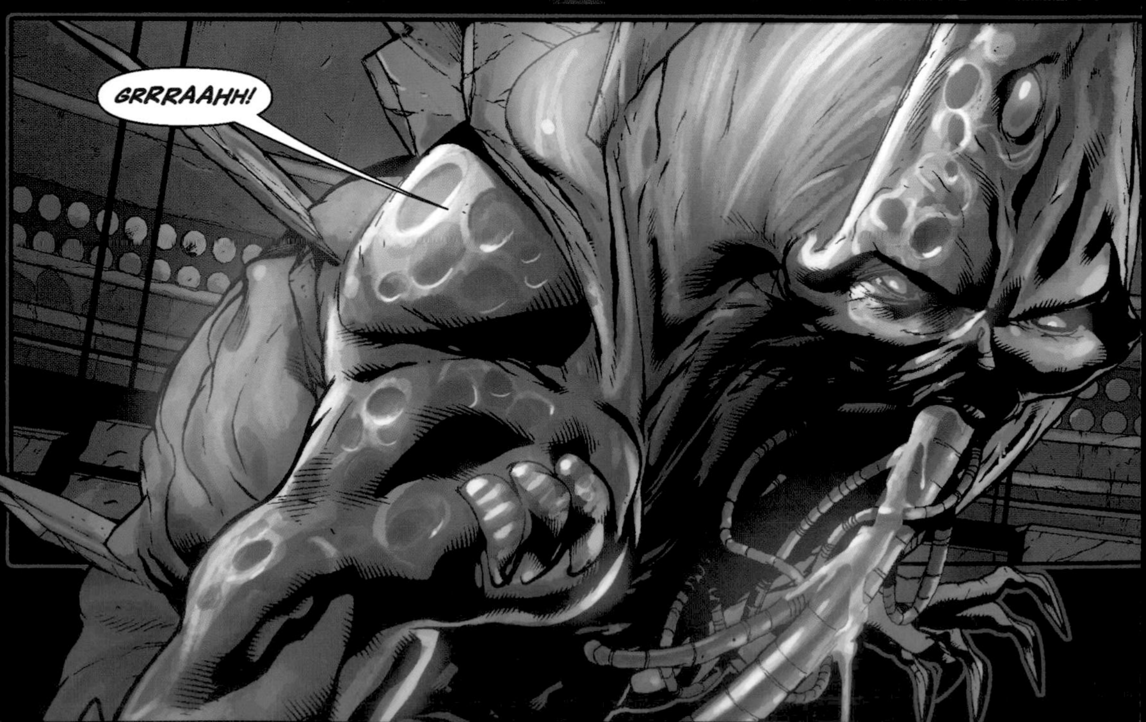
GRRRAAHH!

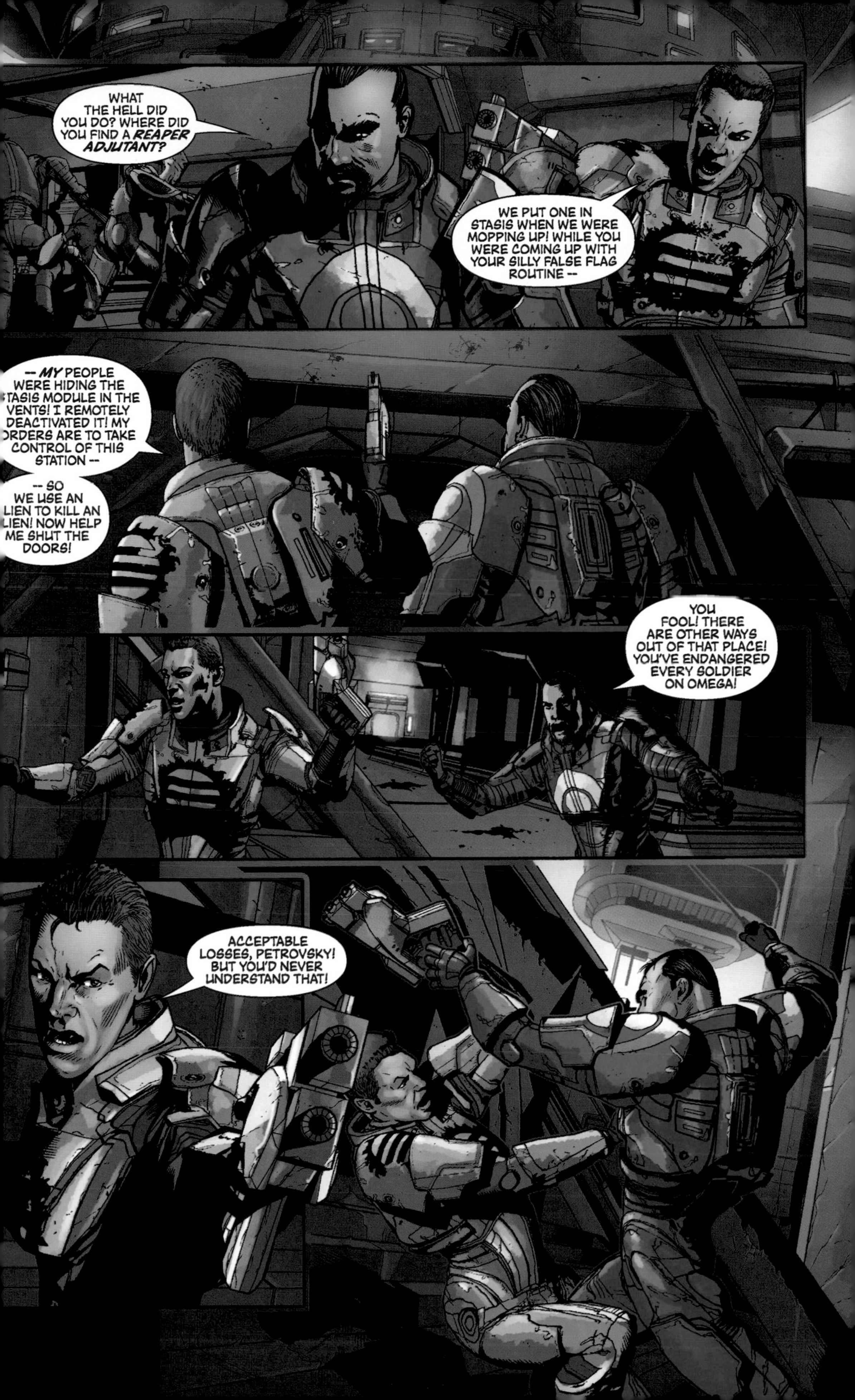
WHAT THE HELL DID YOU DO? WHERE DID YOU FIND A *REAPER ADJUTANT*?
WE PUT ONE IN STASIS WHEN WE WERE MOPPING UP! WHILE YOU WERE COMING UP WITH YOUR SILLY FALSE FLAG ROUTINE --
-- *MY* PEOPLE WERE HIDING THE STASIS MODULE IN THE VENTS! I REMOTELY DEACTIVATED IT! MY ORDERS ARE TO TAKE CONTROL OF THIS STATION --
-- SO WE USE AN ALIEN TO KILL AN ALIEN! NOW HELP ME SHUT THE DOORS!
YOU FOOL! THERE ARE OTHER WAYS OUT OF THAT PLACE! YOU'VE ENDANGERED EVERY SOLDIER ON OMEGA!
ACCEPTABLE LOSSES, PETROVSKY! BUT YOU'D NEVER UNDERSTAND THAT!

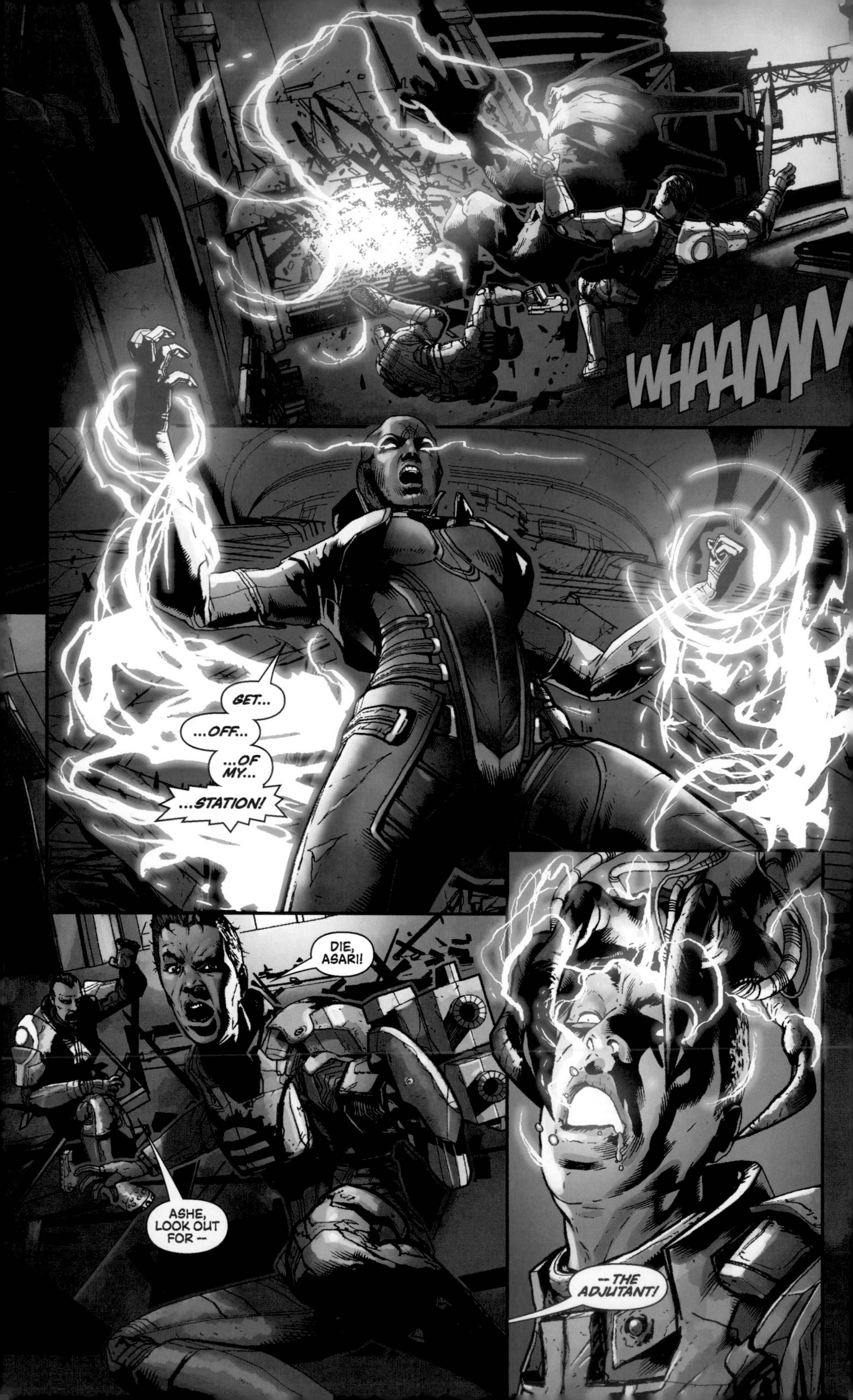
WHAAMM
GET...
...OFF...
...OF MY...
...STATION!
DIE, ASARI!
ASHE, LOOK OUT FOR --
-- THE ADJUTANT!

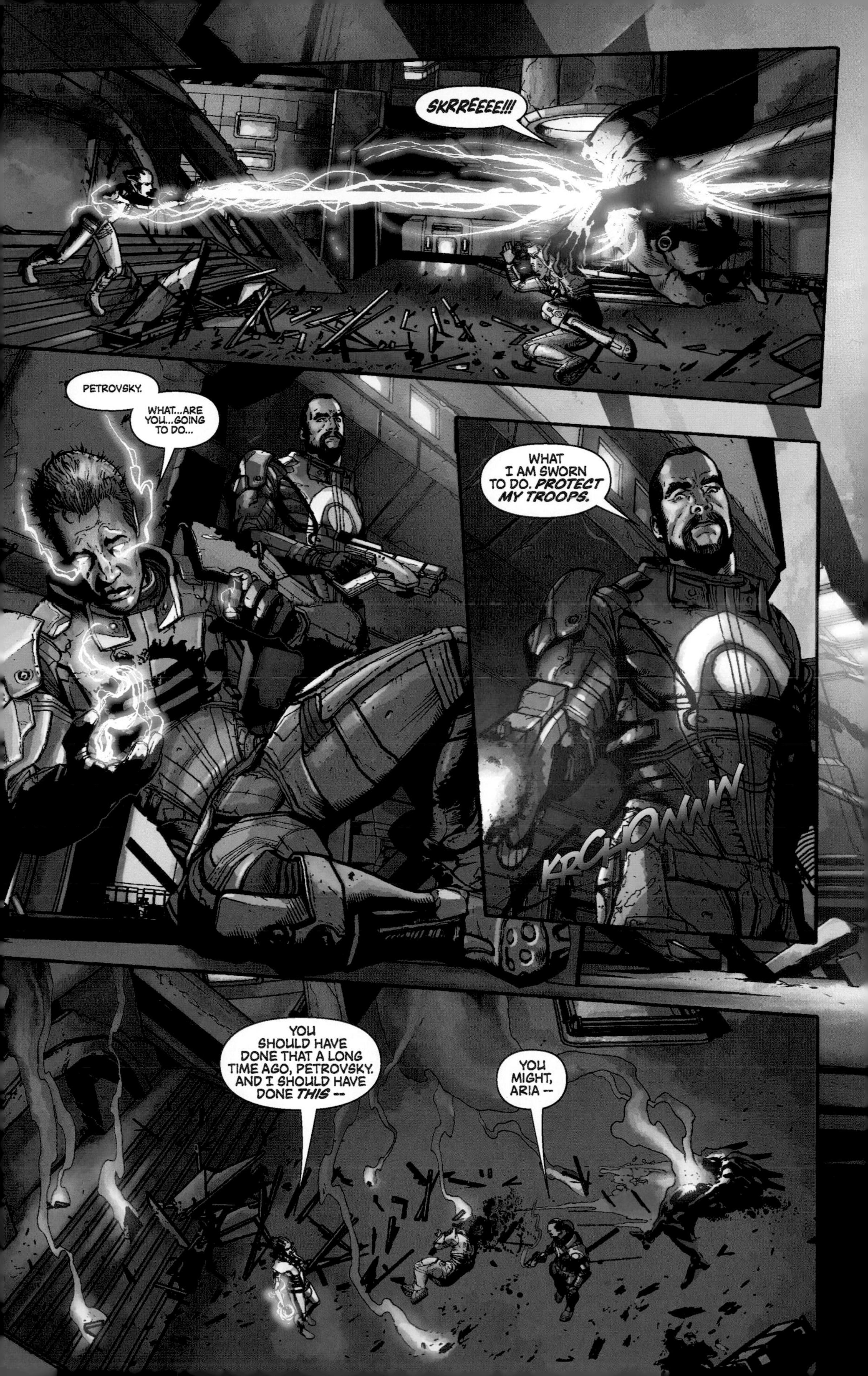
SKRREEEE!!!
PETROVSKY.
WHAT...ARE YOU...GOING TO DO...
WHAT I AM SWORN TO DO. PROTECT MY TROOPS.
KRCHOWWW
YOU SHOULD HAVE DONE THAT A LONG TIME AGO, PETROVSKY. AND I SHOULD HAVE DONE THIS --
YOU MIGHT, ARIA --

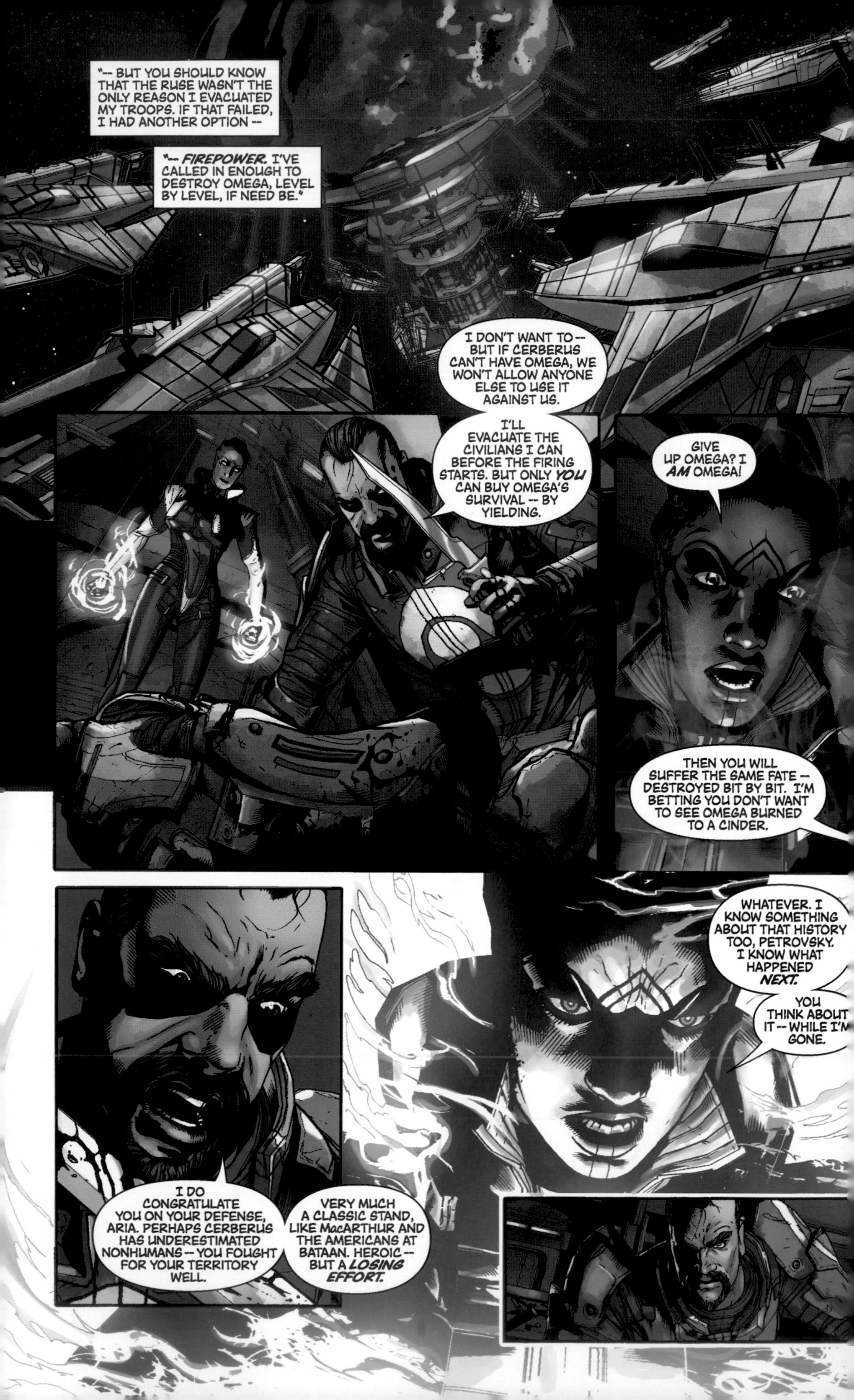
"-- BUT YOU SHOULD KNOW THAT THE RUSE WASN'T THE ONLY REASON I EVACUATED MY TROOPS. IF THAT FAILED, I HAD ANOTHER OPTION --
"-- FIREPOWER. I'VE CALLED IN ENOUGH TO DESTROY OMEGA, LEVEL BY LEVEL, IF NEED BE."
I DON'T WANT TO -- BUT IF CERBERUS CAN'T HAVE OMEGA, WE WON'T ALLOW ANYONE ELSE TO USE IT AGAINST US.
I'LL EVACUATE THE CIVILIANS I CAN BEFORE THE FIRING STARTS. BUT ONLY YOU CAN BUY OMEGA'S SURVIVAL -- BY YIELDING.
GIVE UP OMEGA? I AM OMEGA!
THEN YOU WILL SUFFER THE SAME FATE -- DESTROYED BIT BY BIT. I'M BETTING YOU DON'T WANT TO SEE OMEGA BURNED TO A CINDER.
I DO CONGRATULATE YOU ON YOUR DEFENSE, ARIA. PERHAPS CERBERUS HAS UNDERESTIMATED NONHUMANS -- YOU FOUGHT FOR YOUR TERRITORY WELL.
VERY MUCH A CLASSIC STAND, LIKE MacARTHUR AND THE AMERICANS AT BATAAN. HEROIC -- BUT A LOSING EFFORT.
WHATEVER. I KNOW SOMETHING ABOUT THAT HISTORY TOO, PETROVSKY. I KNOW WHAT HAPPENED NEXT.
YOU THINK ABOUT IT -- WHILE I'M GONE.

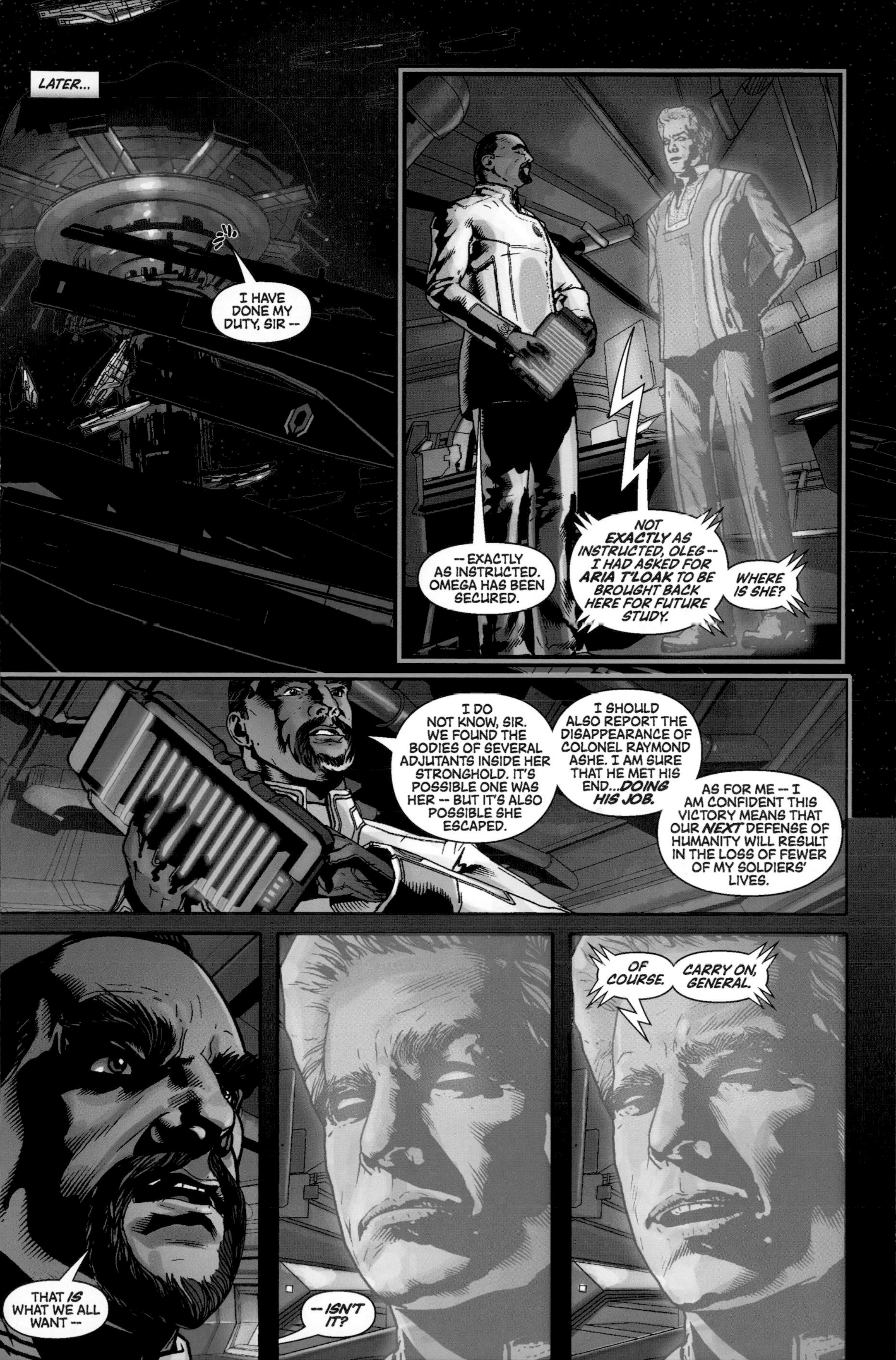
LATER...
I HAVE DONE MY DUTY, SIR --
-- EXACTLY AS INSTRUCTED. OMEGA HAS BEEN SECURED.
NOT EXACTLY AS INSTRUCTED, OLEG -- I HAD ASKED FOR ARIA T'LOAK TO BE BROUGHT BACK HERE FOR FUTURE STUDY.
WHERE IS SHE?
I DO NOT KNOW, SIR. WE FOUND THE BODIES OF SEVERAL ADJUTANTS INSIDE HER STRONGHOLD. IT'S POSSIBLE ONE WAS HER -- BUT IT'S ALSO POSSIBLE SHE ESCAPED.
I SHOULD ALSO REPORT THE DISAPPEARANCE OF COLONEL RAYMOND ASHE. I AM SURE THAT HE MET HIS END...DOING HIS JOB.
AS FOR ME -- I AM CONFIDENT THIS VICTORY MEANS THAT OUR NEXT DEFENSE OF HUMANITY WILL RESULT IN THE LOSS OF FEWER OF MY SOLDIERS' LIVES.
THAT IS WHAT WE ALL WANT --
-- ISN'T IT?
OF COURSE.
CARRY ON, GENERAL.

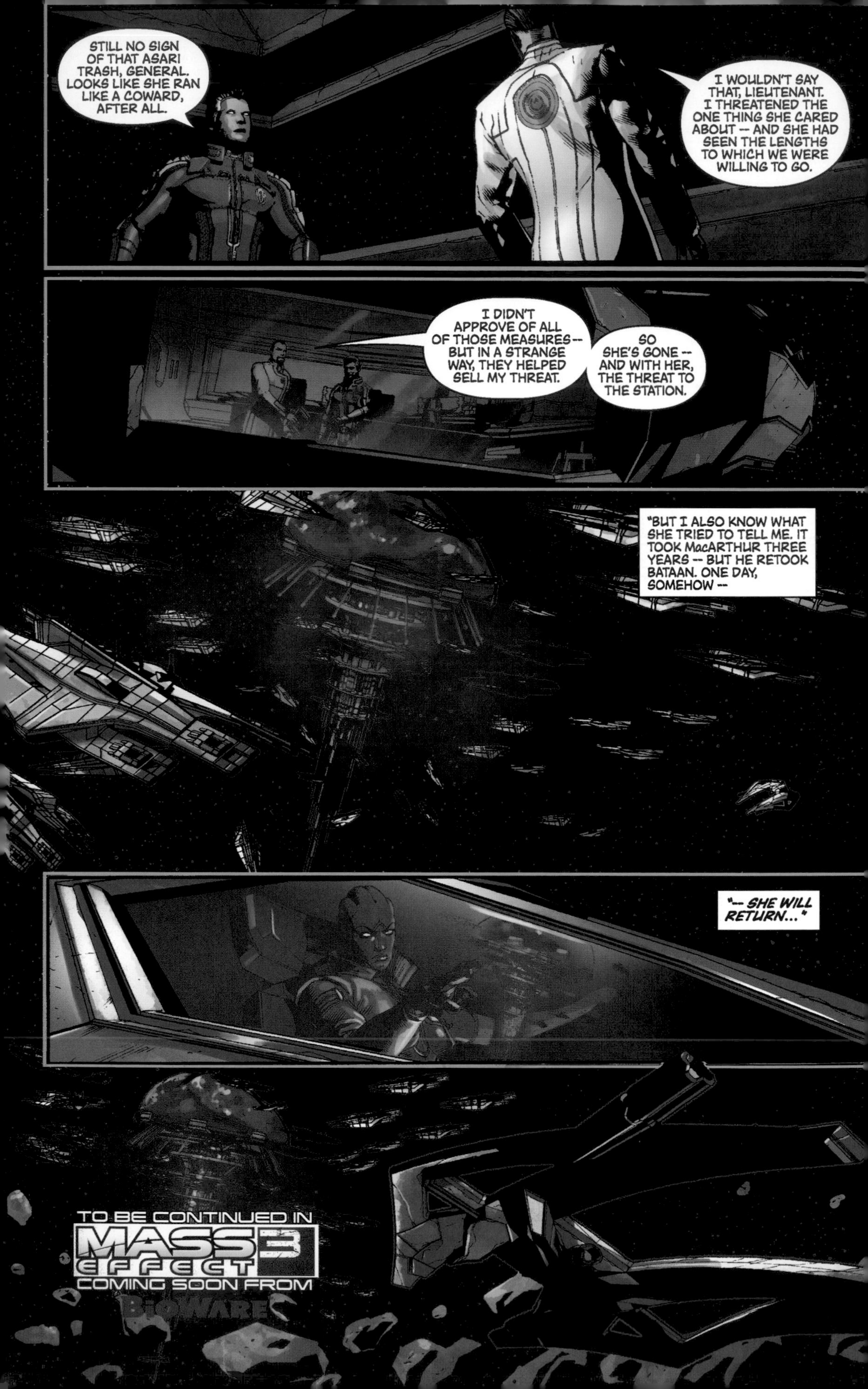
STILL NO SIGN OF THAT ASARI TRASH, GENERAL. LOOKS LIKE SHE RAN LIKE A COWARD, AFTER ALL.
I WOULDN'T SAY THAT, LIEUTENANT. I THREATENED THE ONE THING SHE CARED ABOUT -- AND SHE HAD SEEN THE LENGTHS TO WHICH WE WERE WILLING TO GO.
I DIDN'T APPROVE OF ALL OF THOSE MEASURES -- BUT IN A STRANGE WAY, THEY HELPED SELL MY THREAT.
SO SHE'S GONE -- AND WITH HER, THE THREAT TO THE STATION.
"BUT I ALSO KNOW WHAT SHE TRIED TO TELL ME. IT TOOK MacARTHUR THREE YEARS -- BUT HE RETOOK BATAAN. ONE DAY, SOMEHOW --
"-- SHE WILL RETURN..."
TO BE CONTINUED IN
MASS EFFECT 3
COMING SOON FROM
BIOWARE

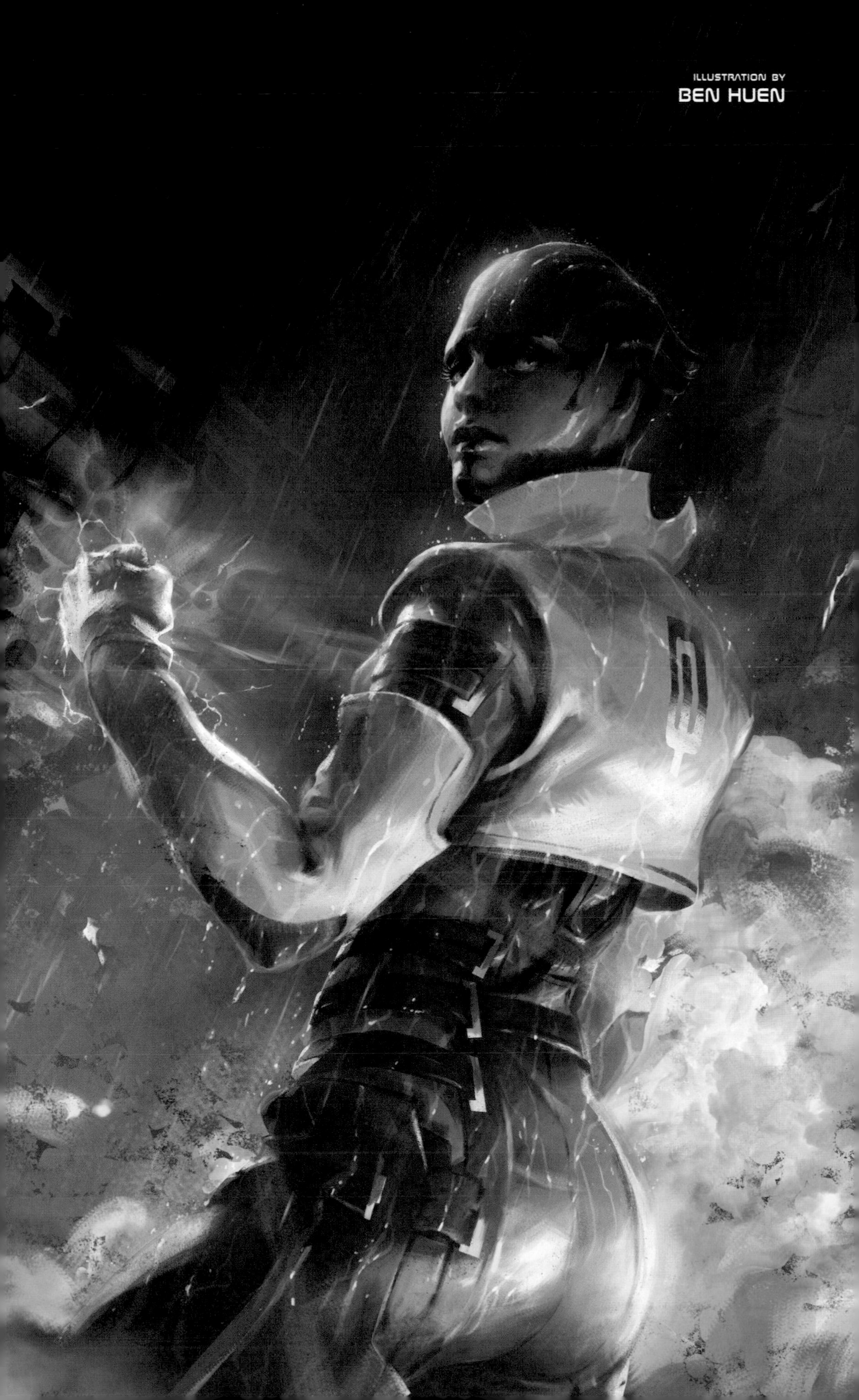
ILLUSTRATION BY
BEN HUEN

CONVICTION

SCRIPT
MAC WALTERS

ART
EDUARDO FRANCISCO

COLORS
MICHAEL ATIYEH

LETTERING
MICHAEL HEISLER

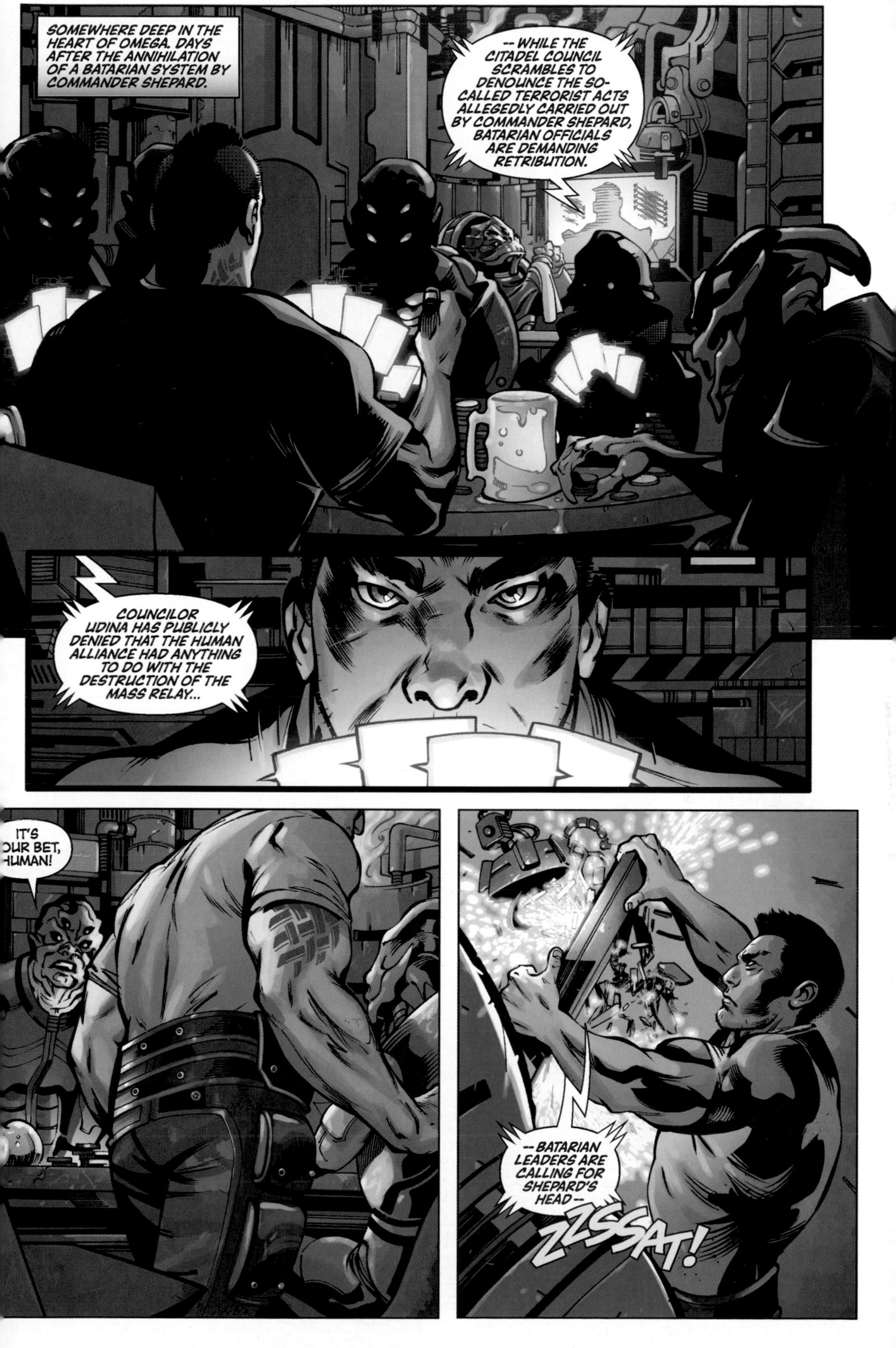
SOMEWHERE DEEP IN THE HEART OF OMEGA. DAYS AFTER THE ANNIHILATION OF A BATARIAN SYSTEM BY COMMANDER SHEPARD.
-- WHILE THE CITADEL COUNCIL SCRAMBLES TO DENOUNCE THE SO-CALLED TERRORIST ACTS ALLEGEDLY CARRIED OUT BY COMMANDER SHEPARD, BATARIAN OFFICIALS ARE DEMANDING RETRIBUTION.
COUNCILOR UDINA HAS PUBLICLY DENIED THAT THE HUMAN ALLIANCE HAD ANYTHING TO DO WITH THE DESTRUCTION OF THE MASS RELAY...
IT'S OUR BET, HUMAN!
-- BATARIAN LEADERS ARE CALLING FOR SHEPARD'S HEAD --
ZZSSAT!

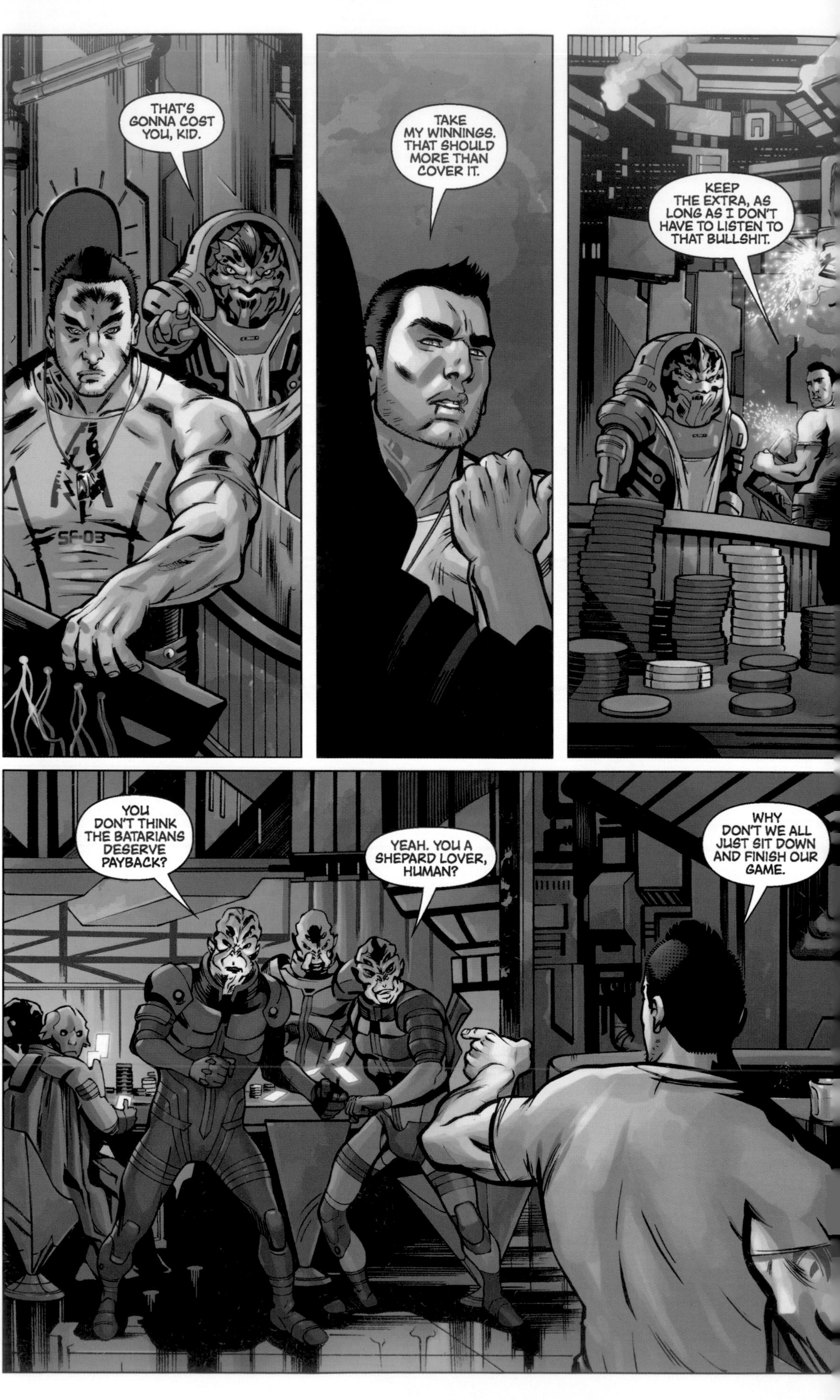
THAT'S GONNA COST YOU, KID.
TAKE MY WINNINGS. THAT SHOULD MORE THAN COVER IT.
KEEP THE EXTRA, AS LONG AS I DON'T HAVE TO LISTEN TO THAT BULLSHIT.
SF-03
YOU DON'T THINK THE BATARIANS DESERVE PAYBACK?
YEAH. YOU A SHEPARD LOVER, HUMAN?
WHY DON'T WE ALL JUST SIT DOWN AND FINISH OUR GAME.

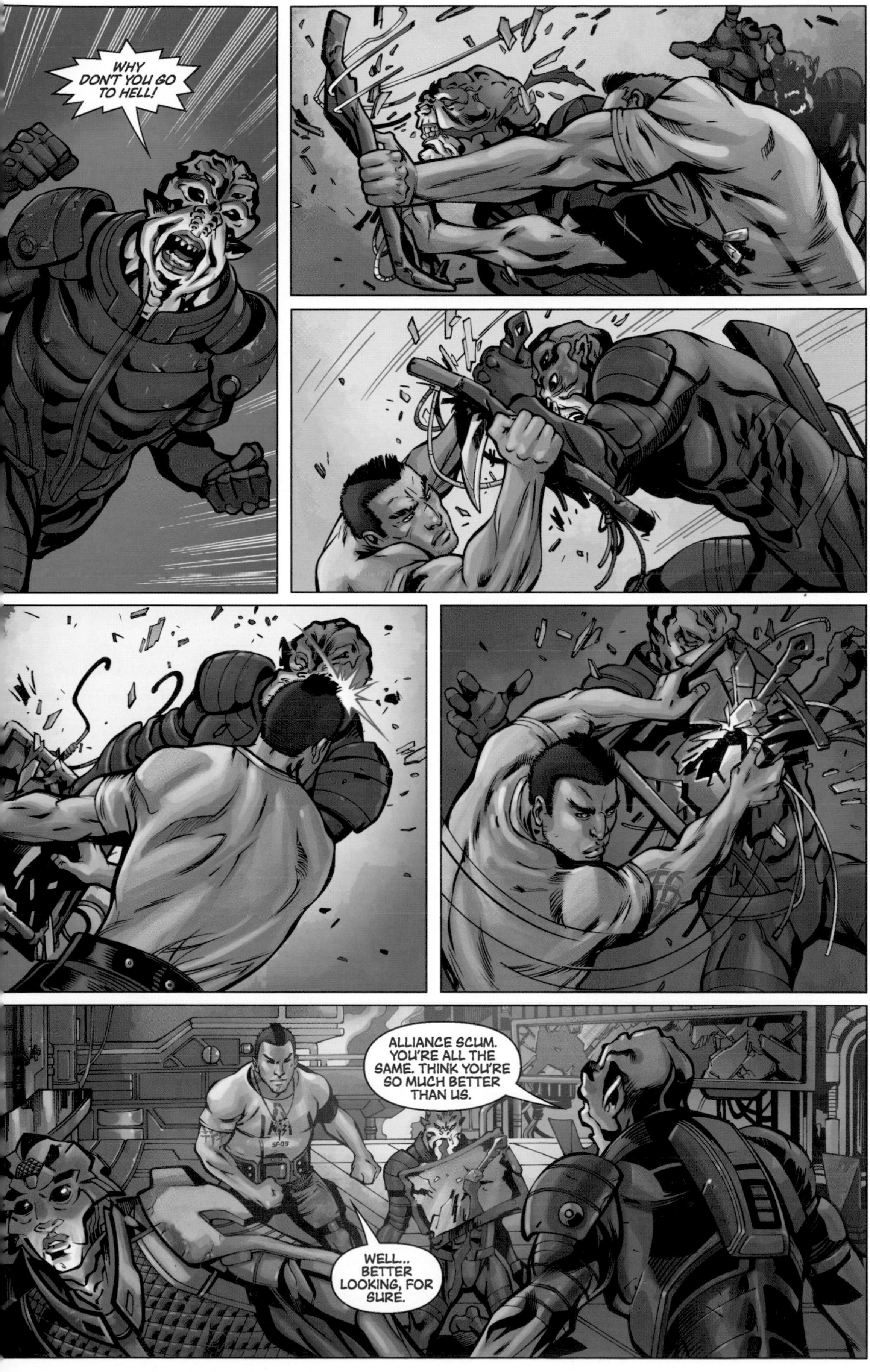
WHY DON'T YOU GO TO HELL!
ALLIANCE SCUM. YOU'RE ALL THE SAME. THINK YOU'RE SO MUCH BETTER THAN US.
WELL... BETTER LOOKING, FOR SURE.

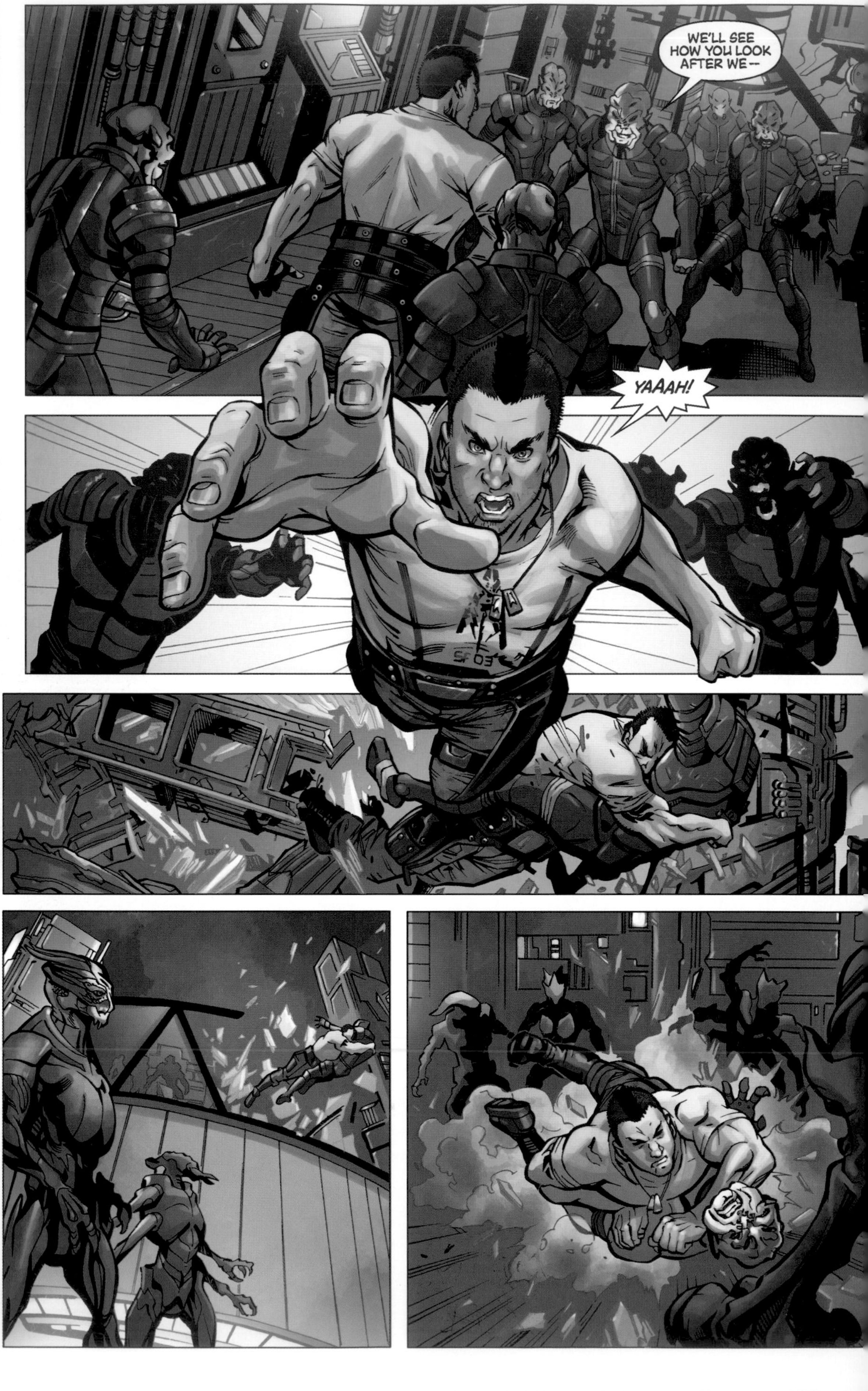
WE'LL SEE HOW YOU LOOK AFTER WE--
YAAAH!

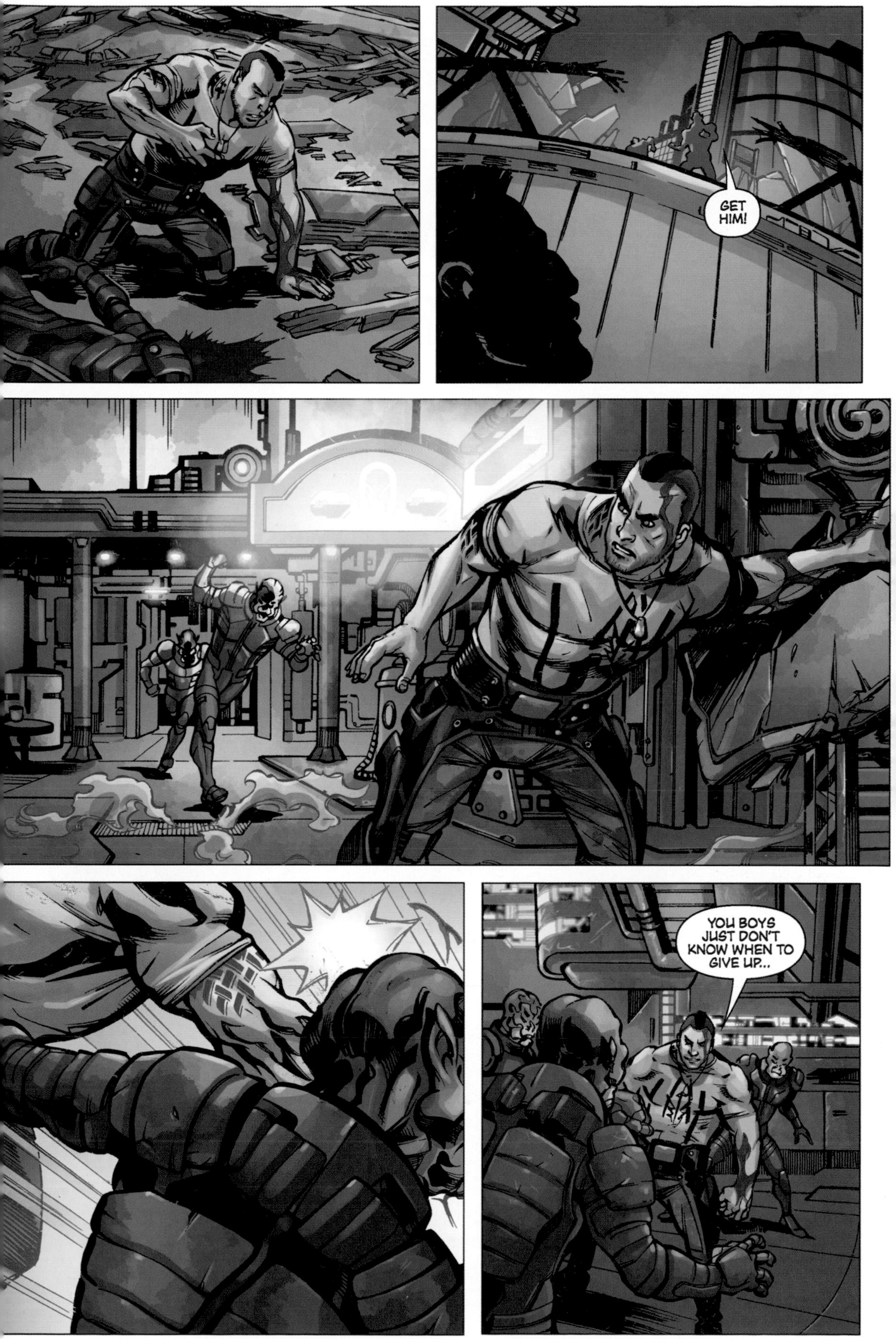
GET HIM!
YOU BOYS JUST DON'T KNOW WHEN TO GIVE UP...

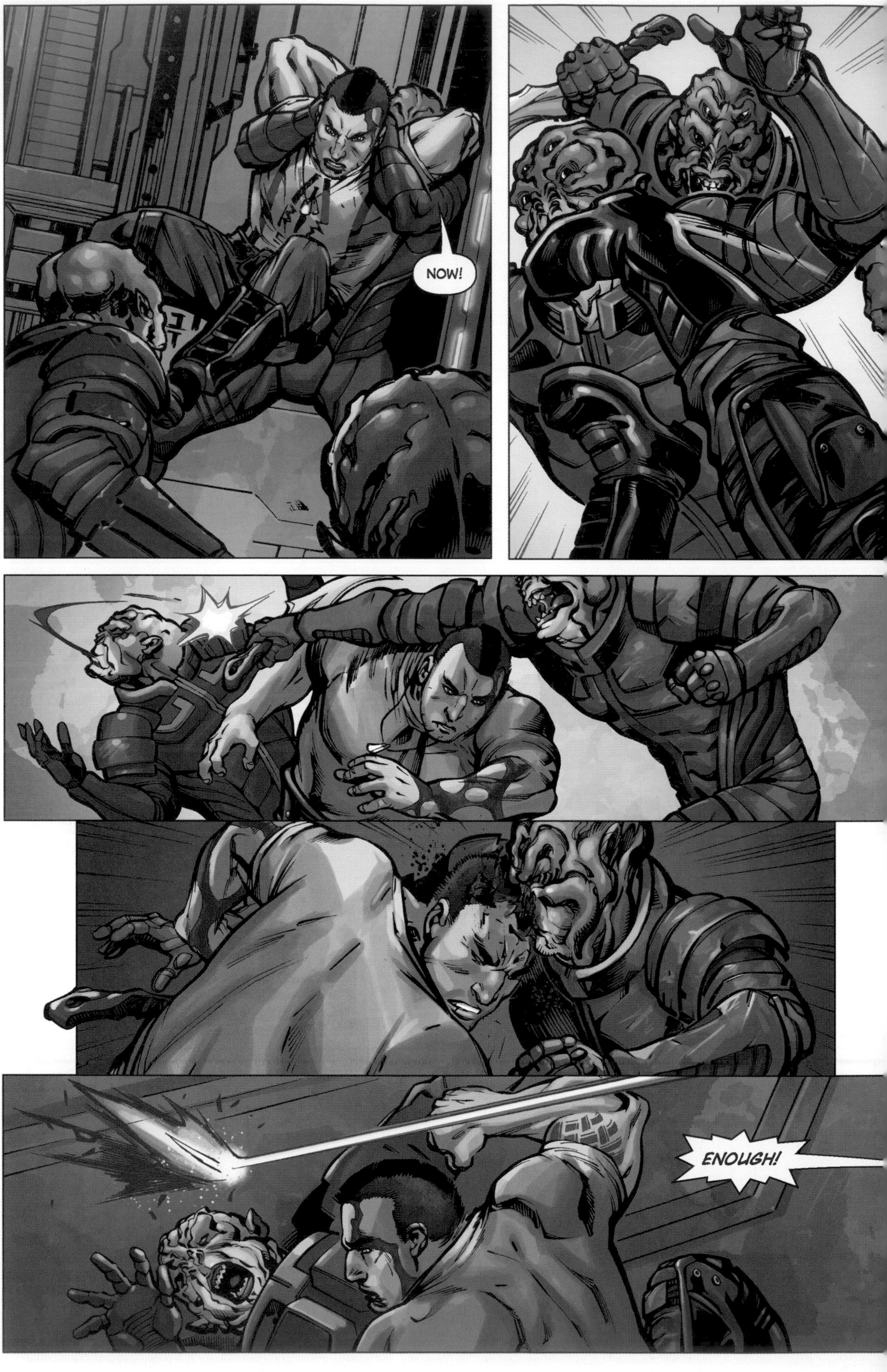
NOW!
ENOUGH!

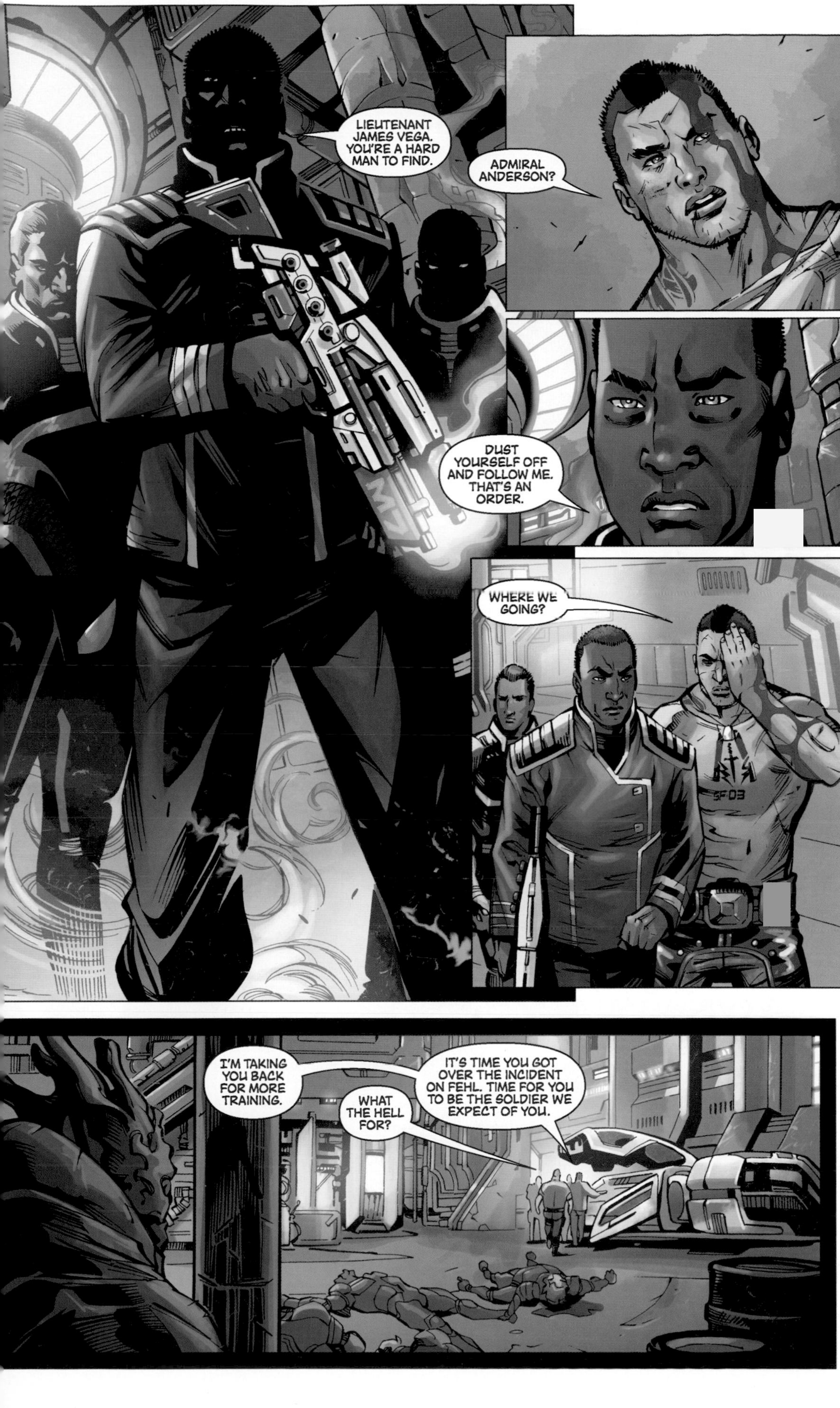
LIEUTENANT JAMES VEGA. YOU'RE A HARD MAN TO FIND.
ADMIRAL ANDERSON?
DUST YOURSELF OFF AND FOLLOW ME. THAT'S AN ORDER.
WHERE WE GOING?
I'M TAKING YOU BACK FOR MORE TRAINING.
WHAT THE HELL FOR?
IT'S TIME YOU GOT OVER THE INCIDENT ON FEHL. TIME FOR YOU TO BE THE SOLDIER WE EXPECT OF YOU.

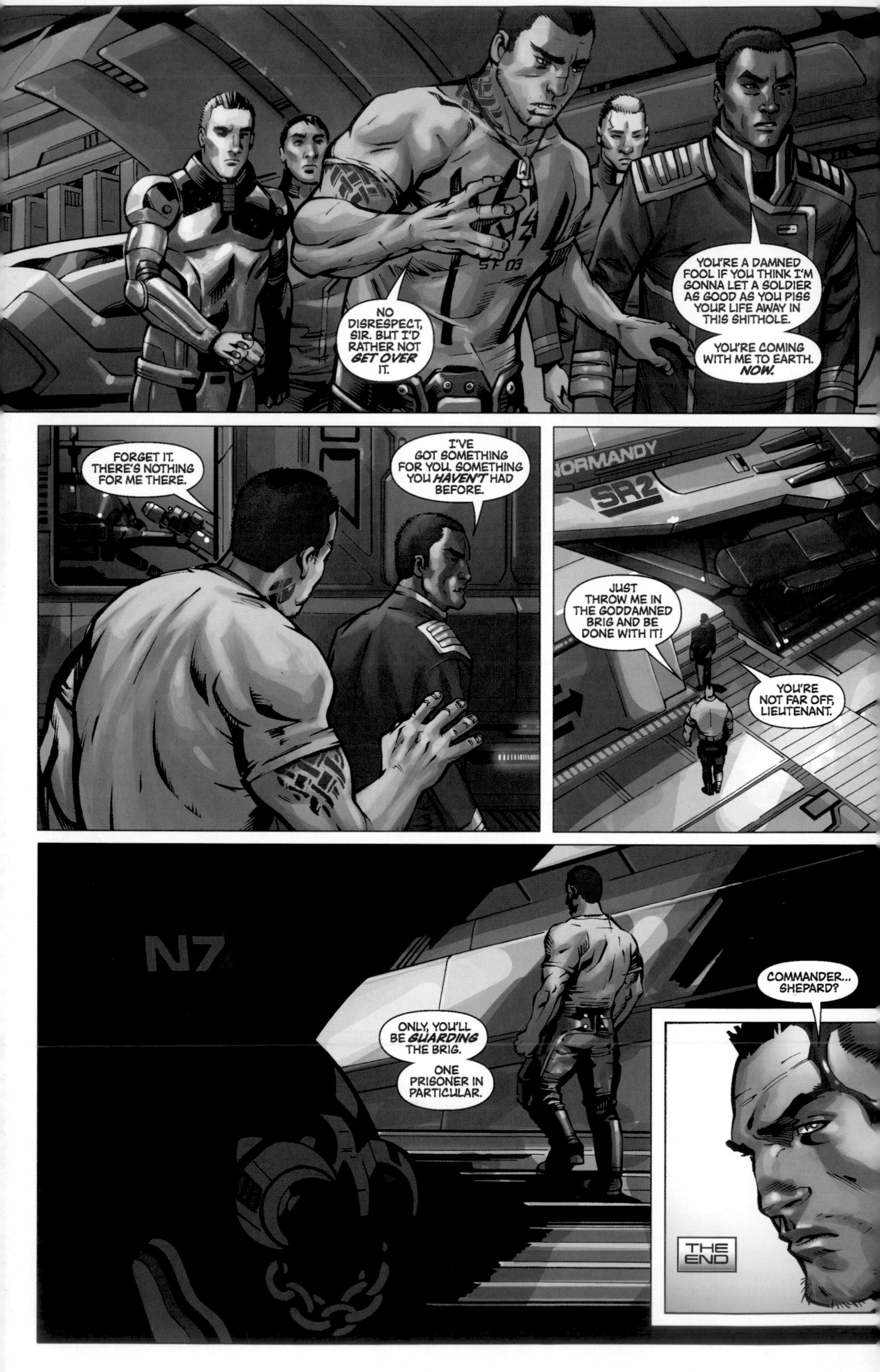
NO DISRESPECT, SIR. BUT I'D RATHER NOT *GET OVER* IT.
YOU'RE A DAMNED FOOL IF YOU THINK I'M GONNA LET A SOLDIER AS GOOD AS YOU PISS YOUR LIFE AWAY IN THIS SHITHOLE.
YOU'RE COMING WITH ME TO EARTH. *NOW.*
FORGET IT. THERE'S NOTHING FOR ME THERE.
I'VE GOT SOMETHING FOR YOU. SOMETHING YOU *HAVEN'T* HAD BEFORE.
NORMANDY
SR2
JUST THROW ME IN THE GODDAMNED BRIG AND BE DONE WITH IT!
YOU'RE NOT FAR OFF, LIEUTENANT.
N7
ONLY, YOU'LL BE *GUARDING* THE BRIG.
ONE PRISONER IN PARTICULAR.
COMMANDER... SHEPARD?
THE END

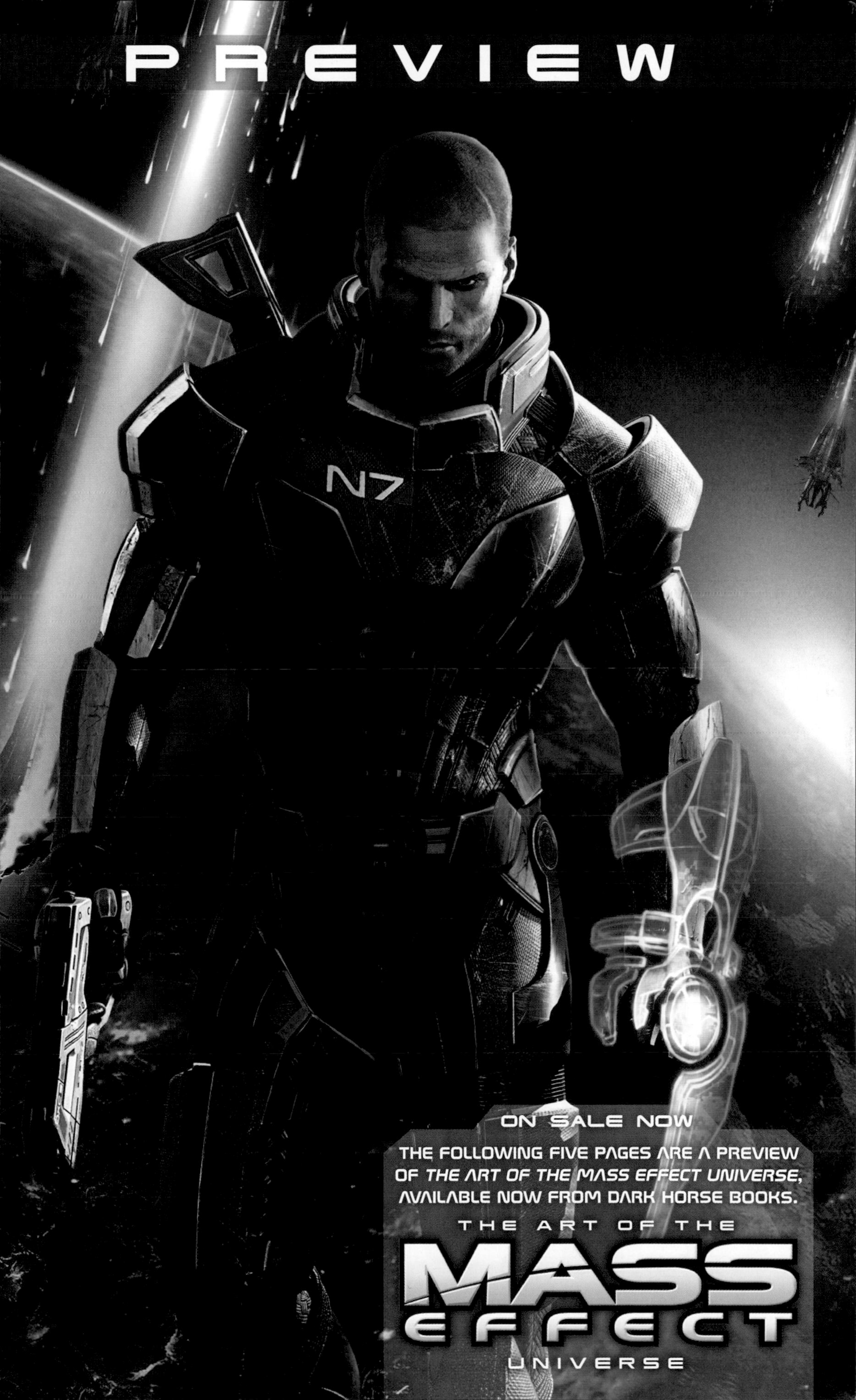
PREVIEW
N7
ON SALE NOW
THE FOLLOWING FIVE PAGES ARE A PREVIEW OF *THE ART OF THE MASS EFFECT UNIVERSE*, AVAILABLE NOW FROM DARK HORSE BOOKS.
THE ART OF THE
MASS
EFFECT
UNIVERSE

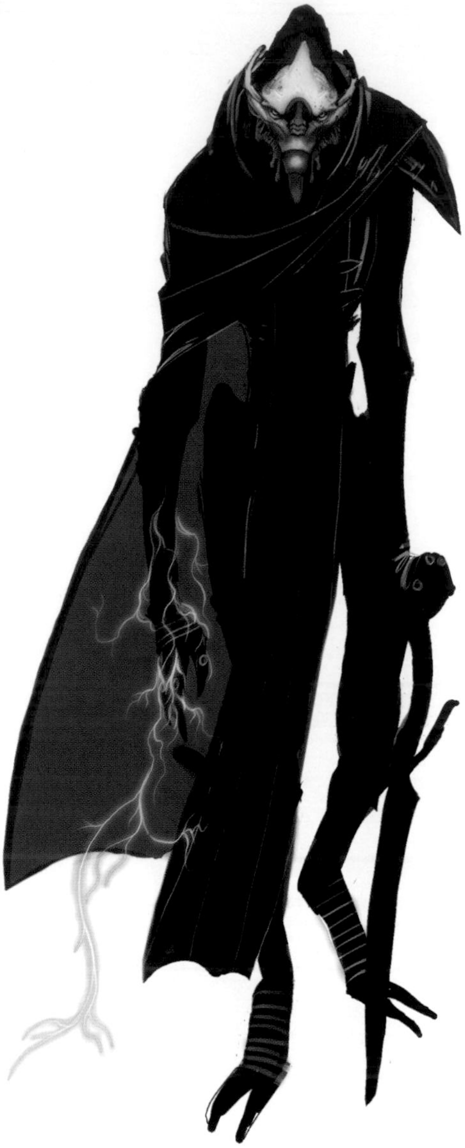

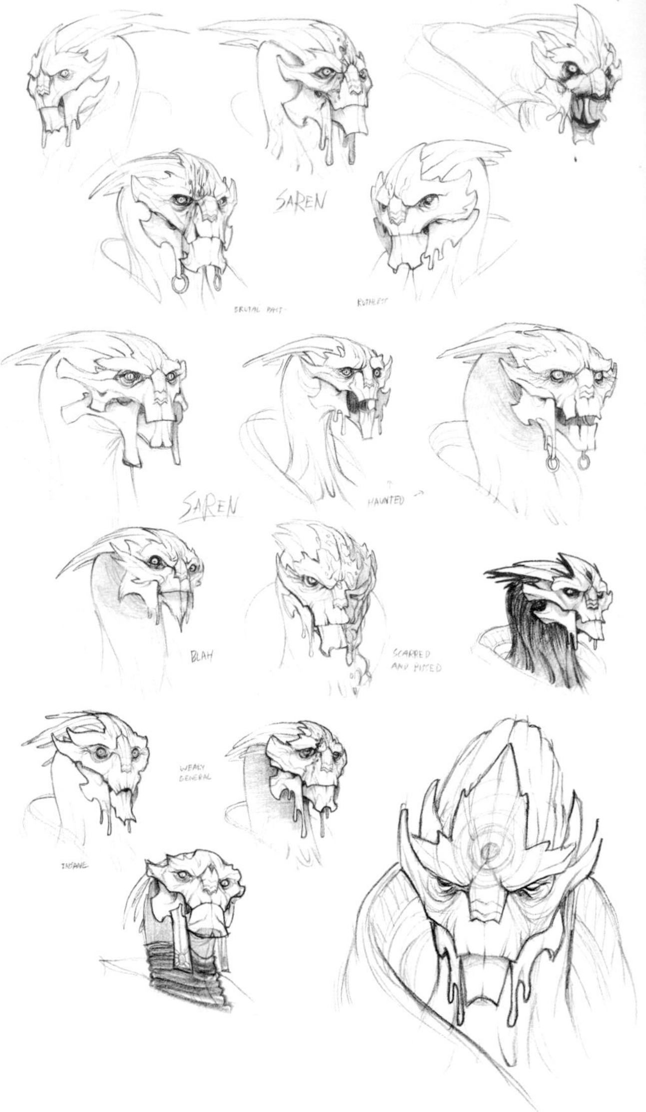

SAREN
SAREN
HAUNTED
BLAH
SCARRED AND PITTED

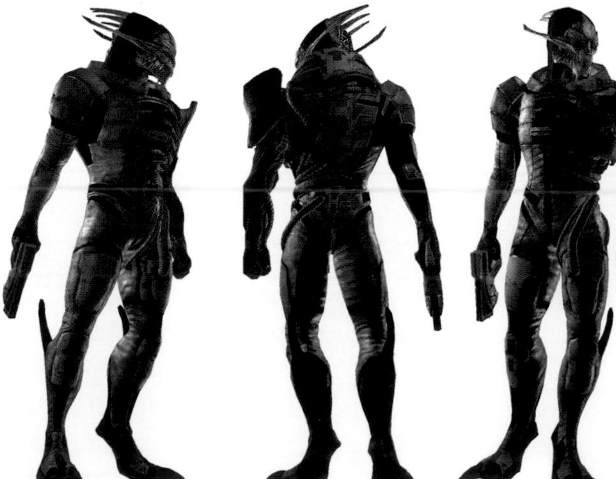

SAREN

At the top left is an early concept for Saren, depicting him as an older, physically weaker character who still possesses incredibly powerful biotics. The concepts on the right are brainstormed images exploring different aspects of Saren's head, experimenting with structure, scarring, and decorations. We ultimately decided that, unlike most turians, Saren would not have tattoos. We went with a distinctive crest and visible Reaper machinery to reflect his indoctrination.

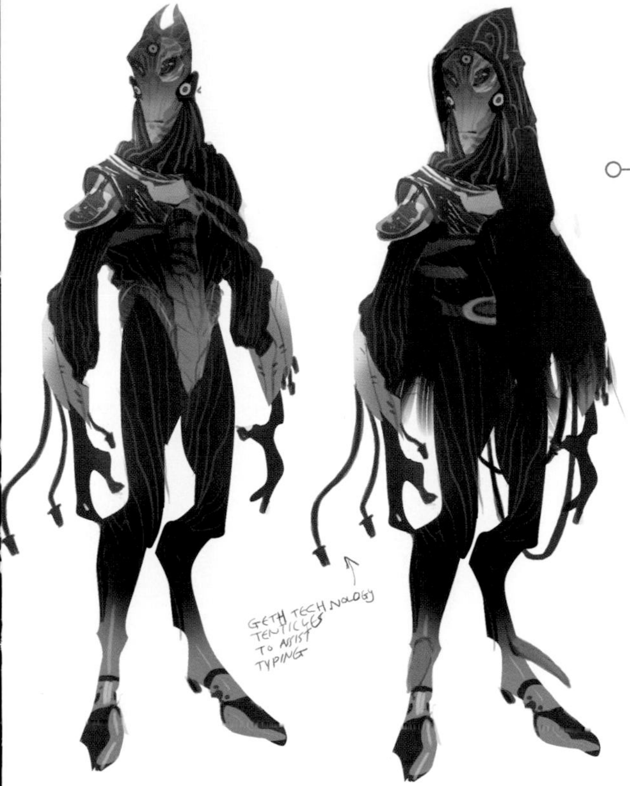
GETH TECHNOLOGY
TENTICLES
TO ASSIST
TYPING

MORDIN SOLUS

Mordin's appearance tried to strike a balance between his scientific background and his time spent in the salarian special forces. Early concepts reflected attempts to make him look unique through variations in head horns and the shape of his eyes.

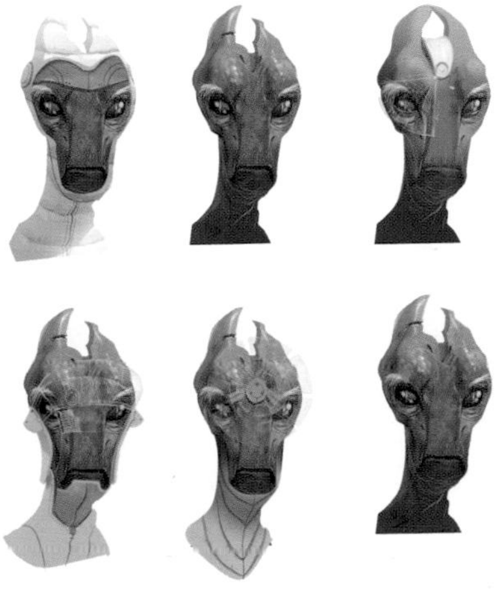

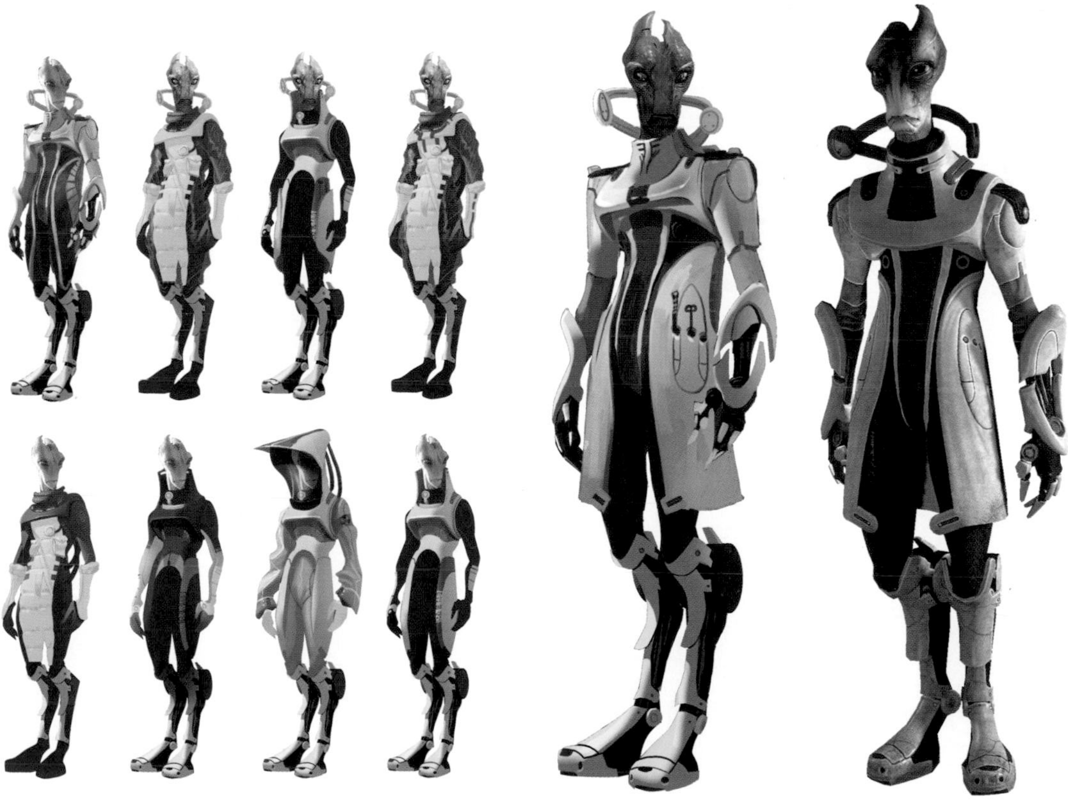

Mordin's appearance hinted at a lab coat and was similar to the outfits chosen for medical characters in the *Mass Effect* universe. The metal collar was added to break up his silhouette—its purpose was never actually explored in the game's dialogue or lore.

ASHLEY WILLIAMS

Ashley, Kaidan, and Liara were meant to be love interests throughout all three parts of the trilogy. After taking them away from players in *Mass Effect 2*, they were ready for a passionate return in *Mass Effect 3*. For Ashley's reappearance in the series, we let her hair down and gave her sex appeal, while keeping her in a uniform that introduced the new Alliance colors. Ashley first bumps into Shepard as an Alliance officer on Earth, so her iconic look is a stylish officer's uniform, but later she will don a full set of armor.

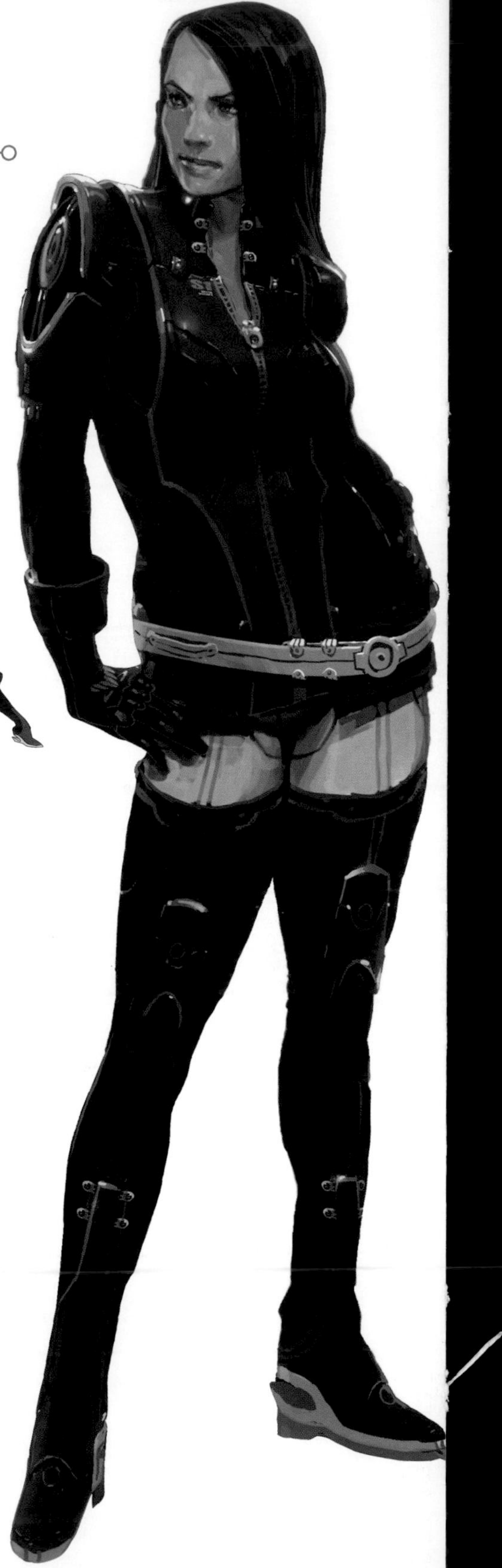

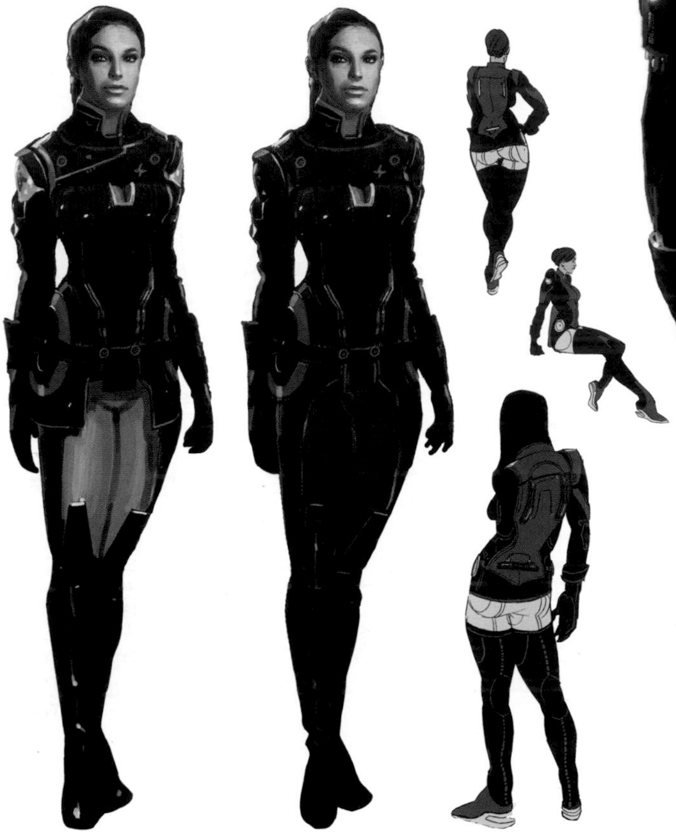

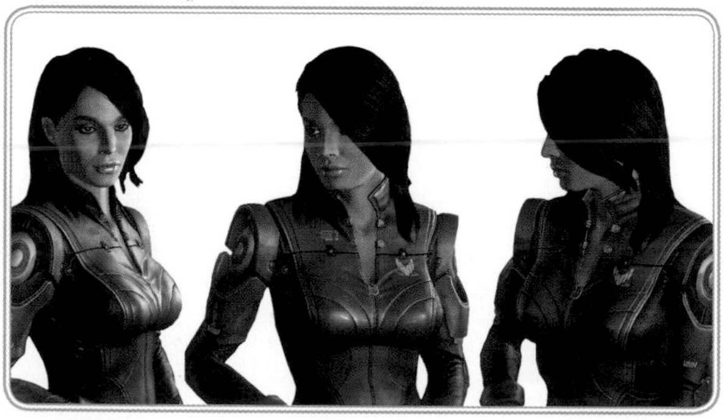

We tried many hairstyles for Ashley. Ultimately the team decided on a less formal look, appropriate since she and Shepard are well acquainted by *Mass Effect 3*.

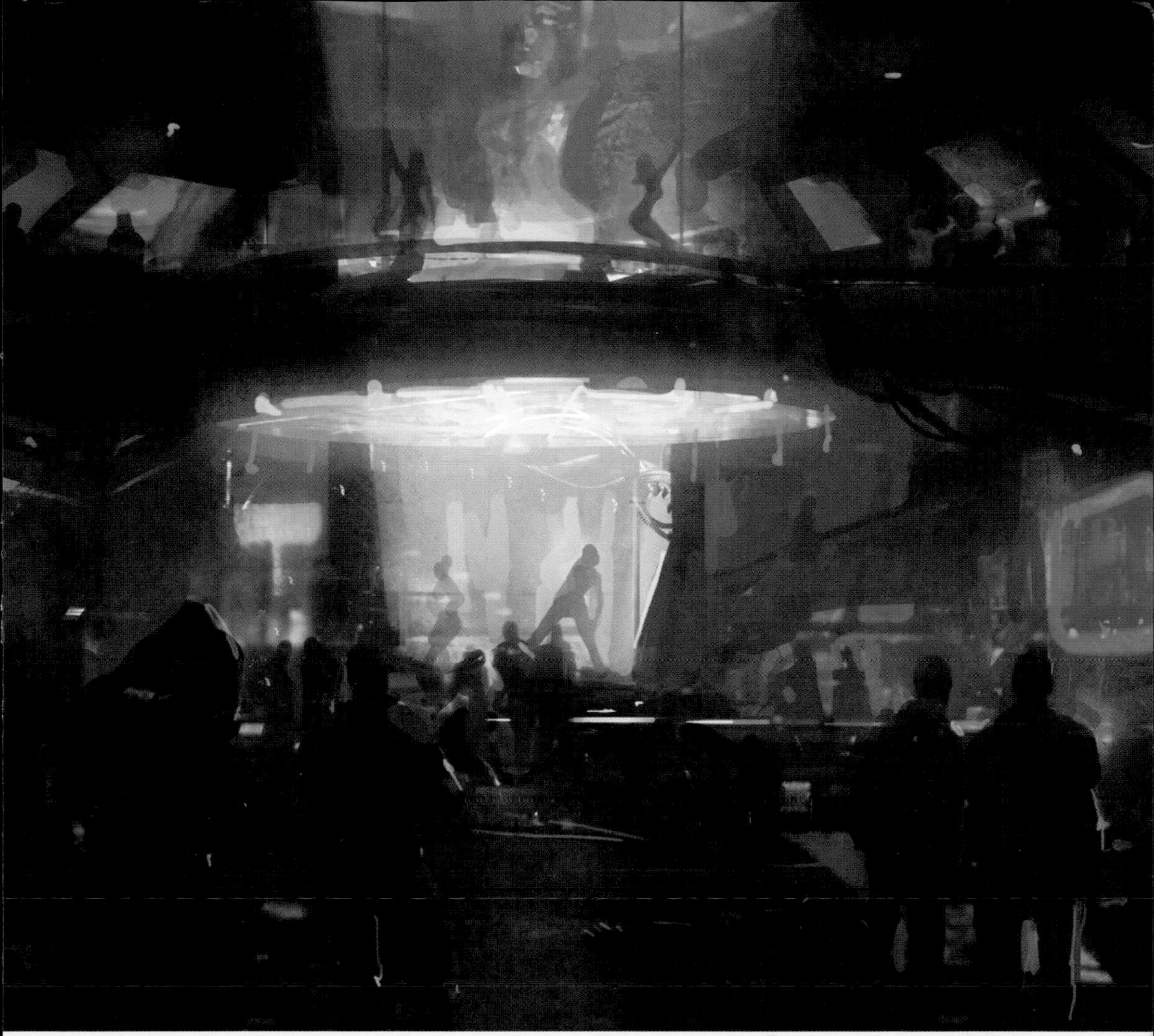

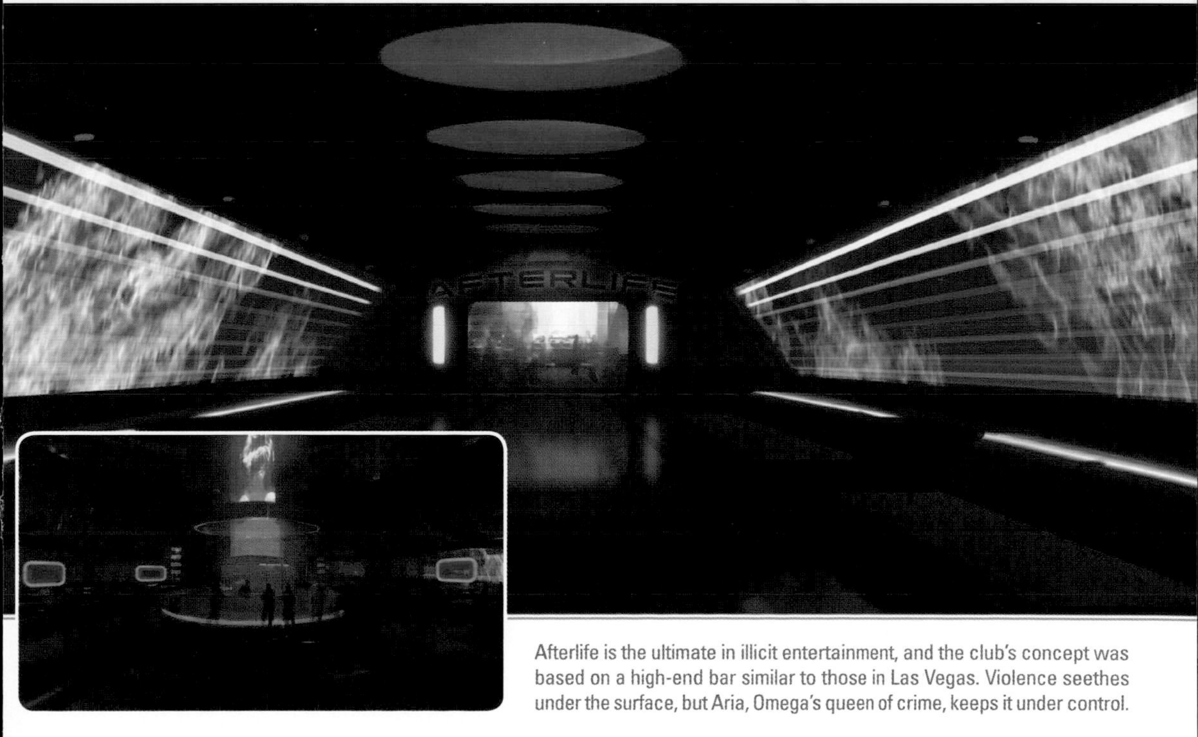
AFTERLIFE

Afterlife is the ultimate in illicit entertainment, and the club's concept was based on a high-end bar similar to those in Las Vegas. Violence seethes under the surface, but Aria, Omega's queen of crime, keeps it under control.

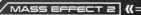

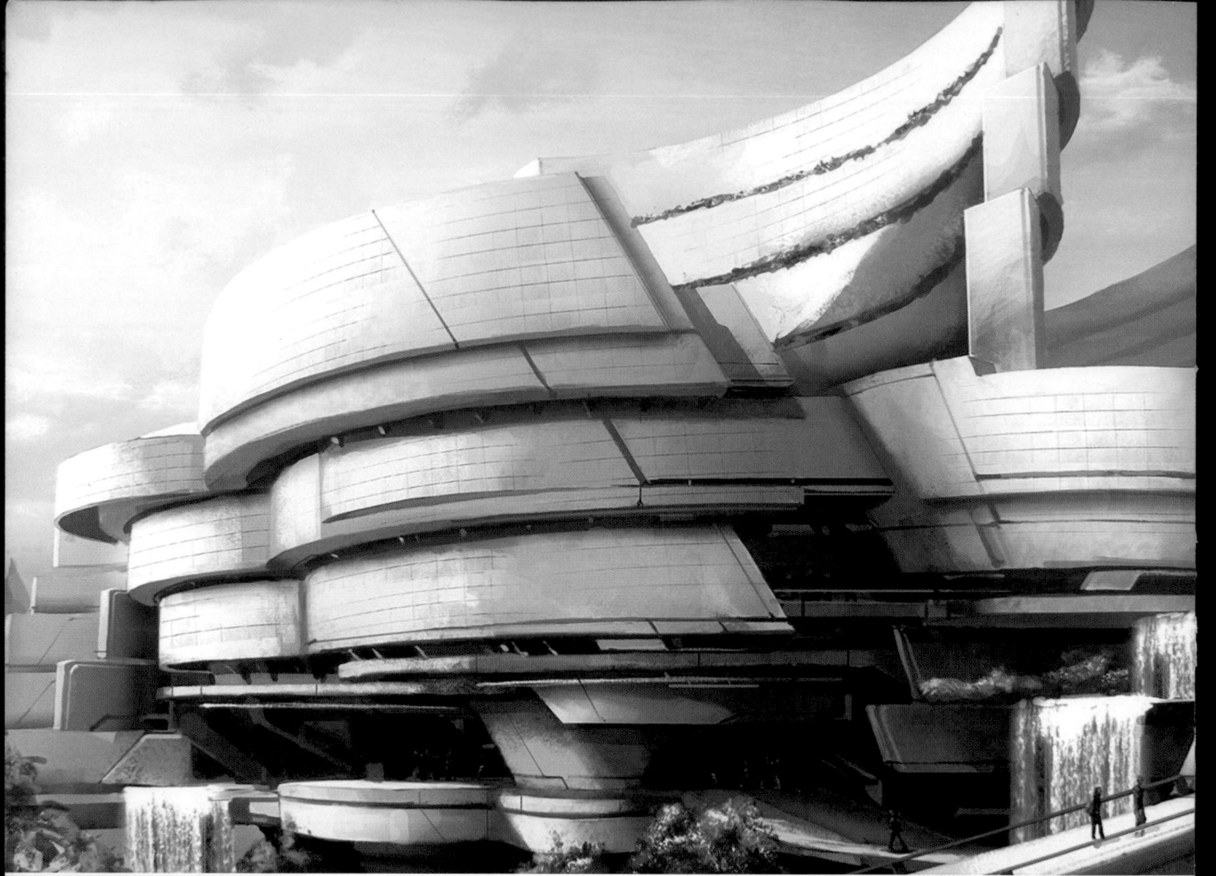

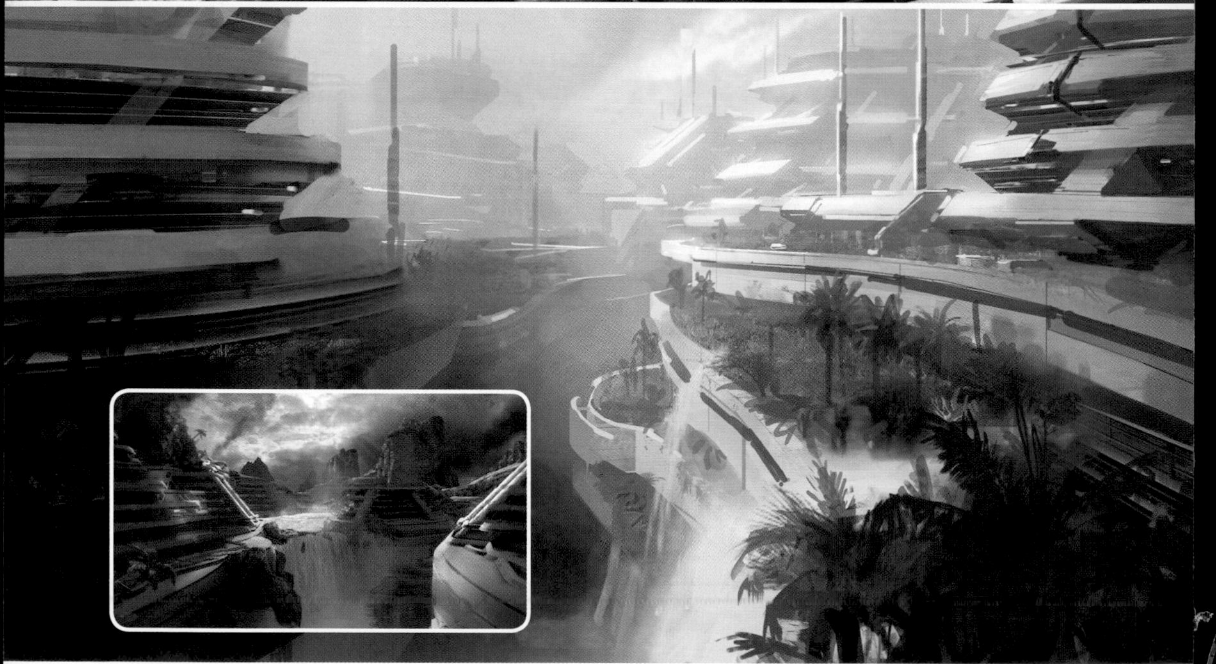

SUR'KESH

Sur'Kesh, the salarian home world, had to harbor an amphibious species. We went with a lush, tropical jungle that implied humidity. We thought the large curves of the structures mimicked some of the more organic shapes in salarian armor and clothing. The actual inspiration for this building was a shopping center in Istanbul. We intentionally designed the interiors to blur the line between the landscape and the structure, which helped give the base a very open and inviting feeling. The rubble is the result of Cerberus dropping in a commando team, turning the idyllic building into a battleground.

EXPERIENCE AN IN-DEPTH LOOK AT THE ART FROM ALL THREE GAMES IN THE FULL-SIZE, 184-PAGE HARDCOVER!

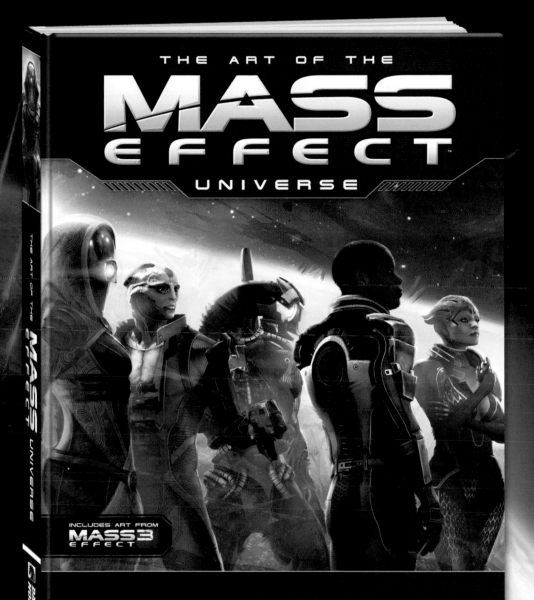

THE ART OF THE MASS EFFECT UNIVERSE

INCLUDES ART FROM **MASS 3 EFFECT**

INTRODUCTIONS BY
CASEY HUDSON AND DEREK WATTS

FEATURING CHARACTERS, ENVIRONMENTS, VEHICLES, AND MORE FROM THE ENTIRE SAGA!

AVAILABLE AT YOUR LOCAL COMICS SHOP OR BOOKSTORE.
TO FIND A COMICS SHOP IN YOUR AREA, CALL 1-888-266-4226

FOR MORE INFORMATION OR TO ORDER DIRECT,
VISIT DARKHORSE.COM OR CALL 1-800-862-0052